THE BEGINNER'S GUIDE TO HYPNOTHERAPY

RORY Z FULCHER

Published by Rory Z Fulcher
www.Rory-Z.com
www.HypnoTC.com

Copyright © 2014 by Rory Z Fulcher

1st edition published in November 2014

Paperback ISBN 978-1502978837

All rights reserved. No parts of this work may be reproduced or transmitted in any form or by any means, electronic or mechanical, including photocopying, recording, or by any information storage and retrieval system without the express written permission of the author, except where permitted by law.

Author Photographs: Ché Ballard
(**www.cheballard.com**)

OTHER BOOKS/MEDIA BY RORY Z

The Instant Hypnosis and Rapid Inductions Guidebook
(Paperback / E-Book)

The Stage & Street Hypnosis Handbook
(Paperback / E-Book)

Hypno-Fasting: The simple, effective way to lose weight but still eat all the food you love
(Paperback / E-Book)

Sam the Sleepy Sheep: The best way to get children to go to sleep
(Paperback / E-Book / Audiobook)

Hypnosis 101 – Learn to Hypnotise Fast – The Beginner's Guide to Instant and Rapid Hypnosis Inductions
(DVD)

Hypnosis 101 – Learn to be a Comedy Hypnotist – The Beginner's Guide to Stage & Street Hypnosis
(DVD)

Hypnotic Language Cards
(Cards)

Core Values Cards (Discover your core values)
(Cards)

ABOUT THE AUTHOR

Rory Z Fulcher (often known as 'Rory Z') was born in Norfolk, England in the 1980s. Having always been an enthusiast of creativity and the power of language and influence, even as a child, hypnosis quickly became one of his great passions. Rory has been practicing hypnosis since his high-school years and currently spends the vast majority of his time working on hypnosis books, videos, live hypnosis training and various other hypnotic projects. For Rory, hypnosis is more than just a full-time job, it's also a passion.

Rory is a successful hypnotherapist, having helped people all over the world with hypnotherapy. He is an adept stage and street hypnotist, and also trains students in all aspects of hypnosis and hypnotherapy. Rory has been featured by (and performed for) various international media outlets, including the BBC, Daily Mail, Lad Bible and Men's Health, to name but a few. As well as bringing hypnosis into the media, Rory frequently travels the world to speak and perform at public and private international conferences and events.

When not busying himself with his hypnosis businesses, Rory spends the rest of his time with his family at their home in Norfolk. Aside from hypnosis, Rory is a (fairly) proficient musician, an expert-novice didgeridoo player, an avid bodybuilding and fitness enthusiast, a cheese and whisky aficionado, a black sheep, a nomad, the class clown, a closet-goth and an all-round English gentleman.

DEDICATION

I'd like to thank my Mum and Dad for putting up with me for all these years and raising me so I could actually string a couple of words together. My Brother for keeping me grounded by telling me I need to "get a real job" – I'm still not going to do that. Both of my Nans, I love you both always. Sara, for supporting all my decisions (stupid or otherwise) and proofing anything that I throw in your general direction. Ché Ballard, for all the creative input, photography, filming and all that jazz (not to mention your witty repartee... *cough*) and Ashley Rayner, for eating all the coasters.

Finally I'd like to dedicate this book to the memory of my Grandad; Brian Garner. Miss you tonnes.

CONTENTS

- FOREWORD

HYPNOSIS INFORMATION

1	SO, WHAT IS THIS HYPNOSIS THING ANYWAY?
3	WHO CAN BE HYPNOTISED?
5	ENTERTAINMENT, THERAPY OR BOTH?
9	MYTHS
14	BRAINWAVES
15	THE CONSCIOUS AND SUBCONSCIOUS MIND
16	SOMNAMBULISM
17	HOW TO TELL IF SOMEONE IS HYPNOTISED
19	SELF-HYPNOSIS

HEALTH, SAFETY & LEGISLATION

21	BEING IN CONTROL (OF THE PERSON/SITUATION)
23	WHO/WHEN TO NOT HYPNOTISE
26	ETHICS/RESPONSIBILITY
27	LEGALITIES, INSURANCES & MEMBERSHIPS
29	PERMISSION/DOCUMENTATION

HOW TO HYPNOTISE

31	HOW TO HYPNOTISE – INDUCTIONS
32	PROGRESSIVE RELAXATION INDUCTION
37	GAZE FIXATION INDUCTION
39	TENSION/RELAXATION INDUCTION
40	HANDSHAKE INTERRUPT (INSTANT) INDUCTION
42	HOW TO HYPNOTISE – WAKING PROCEDURES
46	HOW TO HYPNOTISE – STATE DEEPENERS
59	USEFUL TIPS

HYPNOTHERAPY

71	WHAT IS HYPNOTHERAPY?
72	WHAT CAN HYPNOTHERAPY BE USED FOR?
74	PAST LIFE REGRESSIONS
75	HYPNOTHERAPY SESSION PLAN
80	HYPNOTHERAPY TECHNIQUES
83	SAFE PLACE

Page	Section
84	EGO-STRENGTHENING
86	DIRECT SUGGESTIONS
92	INDIRECT (ERICKSONIAN/CONVERSATIONAL) SUGGESTIONS
92	- ANALOGUE MARKING
94	- COMPLEX EQUIVALENCE
95	- CONVERSATIONAL POSTULATES (COMMAND QUESTIONS)
95	- DOUBLE BINDS
97	- EMBEDDED (INDIRECT) COMMANDS
98	- METAPHORS & SIMILES
99	- MODAL OPERATORS
99	- NEGATIVE SUGGESTIONS
100	- NOMINALISATIONS
102	- NON-SPECIFIC COMPARISONS
102	- NON-SPECIFIC OBJECTS
103	- PRESUPPOSITIONS
104	- SELECTIONAL RESTRICTION VIOLATION
105	- STORIES
107	- TRUISM (YES) SETS
108	- UNIVERSAL QUANTIFIERS (GENERALISATIONS)
113	VISUALISATIONS
128	AVERSION
131	PATTERN INTERRUPTION
136	ANAESTHESIA/ANALGESIA
143	RECONNECTION
145	AGE REGRESSION
156	ANCHORING (NLP)
160	POST-HYPNOTIC SUGGESTION
163	SELF-HYPNOSIS & AFFIRMATIONS
167	DISCLAIMER/CONTRACT OF SERVICES FORM
169	DATA-COLLECTION FORM

- AFTERWORD

FOREWORD

You have picked up this book – hopefully – because you would like to learn how to use hypnosis as a tool to solve problems; both physical and psychological/emotional. Whether they are your own issues, or perhaps you wish to help your family and friends feel better? Maybe you're reading this book with a view towards becoming a professional hypnotherapist or maybe you are one already – I don't know, and it doesn't matter.

I have written this book whilst bearing in mind a couple of possible scenarios pertaining to you; the Reader:

- This could be your first tentative step into the world of hypnotherapy, and maybe you just want to see if it's something that resonates with you, personally…

- You might already be familiar with some basic hypnosis and hypnotherapy processes, but maybe you are looking to expand your knowledge by investigating different views about how best to practice hypnotherapy (always a good idea, in my opinion.)

- How about, the well-read, already-practicing professional Hypnotherapist, looking for some light reading material (or checking out the competition! Haha!)

- Or perhaps you don't have any interest in ever practicing hypnotherapy whatsoever, and you found this book in the store and thought; "ah, Hell, why not? I haven't got anything better to read today."

Whichever category you fit into, you will undoubtedly gain a great deal of positive real-world practical knowledge from this book, and hopefully you will be entertained whilst doing so.

I have not written this book to teach you how to set up and run a successful hypnotherapy practice. I am, however, entirely focussed on teaching you how to become a successful *hypnotherapist in practice*. There's no business start-up info here. If you wish to learn how to set up your own hypnotherapy practice as a career then unless you already have experience being self-employed, you should be investing in a small business management course/book. *This* book wastes no paper explaining the merits and hurdles of self-employment, tax, advertising, etc.

The information contained in this book is the result of my many years spent studying and practicing hypnosis – mostly efficaciously, but occasionally unsuccessfully (even I was a beginner once – so in all honesty you can reap the benefits of both my novice mistakes and of my learned successes as you are learning from this book now.)

This guide serves as an evaluation of my own hypnotherapy experiences and the techniques gained and honed through both professional and personal capacities as a hypnotist. The book also serves as an "instruction manual" so that you are able to achieve the same results that I have personally been striving towards (and successfully achieving) since beginning my career as a professional hypnotherapist – this will be accomplished by breaking down techniques into manageable (and simple) language and including step-by-step "scripts" if you will, for you to utilise and modify to suit your own requirements.

I have personally read a great deal of books on the subject of hypnotherapy, and you quite frequently find the author making simple ideas ridiculously complicated and often barely intelligible to those people that didn't devour a dictionary for breakfast... Though it is wonderful to have a broad grasp of the English language ... I find the unnecessary supposition that those individuals who are striving to amalgamate hereunto ambiguous theories pertaining to hypnotism into a highly developed cogent, strategic model of individual understanding must have been born unto this reality as literary masters from their infancy to be of an entirely pedantic nature...

Or:

...I think it's completely unnecessary to bog someone down with a whole bunch of pretentious words just because they intend to be a hypnotherapist. You don't have to be Shakespeare to use your tongue correctly, and you don't need to be obscure in your choice of words to make lasting subconscious changes in subjects. In fact, sometimes you barely need to say anything at all...

Why make something that is practically a fairly simple subject, difficult? Anyway, I digress.

Throughout the book, I shall refer to subjects in the masculine form (he/him) unless an anecdotal tale requires otherwise, so as to allay unnecessary confusion. This is not due to being in any way "un-PC," simply a matter of congruence and ease of reading. It's best to mention these things at the get-go, I think, in this madly politically correct world in which we live, breathe and more importantly; read, just so that we're on the "same page" so to speak.

If you have already read my book: "The Instant Hypnosis and Rapid Inductions Guidebook" you might recognise certain topics in the first part of this book, but this is simply due to the fact that a lot of what hypnotherapy is, is entirely transferrable and interchangeable with the instant hypnosis model and vice versa – and there's no point in re-writing the stuff that I've already written perfectly, right? Anyway, if you read the other book already, then you already know that repetition is a great way to learn important stuff, and the important stuff is the only stuff you're going to be finding in this book!

Anyway, on with the "stuff"...

WARNING:
If you have no experience with hypnosis techniques, before you even consider trying ANY of the techniques mentioned later on in this book – you must read and acknowledge the information and instructions put forth in all preceding chapters beforehand.

Safety is your number one priority. This means first and foremost the safety of the person that you are hypnotising, and secondly your own safety; physical, emotional and legal.

What is your number one priority?

With this in mind, we may proceed to the first section.

HYPNOSIS INFORMATION

SO, WHAT IS THIS HYPNOSIS THING ANYWAY?

This is a great, simple question that anyone hoping to begin practicing hypnotherapy should be asking. "What is hypnosis?" Though the question does appear to be simple, unfortunately the answer is not quite as simple.

Hypnosis is, by my own definition:

A natural state of altered-consciousness which is conducive to subconscious acceptance of suggested changes in belief or subjective experience.

Try saying that with a mouthful of peas.

Basically, what the above definition means is that hypnosis is a "state of mind" that someone can enter into (with or without the help of a hypnotist) where their mind is more receptive to outside influences and suggestions that can change the way that they think/act.

A hypnotherapist has the knowledge (not power; knowledge) to guide a subject into an introspective state of conscious focus (often accompanied by relaxation) using a variety of techniques and stimuli. Once in this state of "trance" the hypnotherapist is then able to successfully introduce new ideas and habits or remove/resolve any unwanted or negative ideas/habits using various different methods.

If it need be dumbed down further: As a hypnotherapist, you can talk to a person in such a way that they will become "sleepy" or relaxed enough that they "go into a suggestible state" (hypnosis,) where their "conscious mind" is quite distracted. It is at this point that you are able to talk directly to their "subconscious mind" (that part of the brain that does the stuff that we don't even need to consciously think about) and tell it what you want it to do/not do, as the case may be.

If you need it dumbing down any further, I politely suggest you give up before you even begin, because although a skill that virtually anybody can learn, the art of hypnotherapy requires a modicum of common sense and logic for it to be applied successfully. When it comes down to it, you're "messing with people's minds" here, so if you don't manage to grasp (by the end of this book) what you should be doing – then I personally advise that you don't do it, because you might do more damage than good. Don't mess around with that which you do not understand – Until you understand it, that is.

Anyway, looking back, I set out to tell you "what hypnosis is" and I ended up giving you a brief idea of how hypnotherapy works. That was partially unintentional, but it happens. The reason it happens is because hypnosis is a very tricky thing to quantify.

Rather than telling you exactly "what hypnosis is" (for which, I refer you back to the brief-but-pretty-accurate definition at the beginning of the chapter, because that's the best I can do if we're being exact, succinct and not beating around the bush about it); instead I shall tell you:

Hypnosis CAN change physiological/psychological symptoms in a subject to a measurable degree (hypnotherapy would be long-forgotten if this were not the case.)

Hypnosis DOES physically affect your brain. EEG brainwave scans have determined this to be true.

Hypnosis DOES cause/accompany a feeling of relaxation and revitalisation (usually).

Hypnosis IS REAL.

Hypnosis IS NOT REAL.

Wait, what?

Hypnosis is a "nominalisation" of a thing that happens inside our heads – i.e. we've given a name to something that isn't tangible. As an analogy, I'd like you to think about the idea of being asleep and having a dream. We can agree that a dream is a real thing, right? Right... So, go and have a dream, and when you're "having it," grab it and show it to me. Don't understand? Well, what I mean is try pull a dream out of your head, show me the parts of it and how it works. It's impossible to do, because a dream "isn't real," just like hypnosis "isn't real." But just because it's intangible, doesn't mean it doesn't still occur.

Now, not forgetting that last paragraph entirely, you can instead realise that human beings do enter into the state that we often define as "hypnosis" at least a couple of times every day without even realising it. For example, in the morning whilst having your breakfast, you may skip blankly through the channels on TV, later on in the day you perhaps find yourself craving an ice cold can of Coca Cola, but you probably don't remember seeing that split second of bright, red logo on morning TV imprinting that desire into your subconscious mind.

You're driving down the road, daydreaming, and all of the sudden you've jumped ahead 7 miles, completely on auto-pilot, wondering how you managed to not smash your car into a roadside burger stand at some point during this dreamy drive. Your mind was on autopilot for those 7 miles, this means your conscious mind was busy daydreaming about something...anything (probably something inappropriate... no, just me?) and to keep you safe, your subconscious mind took over the process of driving the car. Quite a useful thing to have, that old subconscious mind of yours, eh?

These are examples of what is (for all intents and purposes) a hypnotic state, but with these examples (as with most of these regular, day-to-day hypnoidal occurrences) this state of mind is not being utilised as hypnosis proper... I.e. you are not receiving suggestions from another human being (hypnotist,) directly.

True hypnosis harnesses this natural state, and becomes something akin to "directed daydreaming" or "guided meditation" (the latter a term I frequently use to put therapy clients into a calmer frame of mind about that "scary" hypnosis thing.)

When it boils down to it; you don't really *need* to know *what hypnosis is* to be able to use it successfully, because whether you know what it is or whether you don't, it still exists (apart from it doesn't *wink*.) And whether you believe in hypnosis or not, it still works...Which is handy for us hypnotists.

WHO CAN BE HYPNOTISED?

Amateur hypnotists perhaps believe the statistics that have found their way into the hypnosis world which state something like 70% of people can be hypnotised and 20% of that number are going to be great, responsive subjects.

Professional hypnotherapists, however, know that any human being who has the capacity and intelligence to understand and be understood by other human beings can greatly benefit from a hypnotherapy session. The key to successfully hypnotising everyone that you attempt to hypnotise is "tailoring," and I'm not talking about your suit.

Imagine the state of hypnotic trance as a large, almost pyramid-shaped hill, and as a hypnotist you have to guide people up to the top of this hill into hypnosis (or at least part-way up into a "light" state of hypnosis.) Now, this hill has a different terrain on all four sides; there is a paved path on one side, zig-zagging easily up the hill. Around on the opposite side there is a steep, bumpy, muddy track. On the third side is a very easy incline to the summit, but it is densely populated by trees and bushes. The fourth side is a sheer cliff face.

As a hypnotherapist you cannot assume that your subject will begin his journey standing at the foot of the first, easy path leading up the hill into hypnosis – all people have different experiences and beliefs with regards to what hypnosis is and how it works. Perhaps he will begin standing at the base of the cliff, or the densely wooded incline, or the steep, muddy track. A lot of beginners do make the critical mistake and assume that a "one size fits all" type technique will create that state of hypnosis in everybody. They don't change it up, but simply use the same "script" in exactly the same way, every time with every subject, with the assumption that every subject begins, standing at the start of the "easy path."

You will develop a "one size fits all" technique. That's a fact, there's no way around that, and it's not a bad thing. There's going to be one technique, one method of creating the state of hypnotic trance that you will use more than any other method, and one that you will feel most comfortable and confident with, and that's fine... But to use this one method every time for *all of your subjects*, however, is not a great idea. At best, you will need lots of time and persistence because you may have to guide the subject for a long time around the base of that hill until they even *find* the start of their path into hypnosis, let alone begin to ascend it. At worst, the subject won't even be able to find that path at all, and you as their hypnotherapist can't *force* them to find it, you can only *guide* them in the direction that they are naturally inclined to travel. This is why I always suggest that you need to be prepared and flexible in your approach.

What happens if you are forced to start on the side of the hill with the dense forest? The "one size fits all" wandering up the easy path method isn't going to cut it here... You'd better have another method in your hypnosis-toolbox to cut through the subconscious undergrowth, thereby allowing the subject to carve their own path up the hill.

OK, so perhaps the subject makes it a little way up towards hypnosis, but stops at a plateau and can go up no further. Damn, the second method failed too... Well, then cut back around to the muddy track and get into your 4x4-method and hit the gas until you reach the top of the hill.

And if that doesn't work? Then you're left with the steep cliff side... Well you're going to need to think "outside the box" to get him to the top of the hill. Whip out your climbing gear, call in a helicopter and fly him to the top, or fire him from a cannon...

[Note: if you hadn't realised, these "methods" are not actual hypnosis methods, but simply metaphors – please do not fire your subjects from cannons or drop them from helicopters...especially the ones with a fear of heights.]

The point is; it is beneficial to you to be flexible with your approach with each individual on a case by case basis, and if a method that you are overly familiar with isn't working then you may have to bite the bullet and do something that you are less experienced with. You might have to step outside your comfort zone to get that tricky subject to the top of the hill... Hmmm, perhaps hypnotherapy isn't all comfort, couches and fob watches after all...

To think of it another way, you can compare hypnotherapists to hairdressers: A hairdresser has to know a great deal of different hair-cutting methods so that all clients get the haircut that they desire, if a hairdresser only knows how to do "short back and sides," then this hairdresser isn't going to get very far in the hair-dressing-industry. That's not to say that the hairdresser won't get some *really satisfied customers*, but he would be limiting himself by not learning different methods and techniques to use on clients that required something a little bit different. Woe betides the hairdresser that attempts to give a grandmother a short back and sides... Makes sense, right?

[Note: Assuming that you read this book in a linear fashion, we will focus on the skills and techniques used to induce hypnosis first – the therapy section is closer to the back of the book, because there's no point being a hypnotherapist if you can't actually do hypnosis efficiently first.]

ENTERTAINMENT, THERAPY OR BOTH?

As you are probably aware, hypnotherapy is only one half of the hypnosis coin. Although hypnotherapy is the sole focus of this book, I believe it's worth mentioning the "other side" of hypnosis; adding the dreaded prefix that makes a lot of old, fusty hypnotherapists cringe with thoughts of inappropriate, amoral behaviour, litigious-temptation and the consistent and comprehensive soiling of the so-called "good reputations" of hypnotherapists everywhere: Stage hypnosis ...and to a lesser degree, but becoming more and more common: Street hypnosis

OH THE HUMANITY! But wait... Before you jump on the old, fusty hypnotherapist bandwagon and begin to march against hypnotic entertainers everywhere, I would remind you that the author of this (rather intelligent, morally correct and almost-entirely appropriate) book about hypnotherapy that you are currently reading is first and foremost a professional stage/street hypnotist and prolific trainer of these supposed "hypno-heathens."

Hypnotherapists and stage hypnotists have long been at each other's throats, attacking each other's professions and defending their own, but similar to most religious disputes; a little tolerance, trust and a change of perspective can go a long way.

...Not that I'm suggesting hypnosis is a religion (but maybe it should be, it ticks a lot of boxes – Praise Hypnos! Oh wait, that's Greek Mythology, never mind.)

Anyway, a *good* hypnotist is going to be conscientious, lawful, ethical and engaging whether he is in the therapy room, removing a severe case of claustrophobia for a single subject or making a group of people believe they are chickens in front of a large auditorium of paying spectators. When we get to the bottom of the issue, we realise it isn't about which *use* of hypnosis is right or safe or morally correct. Can you guess what *my* opinion is? Can you figure out why *I* think relationships between therapists and entertainers have been out of sync for so long? No?

The answer is PIE! Mmmmmm PIE. Breaking down the acronym:

People + Integrity + Education

All of us are different characters, no two humans the same. We may well be in the same profession, but that doesn't make us the same person. By nature and by nurture, we are all different PEOPLE.

We weren't brought up by the same parents/guardians, we have learned different models of the world from these people, and we have then gone on to modify those models again until they resonated with us, until we felt that the way in which we act and behave fits in with our own internal standards of honesty and INTEGRITY.

And though we might be learning the same basic skills, we individually process information in different ways, placing more emphasis on certain points than other people perhaps do, sometimes disregarding a piece of information that we feel is relatively unimportant, whilst a colleague might believe the exact opposite, believing said piece of information to be of highest priority, thusly this affects the individual teachings we take away from our EDUCATION.

Picture Danny, a restaurant worker, flipping burgers since he left school. He was brought up by his respectable family to care about himself and others, to show respect, be polite and to strive to be the best he can at whatever he chooses to do. This translates to his work.

Danny's colleague Jeff was not brought up this way, and as such does not have the same set of moral values and personal standards as Danny. Jeff turns up to work, unwashed, untidy, and unpleasant. He drops food on the floor, picks it up, dusts it off and puts it back on the sale rack, he coughs in customers' faces. He shouldn't be working in a restaurant... But he is. Jeff is the same age as Danny, doing the same job, wearing the same (albeit dirtier) outfit, but he is entirely different. The same goes for any employed person, hypnotists included.

Jeff didn't care, and so perhaps in the eyes of some customers he set a bad example for all of the other restaurant staff, just as some stage hypnotists in the past (and probably in the present too) do not care about their subjects, do not care for safety, rapport, compassion... Maybe all they care about is getting paid at the end of the show, screw the subjects, screw the onlookers and look after number one, and you have to realise that that's just how some people are. It's a hard fact of life, but one or two bad eggs shouldn't cause us question the chicken, if you get my drift. When I personally train a person in the art of hypnosis, the primary focus is the fact that the well-being of your subject(s) is the #1 priority above everything else, and this goes for hypnotherapy too, in equal measure.

And flipping back to the other side of the coin; it's not just the odd stage hypnotist that can be morally-corrupt. I have heard a few stories of hypnotherapists acting inappropriately, rushing through sessions as if they didn't want to be there, checking their phones and texting during therapy sessions, giving improper and dangerous suggestions... Sometimes you even hear news of a hypnotherapist having tried to sexually assault a subject whilst in trance – These things can and do happen, it's sad, but it happens whether we like it or not.

Like I say; we are often defined by what we do, instead of how we do it, and a whole profession of people can end up being tarred by the brush of one or two idiots, and this is wrong, but this is life – suck lemons or make lemonade.

Stage (and street) hypnosis is great fun and the practitioners are always striving to bring hypnosis into the public eye (their healthy egos demand that they do so.) This benefits *hypnotherapists*, because as a rule, most people don't know that hypnotherapy and stage hypnosis are different creatures entirely (as a stage hypnotist, I quite frequently get emails asking for details of my "hypnotherapy show"...) so clients often ask a hypnotherapist if he does any stage performances, and if he doesn't (and assuming he isn't prejudiced, *wink wink*) he can refer the client to a stage hypnotist that he knows and respects and vice versa, the same for the stage hypnotists referring prospective therapy clients to a hypnotherapist.

All publicity is good publicity, or so they say, and I'm inclined to agree. I wholeheartedly recommend stage hypnotists and hypnotherapists to engage with each other, because networking is networking and that's how you get ahead in business (don't take my word for it, go out and speak to any self-employed individual.)

I am of the new breed; a crossover, if you like. I have my fingers in many hypnotic pies, and I believe that this benefits me immeasurably; giving me many more tools to work with than:

The average hypnotherapist
Example: I use instant stage hypnosis-style hypnosis with my hypnotherapy clients, but I can always dip into the "old-school hypnotherapy bag" if a subject requires more subtle treatment. Also, I'm not held back by the incorrect belief that a lot of hypnotherapists have; thinking they need a quiet office environment to perform hypnotherapy...

Or the average stage hypnotist
Example: I know how to properly deal well with unexpected emotional reactions/regressions during stage shows. Also, you often find that people who attend a hypnosis show become very interested in self-improvement using hypnotherapy...

I'm talking about myself here, only because I am able to see things from both perspectives, I can see where hypnotherapists are coming from when they say "stage folk are dangerous philistines," and I can appreciate the sentiment... But I also know that *they are wrong* on most counts regarding 99.9% of hypnotic entertainers. Just the same as I can see where stage guys say that hypnotherapists usually bore people to sleep with outdated and unnecessarily long inductions, which, again, can be true (especially if the hypnotherapist wasn't trained by me!) but is definitely not always the case.

The simple fact remains; some people don't want the pressure of performing on stage in front of a huge crowd of strangers, just the same as some people don't want to be tied to a therapy room full of clients five days a week. Different strokes for different folks. Everybody is different, and you have to do what feels right for you. By being happy with what you do, you will automatically enjoy it more and henceforth perform your role better than any so-called-hypnotherapist who is only in it for the money.

If you, like me, *are* interested in trying your hand at both disciplines, you have to remember they are very different ballparks with extremely varied clientele who all have polar-opposite expectations of what you should be doing for/to/with them. But I am living proof that it *is possible*. And that it is perhaps even lucrative...

(And if you *are* interested in trying your hand at both, you should get in touch with me for some hypnosis training! – Hey, I can plug if I want to – It's my book!)

MYTHS

Can you get stuck in hypnosis?

Aside from "abreactions" occurring (which we will cover later,) becoming "stuck" in hypnosis is not going to happen. Hypnosis can be induced to last for a long time, hours, probably even days, but the subject will need regular "maintenance" from the hypnotist to allow them to remain in this hypnoidal state.

Ormond "the Dean of American Hypnotists" McGill famously used a "window sleep" stunt to advertise his hypnosis show. To perform this, he would commandeer a shop window, have a bed placed there and at 3pm on the day of his show he would hypnotise a young woman, suggesting that she would remain comfortably asleep until show time at 8pm, at which time she would then be transported by ambulance (still asleep) to the auditorium where he would awaken her from the bed at the very start of his show, for all the crowd to see.

During this 5 hour period of hypnosis, McGill would return to the window on an hourly basis to reinforce suggestions and to allow the woman to alter her position if she'd become uncomfortable. He maintained that whenever he performed the stunt, five hours was the maximum time he would allow the subject to remain in hypnosis.

Although there are (perhaps questionable) records of longer spans having been achieved in the past, regular maintenance was almost always required to keep the subject entranced.

So no, it is impossible to get "stuck" in hypnosis.

Is hypnosis dangerous?

"Hypnosis is dangerous!" – Many hypnotists and hypnotherapists will immediately deny the credibility of this statement, but I personally agree with it entirely: Hypnosis IS dangerous.

Hypnosis is like a box of matches. In the right hands matches can provide heat for warmth, light to see in the dark, fire to cook, etc. but in the wrong hands those very same matches could cause blistering of the skin and burn down buildings.

In comparison, hypnosis in the right hands can provide cures for various conditions and ailments, it can produce wonderful, original entertainment and it allows for essential deep relaxation, etc. but in the wrong hands hypnosis could cause mental anguish, create psychological distress, worsen pre-existing physiological disorders, and I believe if *seriously* abused – think black ops military brainwashing scale – could even perhaps result in death (albeit probably indirectly.)

Now, as you can probably guess; this is not the opinion that professional hypnotherapists the world over want to hear, and it's certainly not an opinion that they would choose to voice when a potential subject asks them the question.

Yes, *obviously people want to feel that they are in safe hands*, but I'm sure they would much prefer to know the truth and have the option to *choose* to trust you as a hypnotherapist, rather than being tricked into it (I know I would.) This is why, when anyone asks me, whether at a stage show, or on the therapy couch, I will always admit that yes, hypnosis could be dangerous… in the wrong hands!

You wouldn't let a 17 year old trainee-bricklayer who read a book about cardiovascular surgery give you a double bypass operation, surely? This same guy also skim-read a book about hypnosis by the way, "hypnotherapy for idiots" I think it was… Would you feel comfortable letting this avid reader mess with your subconscious mind and all the valuable information and intricacies held therein? I know I wouldn't… But I also know he's probably a real person, out there somewhere doing exactly that… So be careful.

Do hypnotherapists have magic powers?
Find your nearest hypnotist and throw him off the top of a multi-story car park and see if he flies away*. Odds are infinity to 1 against that he won't.

(* Don't actually try that, because odds are high that it could be me ending up getting chucked off a roof)

As a hypnotist, I do not have magic powers (aside from my magical boyish good looks, obviously.) There is nothing inherently magical about hypnosis. The word magic implies that "supernatural forces" (or if you're a sceptic; "highly improbable forces") are at work, when in fact they are not. Hypnosis is definitely mystical, rather than magical.

I choose to refer to hypnosis as an esoteric art because although readily available, relatively few people actively search out the information that would allow them to become hypnotists, even though virtually anyone on the planet – especially in this age of the mighty www. – has it within their power to do so (and by power, I obviously don't mean levitating-a-teacup type power, more like the switching-on-a-computer-and-surfing-the-web kind.)

I've met a few hypnotists that like to shroud themselves in mystery, myths and "magic," and sure, if that's your bag and if it helps to pay the bills then go for it, but it's definitely not mandatory.

Maybe people will admire and revere you more if you introduce yourself as "*Jacque the Magical Mesmerizer of Mystery!*" rather than saying "Hiya, I'm Jack... Oh, and by the way, I'm a hypnotherapist," but one can quite imagine it'll be a lot easier for regular-Jack to build rapport and trust on an interpersonal level.

Does hypnosis only work on certain people?
Completely 100%... wrong. Almost anyone in the world can be hypnotised to some degree. The "depth" of the hypnotic state is variable from person to person, but the ability to be hypnotised is not.

A lot of people think that just because they didn't *actually see* something that the hypnotherapist asked them to visualise or because they didn't react well to a suggestion means that they can't be hypnotised, but this is untrue because like I said, almost everyone in the world can be hypnotised. This is a fact.

This myth of hypnosis only working for part of the population probably came about due to the proliferation of stage hypnosis shows (sorry, again.) The reason somnambulists and highly suggestible participants are chosen during stage shows is because the stage hypnotist wants to get the "inductions" and "deepening" over and done with as quickly (and with the highest success rate) as possible, so he can get onto the show itself. If time is not an issue, most (if not all) people can enter a level of hypnotic trance where fascinating "deep-state" phenomena can be demonstrated, assuming they follow instructions and do not actively resist the process.

As mentioned earlier, if a hypnotist is only using one method to hypnotise – as a fair amount of hypnotherapists do, with our old faithful "progressive relaxation" induction – the results will often be limited. Some subjects need to relax into hypnosis, others need to be shocked into it, others confused and bamboozled into it, covert conversational hypnosis is another option for those people who are adept at NLP tricks 'n' phrases, and so on. A hypnotherapist must adapt to the subject, and not the reverse, make no mistake!

"There are no poor subjects – only inflexible hypnotists." – Milton H. Erickson*

(* If you are interested in "conversational" or "covert" hypnosis, check out works by Milton H. Erickson. He was the very best in his field - period!)

Is hypnosis the same as sleep/unconsciousness?

Even though the word "sleep" is used frequently in modern hypnosis, hypnosis is definitely not sleep. Here's a little hypno-history for you:

Hypnosis started out life in the 1700's as "Animal Magnetism" alternatively known as "Mesmerism" after its creator Dr Franz Anton Mesmer. Magnetism basically consisted of passing magnetized objects over an affected area, thereby "curing" the ailment.

Benjamin Franklin was asked by the scientific community to test and validate/disprove this theory, which he did successfully by exposing a blindfolded patient to both a magnetized tree and a regular tree. The patient did indeed react, but he reacted in exactly the same way to both trees, thereby disproving magnetism and in essence validating the idea that the mind can achieve incredible feats when it comes to altering a person's physiology/psychology/overall health – even without the person's knowledge or direct intention.

This might not all seem entirely relative to the subject in hand, but now consider that many patients upon encountering Mesmer's tree automatically fell into a trance like state. This trance was not provoked or suggested in any way by Mesmer. After having initially heard of this "miracle tree," the patient formed a notion of what would happen upon touching it before he even got there, and his mind developed the idea that something spectacular and strange would occur upon contact with the tree. The subconscious minds of the patients decided not to let them down in this regard, and once one subject was seen reacting, the rest then followed suit because it had become socially acceptable to do so.

So, hundreds of people were hypnotised by a tree, and the word "sleep" was not uttered once. Is that proof enough for you that hypnosis is not sleep? If it's not, take a look at the "brainwaves" chapter for some modern scientific evidence proving once and for all that hypnosis and sleep are mutually exclusive.

I frequently hypnotise people without mentioning "sleep" or "going deeper" or "dreaming," but because these words are commonly associated with hypnosis it makes sense to utilise the belief systems of your subjects to get them into that state of hypnotic trance. If someone believes that to be hypnotised, the hypnotist must look into their eyes and suggest "you are getting sleepy..." then that's what a good hypnotist would do.

[Note: Aside from the word "sleep" itself, there is really only one actual link between hypnosis and sleep and it is this: It is entirely possible to lead a subject from a state of hypnosis into true natural sleep and vice versa from genuine sleep directly into hypnosis.]

Will a subject forget what happened during a hypnotherapy session?
It is entirely possible to suggest to a subject that "when you wake up, you will not be able to remember anything that has happened during this hypnotherapy session, no matter how hard you try." This works really well, and the subject truly won't remember the comings and goings of the session.

If, however, you *do not* apply a "post hypnotic suggestion" (i.e. a suggestion that will activate when the hypnotherapy session is finished) of amnesia, most people will have at least some hazy recollection of the experience, whereas others will remember the whole thing, almost word-for-word. Everybody reacts to/remembers their hypnotherapy experience in a slightly different way unless they are "programmed" to react in a different manner.

Is it true that only weak-minded people can be hypnotised?
"Weak-minded" is a term that is open to way too much interpretation. But to go back a couple of steps; you will recall we covered who could and could not be hypnotised... Remember? That's right, *practically everyone* can be hypnotised. Some people are just better at following suggestions than others.

Soldiers and emergency service workers for example are used to following instructions to the letter as they've been trained to do so.

Creative people such as artists, musicians, designers, fiction book readers, are more adept at using their brains to imagine and visualise situations which means they will perhaps have a more vivid experience. That is not to say a "better" experience, because all experience is entirely subjective.

Logical people, mathematicians, accountants, administrators, scientists are good at following instructions, but also are rather analytical and so question the whys and wherefores more than the creative folk, so they respond well to confusion techniques and information overload to take away that critical-thinking aspect of the hypnotherapy session. What it comes down to is:

If you are willing and you're open-minded, you can be hypnotised.

If you're not really willing to try and you are sceptical of hypnosis, you can be hypnotised.

If you don't know that you're about to be hypnotised and you don't even know of the existence of hypnosis, you can be hypnotised.

Get the point?

BRAINWAVES

As a human being, your brain is consistently producing electricity all the time. These electrical currents are referred to as "brainwaves." Now, we don't need to get into too much detail here because I'm not training you to be a neuro-scientist, but a brief overview is always helpful to know, because although you might not be thinking about brainwaves during a hypnotherapy session, you sure will be affecting them. ...I find we hypnotists are always making waves.

(I know, that was a terrible joke. I'll repent for it on my deathbed... Probably)

Anyway...

You can hook a subjects up to an Electroencephalograph (EEG) machine (if you happen to have one lying around) to monitor the electrical activity occurring in their brain. The electricity is measured in terms of frequency, and this frequency changes depending on the "conscious-state" of the subject; fully alert being high frequency, deep sleep being low frequency.

There are 4 accepted measurements of brainwave activity, they are:

Beta (14-40Hz) – Awake/Fully Conscious
Alpha (7.5-14Hz) – Light Trance/Daydreaming/Distracted
Theta (4-7.5Hz) – Deep Trance/Introspection
Delta (0.5-4Hz) – Deep Sleep/Unconsciousness

Most of the time, a hypnotised subject's brainwave pattern will fluctuate somewhere in between alpha and theta.

The delta state is arguably never achieved in hypnosis, as this is the brainwave prevalent in dreamless sleep and complete mental and physical inertia. The REM (or dreaming) cycle during sleep occurs at the Theta level.

Although the subject of brainwaves and their relation to hypnotic trance is a very interesting one; it does not necessitate in-depth study for our goals at this level of expertise, and is probably just confusing you for no good reason. Don't fret, it's not vital knowledge, so you can commit to memory or not… Let's move swiftly on.

THE CONSCIOUS AND SUBCONSCIOUS MIND

Your mind is a very interesting mechanism, and one that is entirely focussed (subconsciously at least) on the welfare of its host body; that's you. Sometimes the mind can cause us to do things that consciously we think are not in our best interests, when in fact they may actually "subconsciously" appear to be so. For example, perhaps as a child John choked on a baked bean whilst sitting in his high chair, and mummy and daddy had to come and lift him out and give him a baby-sized Heimlich manoeuvre to dislodge the pesky bean, temporarily traumatising poor little baby John in the process. This incident is obviously so far back in his life that it is a long forgotten memory… But to this day, for some reason John has an "unexplainable" phobia of baked beans, and can't even say the name of the food without experiencing phobic symptoms, let alone eat a spoonful!

The reason that this phobia persists, even though the subject cannot even remember the initial event, is that the subconscious mind learned from that experience all those years ago, and the subconscious took it upon itself to decide that to "protect" John from ever having to go through the terror of choking on a bean again that it should just make John afraid to go near beans again instead. It's sound logic, really, when you think about it… But unfortunately, although it's going to stop John from choking on a bean, it's not going to stop him from choking on all food, and is therefore probably not the best course of action for John to take.

It's the same as a child that grows up with his parents telling him something along the lines of "you are worthless," "you'll never amount to anything," "why don't you just quit, you're too stupid to do that" … the parents, in essence are hypnotising their child into believing those "suggestions" that they are giving him, through the medium of constant repetition, or a single, traumatic event/suggestion that just "sticks" into the boys subconscious mind permanently.

If these suggestions only went into the conscious part of our brain, there wouldn't be so much of an issue, seeing as the conscious mind only has the capacity to do a very small number of things at one time (research suggests most people can actively successfully remember between 4-7 things at one time,) and the conscious has next to no capacity for long-term memory. These suggestions go in and out of the conscious mind in a jiffy… Sometimes though, we consciously dwell on these negative suggestions, and work ourselves up into an emotional state, and the more we focus on the suggestions and the more emotion we associate with them, the more those possibly harmful suggestions work themselves into our subconscious minds, to trouble us at a later date.

The subconscious mind learns without thinking, without rationalising, it simply learns from experience. The subconscious is that place in your brain where you store all of your memories and everything you ever learned, it's where your knowledge of basic language and human interactions resides, it's where your innate understanding of your own physiology resides (how to breathe, things that cause you pain to touch, etc.) Your subconscious mind is basically your human "operating system." A nice metaphor to explain this would be to imagine yourself as a laptop computer, your body is the laptop itself, made up of many complex parts, all neatly designed and placed together at the laptop factory by your loving factory-worker-parents, and all of these complex parts work together in unison to run the operating system which makes the human-laptop actually function.

The conscious mind is simply what you see on the screen; it's the display. Once you've opened a program on a laptop you can consciously use it, you can play around with it, but just because you opened it once doesn't mean it's going to stay there for you to see it on the screen forever... Once you're done with it, it will go away, to wherever it is that the programs go once you've stopped consciously using them... (I wonder where that could be...) But, after you finished using the program, there's probably a log somewhere in the computer that remembers exactly what was opened, and when and how and for what purpose... This log is a memory and it has joined all of the other memories that the computer has had since it was first turned on, in the computers "subconscious."

Just like with human memories, if you know the right way to access the computers subconscious memory banks, you can find all of these memories and use them, change them or delete them. If you don't know how to do that, and you're running the computer at a completely conscious level (a standard computer user, just dealing with the programs themselves, and not the programming that lies beneath,) usually the computer will work fine anyway, but sometimes you might have inadvertently done something to the computer's "subconscious" without realising it, which could later cause unwanted effects to your "conscious" display on-screen, at which point you can either live with your glitchy programming, work around it... or call out a computer technician (or "computer hypnotherapist") to fix that part of the subconscious programming that is not meant to be there, or is no longer of use.

Get it?

SOMNAMBULISM

What is a somnambulist?
The origins of the word somnambulist can be traced back to the Latin "somnus" which means sleep (and originally was the name of the Roman equivalent of Hypnos the Greek god of sleep) and "ambulare" which is the Latin equivalent of the term "ambulate" which means to walk. Put it together and what do you get? That's right: your every day, garden variety sleep walker.

People that are prone to nocturnal activities during sleep, whether sleep walking, sleep talking, sleep accidentally-kicking-your-partner-in-the-crotch, often make brilliant hypnotic subjects. Their subconscious mind is more in-tune with their psychological and physiological responses than the rest of us, this simply means they accept and react to suggestions more easily and more intensely than most people would.

These are the people that a stage hypnotist aims to get up on stage at the start of the show, but for the purposes of hypnotherapy, the somnambulistic trance state is unnecessary (but if you do get one, don't worry, hypnotherapy works just as well with a somnambulist as it does with a nonmnambulist ... yeah, I just made up that word... doesn't quite flow off the tongue... go on, try it.)

Fun fact: It's not just humans that are somnambulistic by definition... I'm sure you've seen a dog, fast asleep, dreaming away happily and twitching his legs as if he's trying to run after a cat in his dream... That said, you probably won't succeed at hypnotising a dog, but by all means feel free to try it – and if you succeed, I'll eat my hat (or at least hypnotise you into thinking I did.)

HOW TO TELL IF SOMEONE IS HYPNOTISED

There are a variety of naturally occurring phenomena (or physiological tell-tale signs) that will let you know if a person is actually hypnotised. It's a good idea to always pay close attention to your subject's physiology, you will learn to recognise (roughly) how "deep" the subject is in trance, and you will then be able to tailor the session to work better by feeding back the subjects experience, timing the suggestions in unison with respiration, etc. (we'll go into that more a little later.)

Blank expression/relaxed facial muscles
When a person is hypnotised and left "under," their facial muscles will usually be completely relaxed and inactive, as if they are oblivious to the world around them. If their facial muscles are tense or they are smiling, frowning, etc. this can

be a sign that they didn't go into trance yet. The same goes for the person that laughs or tries hard to not laugh during hypnosis. Occasionally, though, a hypnotised subject may genuinely laugh when deep in hypnosis, so it's a judgement call, and the more you practice, the more you will learn to recognise the signs of a hypnotised subject.

If someone does start to giggle a little, you can simply say "that's right, laughing feels great and allows you to comfortably relax even more. The more you laugh, the deeper you can go into hypnosis now." Easy as pie.

Slumped posture

If a subject that you have attempted to hypnotise is sitting with arms folded and a straight back, the odds are high that they're not "under" or not "surrendering" to the hypnotic process. In this case you can have a go at re-hypnotising the subject a couple of times (the technical term is fractionation,) and manually have them relax. Or you can just keep going with your deepening methods... It's up to you – another judgement call. The ideal posture you are looking for is one of comfort and relaxation. Stiff limbs are not regularly conducive to a relaxed state (unless you cause them with direct "catalepsy" suggestions.)

Blushing

Some people blush (or pale occasionally) when they are hypnotised, but not all people, and as such this is not the most reliable way to test for a state of hypnosis in your subject, but don't be alarmed if one of your subjects looks a bit redder than normal (unless of course their airway has become blocked, then perhaps you should be alarmed) because change of skin-tone during hypnosis is a relatively common, normal occurrence.

Relaxed breathing

It might seem like an obvious one, but a lot of people forget that you can see how relaxed a person appears by monitoring the rise and fall of their chest or their inhalation/exhalation speed (whichever is easier to see, it will vary.) If your subject is breathing like they just ran a half-marathon, you might take a while to have them manually focus on their breathing, working to slow it down to a relaxing, deep tempo.

Rapid eye movement (REM)

This is pretty much the number one natural indicator that someone is deep in a state of hypnotic trance. Rapid eye movements usually happen during the sleep cycle when a subject is dreaming. As you may know, we do not dream constantly during sleep, but dreams come intermittently; the earliest dreams of the night being very short and the dreams closest to morning and awakening being the longest.

As the subject imagines these dream images, the eyes rove around "seeing" the dream, whilst the body (usually) remains paralysed to prevent injury. The same phenomenon happens during hypnotic trance when the subject is made to use his powers of imagination and visualisation.

So, if you tell your subject to "picture a meadow lined with trees, with colourful flowers everywhere and birds drifting in the sky on a warm breeze" and his eyes begin to flutter and flicker, you've got a live one, so reel him in!

SELF-HYPNOSIS

There is a school of thought that suggests "all hypnosis is self-hypnosis," and I am of the opinion that this is a correct theory. Try this quick test:

Sit down and actively relax your entire body, focus on achieving a state of deep muscular relaxation by simply relaxing all the muscles in your body from the tips of your toes to the top of your head, do this section by section and repeat the process a couple of times, until your entire body feels really heavy and relaxed. Take as long as you need 2 minutes... 5... 10 minutes, however long it takes to achieve a state of great relaxation. Once you're relaxed I'd like you to then suggest to yourself that all of that relaxation is flowing to your face and focussing around your eyelids, all of that relaxation completely relaxing all of your eyelid muscles until it's as if they no longer work at all, and they are completely stuck together, and you'll find that the more your eyelids relax, the better you feel, and the better you feel, the heavier and heavier they become. Allow yourself to believe that the muscles don't work, and that they are stuck, pretend they are, know that they are, believe that they are, because you are in control of the way that you physically react to your own thoughts. And when you try to open them, they *will be stuck*.

Once your eyelids are immovable and you have tested them, you can count from 1 to 5 to bring yourself all the way back to this level of consciousness, now, and your eyes will unstick.

Put the book down and take a moment to do this now...
(Again, if you try this test whilst trying to disprove it then obviously it won't work, so approach the test with an open mind and a firm, confident belief that it will work, and it will.)

The simple test above is one of self-hypnosis. If you try it and it doesn't work, it just means you didn't really want it to work, or that you didn't *believe* hard enough. The test is also something that a hypnotherapist can use to test susceptibility in subjects, and even to induce a state of hypnosis... The fact is; hypnotherapists are selling self-hypnosis to the masses.

Someone that wants to stop smoking is completely able to achieve this on their own using self-hypnosis. A daily session of meditation interspersed with correctly framed positive affirmations to "allow yourself to see smoking being left behind, to know you are strong, to feel that you have strong will power, to let nothing stand in the way of your health," would have an effect on the subject that is very similar to hypnotherapy. It's just that most people *don't know* that they can do this or even how to go about it. It's not something that is taught in school, and most people wouldn't even know to research it, so we can't blame them really. But *we* know that people have the ability to achieve those things that they desire, to change habits, realise dreams and conquer fears. We're simply here to give them a gentle, relaxing push in the right direction.

If you are looking to help yourself overcome an obstacle by using true hypnosis (rather than simple meditation and affirmations – which is what "self-hypnosis" basically amounts to if you do the whole process in your head) you will be able to simply use the information given later on in the book to create a self-hypnosis session which you will either be able to run through in your head (if you have a good memory,) or, the way that I usually do it for *myself*; record yourself reading out your entire self-hypnosis "script," then lay back and play back the recording.

Using yourself as a "Guinea Pig" is a great way to get to know what works best for you (as a hypnotist, and as a subject,) *and* you can work on any issues that you might want to resolve at the same time. Win/win! So give it a shot. These days most phones have a sound recorder built in, so you have no excuse to not try it. There's nothing to fear, because as you know:

All hypnosis is self-hypnosis, so you are in control.

I personally began my hypnotic journey wanting to be a hypnotherapist, and I started by recording myself, just like you should, by recording and listening to basic hypnosis inductions, seeing what worked, improving, re-listening, re-improving... Once I nailed that, I began to make hypnotherapy recordings for myself to stop smoking, build confidence, and even to pass my driving test without being nervous (I failed the first time, nearly crashed into a Volvo due to nerves)... And guess what? They all worked! So practice on yourself – it's the easiest way to get started and to improve your technique and confidence (not to mention improving your life in the process.)

It's beneficial when performing self-hypnosis that you do it at least once per day (I suggest either when you wake up or just before bed,) because repetition of these positive suggestions will help your subconscious to successfully integrate the information much better than just doing it as a "one off." I have included a section on self-hypnosis at the end of the book, as it is a useful tool to teach to your subjects – it will also improve your success-rates.

HEALTH, SAFETY & LEGISLATION

BEING IN CONTROL (OF THE PERSON/SITUATION)

Prepare your workspace
Wherever you are going to be performing your hypnotherapy sessions, it's best to have some control over the environment. You do not particularly want to be interrupted halfway through the session by a family member bursting into the room, a loud telephone going off or a pet cat jumping onto your subject's hypnotised face (these things happen.)

I always ensure that before starting a session at a subject's home, all phones are turned off/unplugged at the wall and anybody else in the house is informed that they should not interrupt the session for any reason. If there are pets, have them put into another room/outside, if possible. Basically, you are trying to cut down the possibility of anything that might interrupt the session – and although you can't guard against every eventuality, these tips form a strong starting point.

If you are planning to have your own therapy room, it's obviously nice to have it arranged pleasantly so when people come in to see you, your room gives a professional impression. Clean, tidy, nice smelling and not too hot/cold are some of the main considerations. It's nice to have a comfortable hypnosis-chair for your subjects too (it's not necessary, but obviously comfort begets relaxation – so make 'em comfortable.) Anything other than those things just mentioned are not necessary, but I'll mention a couple of other things that are nice to think about.

I know some hypnotherapists who always make blankets available for subjects in case they are cold in the room, or to cover up the legs of any female subjects wearing short skirts if they should desire it. Some therapists like to have their certificates and credentials displayed on the walls of their room and this is a good way to "instil faith" in your subject, as you will appear more professional if you have some pretty certificates with your name on them (but in reality, that's about all they're useful for...we'll cover that a little later.)

I love to walk into a hypnotherapists room and find a display of hypnosis/hypnotherapy books – again, it furnishes your appearance as an educated therapist (and if you've actually read them, then that probably helps too you know) and also it gives your subjects the opportunity to have a little flick through the books too, which will probably help to build up their expectation of what's to come...

A music playing device, whether a stereo, computer or mp3 player with a portable speaker – some hypnotherapists are huge fans of using relaxation music in the background during their hypnotherapy sessions, you can find a great many instrumental tracks that are perfectly suited to meditation and hypnosis, it's up to you if you want to use music or not – I don't bother, personally. Maybe the music helps people to relax, maybe it doesn't... It's all down to each individual's subjective experience and your own preference.

All of that said, you don't need to be in your own therapy room to do hypnotherapy. You don't need to be in someone's home to do hypnotherapy. Hypnotherapy is a skill that at the most basic level only requires two things; thing 1 is the hypnotherapist. Thing 2 is the subject. You can be in the middle of a busy street, sitting up the pub, travelling on a plane... It doesn't matter as long as *you* are there, because you have everything you need to do hypnotherapy. It's all up there in your head (or it will be, by the end of the book.)

Vigilance
Unexpected things can happen during a hypnotherapy session, the number one of which being "abreactions" (which we will cover in detail later.) I implore you to always stay vigilant and *watch* your subject. If you're not paying attention to the subject, they could be having a seizure, having an abreaction, falling off their chair... Anything can happen, so you must always keep watch. This is also why I dislike the idea of experienced hypnotherapists who read their entire hypnotherapy session from scripts (when you're just starting out, it's forgivable – don't worry) but if you've got your nose in a script, how are you supposed to watch your subject *and* read a script at the same time? Unless you're a chameleon and have your eyes on stalks, you can't, to put it bluntly. I'll talk more about scripts later, but for now: keep your eyes peeled, and on your hypnotic subject!

Assert confidence with non-participants (general public)
Not very often, but occasionally you might have to deal with friends or family of the subject or even members of the public, interrupting a session and being inappropriate (trying to wake up the subject, or testing if they're "faking it,") you must put your foot down straight away. Tell them to stop and to step back, because they don't know what they're doing and that they could do a lot of damage without even realising it. If that fails and your antagonist didn't get the gist, another route is to use a metaphor. Suggest if they were watching their friend getting surgery under anaesthetic, maybe they would they try to wake him up or make a few incisions themselves? There's equal opportunity to cause damage in hypnosis, even if it is not so overtly apparent.

That said, in a therapy-setting, you shouldn't experience too many instances of this happening, but it's best to be prepared for any eventuality. Just remember, you're in charge of this person when they're "under" so ensure that they are safe and that you are in control of the situation.

Self-confidence/Believe in your abilities
Confidence and self-belief should become very important to you as a hypnotist. You wouldn't feel comfortable if your dentist had to refer to notes during a check-up to make sure she was doing the right thing, the same applies with hypnotherapists. You need to know what you're doing, and more importantly you need to always *appear* to be confident in your abilities (even if, on the inside, you might be terrified – which isn't unheard of, especially when you're just starting out as a hypnotherapist.)

If you *are* inexperienced, the need for an image of self-confidence is doubly important from a subject's perspective. If the subject sensed that you didn't believe in your abilities as a hypnotherapist, then you're going to be fighting a losing battle. Luckily for you, other people can't tell real confidence from fake confidence, so like I tell all of my new students, if you don't have the confidence yet: Fake it 'til you make it! Seriously. No one but you will know the difference, and if you fake this feeling of confidence, eventually it *will* be replaced with the real thing...permanently.

Sounds easy, right? That's because it is.

WHO/WHEN TO NOT HYPNOTISE

Drug & alcohol abusers
If you can tell that a prospective subject is high/drunk then do not touch them with a barge pole. Drugs and alcohol cause people to do some very strange things, so you can never quite predict how they would react to/during hypnosis.

Example:
You have a woman who has come to your practice because she wants you to cure her alcoholism. The problem is, she's drunk right now... Let's say you let it slide this once because you need the money to pay for some glitzy new shoes you just bought on EBay. You're about half way through the session, and though you believe you are "in tune" with the subject, you are still oblivious to the fact that in her head for the past 5 minutes this inebriated subject has been feeling like the room was spinning and spinning. This results in nausea, and before you know it, she's lurched forwards and thrown up all over herself, all over your hypnosis-

chair and your brand new shag-pile carpet (which you will now have to get professionally cleaned/incinerated – depending on what she'd eaten that day.)

Is it worth it? No. Don't do it. If there's any sign of intoxication, ask the subject to come back when they're in a clearer frame of mind, for their own safety and wellbeing.

Epileptic/Fit-prone
Fits and seizures can be triggered by emotional situations and an individuals' response to said emotive trigger. Now, as far as I can remember, hypnotists take great pride in being able to elicit highly emotional reactions at the click of a finger... I take it you can see where I'm going with this. I don't think we even need an example for this one, it's pretty self-explanatory. I would suggest that you always ask about this, and always politely refuse the possibly fit-prone. That is my preference.

Pregnant women
Hypnosis has *no* adverse effects on pregnant women, in fact many women give birth whilst in hypnotic trance as it helps them to control and alleviate a great deal of pain, so obviously when performed in a safe, controlled environment hypnosis is entirely beneficial for pregnant women. We're not worried about the effects of hypnosis itself in this case, but I like to add pregnant women to this section just to ensure that if you *do* hypnotise a pregnant woman, that you take utmost care to have her seated/lying down where there is 0% chance that she could fall or in any other way injure herself.

Common sense is an important hypnotherapist's tool.

Injured parties
Example:
You have a subject who wants to give up smoking, and you decide to hypnotise him using a "handshake interrupt" induction (which involves physically manipulating his arm/hand.) You grab the guy's wrist with a regular-moderate grip. Now, the part where you give him the command to go into hypnosis is replaced with the sound of; "argggghhhh" emanating forcefully from his mouth – unfortunately, you didn't know that *this subject is recovering from a sprained wrist that he sustained 2 days ago whilst playing football.* If you plan to use a physical induction, always ask about injuries/ailments.

If someone has a minor niggling pain/old injury, it's down to your discretion to choose whether to use a rapid or progressive induction. Whichever you choose, remember what and where their problem is and ensure you don't do anything to aggravate it. If someone has an outright broken limb or any other more serious condition, obviously do not hypnotise them using any physical methods.

Psychological instability
A similar situation here to the alcohol/drugs situation. Never hypnotise anyone with serious mental disorders; schizophrenia, manic depression, psychosis, etc. Always ask. If you suspect that someone might not be "all there," it is your right and your duty as a hypnotherapist to decide to not hypnotise him. Yes, he might be offended if you suggest that you don't think he's "in the correct frame of mind" to have a positive hypnotic experience, but at the end of the day, you have to look out for yourself and you have to respect your subjects. Treating a subject when you know that there is a chance you could end up damaging them even more is not respectful.

Respect given is respect earned, if you are respectful you will earn a great reputation, if you are not, the opposite will surely happen and your career as a hypnotherapist will be a short and volatile one.

Look in the mirror…
Would YOU want to be hypnotised by some drunk guy? I highly doubt it. Some of us enjoy an alcoholic beverage, others like to have a drink to calm the nerves – that's just fine, but not whilst you're working! If you have a heavy drinking session on a Friday night, ensure that you don't have any clients booked in for the next morning. Turning up dishevelled and hung-over to a hypnotherapy session is unacceptable – don't do it.

If you like to go out drinking with your friends and someone asks you to perform a hypnosis demonstration, it's down to your discretion. I suggest that if you've had more than a couple of drinks (i.e. 2,) don't do it.

I have been out in a bar, and I ended up chatting with a friend about hypnosis for a while. Then, all of the sudden he shouted out to the whole bar:

> "This guy can hypnotise anyone, come and let him hypnotise you"

Now obviously he had the best intentions (and just wanted to see some hypnosis,) but I'd been drinking steadily for most of the afternoon/ evening, so I had to turn away half a bar-full of hypnosis requests. Some of the people were literally begging me to hypnotise them!

(I hope you want to be popular, because we hypnotists always seem to be the centre of attention...)

It was hard to refuse these requests (simply because I was brimming with alcohol-fuelled confidence and I wanted to entertain) but when you're not in full control of yourself – even though you may drunkenly think you are, you're probably not – you should straight up instantly and honestly refuse. Anyway, nothing's stopping you from giving out your business card and coming back to meet them next week to give them a professional, sober demo!

Similarly if you are seeing a subject to help him to stop smoking, it's probably best if you don't wander in stinking of smoke yourself... Makes sense, right?

Finally, personal hygiene is a must. If you're running your own hypnotherapy business you are your own best (or worst!!!) advertisement. So if you maintain a professional, clean, friendly appearance, it can only help. Would you want to go see a therapist if they were wearing a dirty, sweaty t-shirt, had filthy, soiled fingernails and spoke to you breathing garlic-breath from the pasta they had at lunch time? I wouldn't...

Remember: It's up to you to cultivate and maintain a professional image (at all times, if possible.)

ETHICS/RESPONSIBILITY

Hypnotherapy is not a light-hearted career choice. To paraphrase some famous movie quote or other; "with power comes great responsibility." By the time you finish reading this book, you will have the "power" of hypnotherapy (it's a skill, not a power.) You will be able to go out an actually affect a positive change in people's behaviour and subconscious processing. I would say that *definitely* comes with a great responsibility.

- You are responsible for the safety of your subjects.
- You are responsible for acting appropriately with your subjects whilst hypnotised or otherwise.
- You are responsible for striving for excellence in your own hypnotherapy practice, and not just settling for the bare minimum.
- You will be the face of hypnosis to your subjects, so you are responsible for ensuring that you give them a positive experience with hypnosis for the benefit of yourself, and hypnotherapists everywhere.

You have to look at hypnotherapy from a customer service point of view, because hypnotherapy wouldn't exist if there were no customers that needed fixing. I'm not saying "the customer is always right" but what I am saying is *you must always treat the customer right*.

Got it? Good. Now let's move on to the exciting stuff...

LEGALITIES, INSURANCES & MEMBERSHIPS

Haha, fooled you! I bet you thought we were getting to the hypnosis part! (Almost there, don't worry. Just a couple more important bits to cover first.) With regards to professional body memberships, certification and accreditation: In the UK, anybody is (legally) free to set up as a Hypnotherapist *without any formal training/certification whatsoever*. Crazy, but true.

At the time of printing, there are no regulations or laws stipulating that you *must* complete any type of hypnotherapy training before setting up your own practice. Likewise, there are no regulations or laws stating that you *must* hold hypnotherapist insurance. That said, if you *are* considering hypnotherapy as a career choice, I would wholeheartedly advise that you *do* enrol on a comprehensive hypnotherapy course (NLP too, for good measure.) I also advise that you *do* get hypnotherapist insurance, for these reasons:

1 – People want to hire professionals. Professionals have top-credentials and insurance. Fact.

2 – You want to protect yourself from any possible legal issues that might arise. This society is growing ever more litigious, having no insurance is just tempting fate. Fact.

3 – The more you learn, and the more techniques you have at your disposal, and the more practice you get, the better a therapist you are going to be. Fact.

4 – Yes these things *can* be expensive, but think of them as investments. They will eventually bring in more business than you'd get if you didn't have them. Fact.

There are a great variety of different organisations that provide accredited hypnotherapy qualifications. Whether it's a council of professionals, international society or general register, none of these "professional bodies" are technically regulated or legally enforced by the (UK) government. They are there of their own right and under their own regulation to ensure "good, professional practice" and as a label of "excellence" so that hypnotherapy clients can "know" that the hypnotist is well-trained, knowledgeable and professional.

Please excuse the over-use of sarcastic quotation marks in the previous paragraph, but I feel their usage was entirely valid because due to the fact that our profession is not externally/legally regulated, it could be very easy for these organisations to suggest that their members are "good, well-trained professionals" without ever having to actually validate those claims!

So take your pick. In reality, it doesn't really matter which body/organisation you belong to, or even if you belong to one at all – the thing that matters is that you get the *correct training*, and enough of it. I am personally registered with the National Guild of Hypnotists (NGH), that said, I practiced successfully as a hypnotherapist without these qualifications for years. I used hypnotherapy and NLP techniques that I learned from reading books on the subject, and as such I told people that I was a qualified hypnotherapist and NLP practitioner...because you can, there's no law to state that you can't do that...

When you train on a good course, however, you often get to learn a lot of stuff that you just can't get from reading books. Imagine if you didn't know how to ride a bike, and you read the "Bike Riding for Beginners" book... Do you think you could automatically get on the bike and ride off into the distance? Odds are...no. Doing a hypnotherapy course is therefore a great idea, assuming your trainer actually knows what he's talking about. There are a lot of people out there "teaching" hypnotherapy courses who have only read a book on the subject themselves... Some of these charlatans don't even do hypnosis as a job!!! Buyer beware!

Do *a lot* of research before you spend money on a course, because some of these courses can cost up to £4,000 (and more in some cases). Don't waste your money joining a course if the instructor is not credible. It'd be like the blind leading the blind... If, after finishing this book, you intend to train to a professional level, I personally provide comprehensive, bespoke hypnotherapy training (including international accreditation with the NGH). For more information and course dates visit the **Hypnotherapy Training Company** website: *www.HypnoTC.com*

With regards to hypnotherapy insurance in the UK, there are various providers and I won't name them here, because it is up to you to find the best policy for yourself by doing research. At time of writing, a 12 month hypnotherapy insurance policy will set you back around £45-80 and this will cover you for public liability as well as psychological damage claims – Don't worry, you don't frequently hear of hypnotherapists needing to claim on their insurance, but it's better to have it and not need it, right?

In the USA and other countries, there are different laws, often on a state-by-state basis and I'm not going to go into them here, so if you are looking to practice hypnotherapy in another country I would first suggest that you contact the local council/government office for information on current laws, legislation and insurance requirements. For example, if you are in Norway, I believe you have to be a qualified psychologist to perform hypnosis and if you are not, you run the risk of a large fine or even a prison sentence! Always check beforehand!

PERMISSION/DOCUMENTATION

Get permission from ALL subjects

Many hypnotherapists use a standard disclaimer/contract of services for every client treated. This is a document that sets forth a brief description of your services, costs and other client-specific information. The document can also include a waiver, i.e. "by signing this, you agree to undertake this hypnotherapy session entirely at your own risk" etc. (I would advise against this last part, because it gives the suggestion that something *could* go wrong, which not-so-subtly suggests that you don't know what you're doing as a hypnotherapist – also, if you have insurance, why would you need a disclaimer? Duh.)

Also, you can use this form (or a separate one) to gather client-specific information (which is very useful to have during a session, and in reference for future sessions, rather than having to ask all of the questions over again – you often find that you get repeat-clients who come back for more than one issue, so this can be a real time-saver.)

I have provided an example of a basic disclaimer/contract of services form and also a list of information that might be worth including on a data-collection form at the very end of the book. You can copy these verbatim and use them for yourself, or you can simply use the information presented as a template upon which to base your own individual "client pack."

Keep documentation until long after the session

You never know when an ugly little woodworm is going to crawl out of the woodwork to try and cause you much unwanted trouble, so I personally advise that you keep all of your contract of service and data gathering forms (and any other records – video, audio, photo, whatever you choose to use) for at least 4 years (if not indefinitely.) If nothing untoward has come up in 4 years, the chances are very slim that it ever will, but as with most things in life; you can never quite guarantee that it won't happen!

I still personally have the documents and videos from my very first hypnosis shows and hypnotherapy sessions, and I will probably keep them stashed away until I pop my clogs (then they can sue me all they want, because it probably won't bother me quite as much by that point.)

It doesn't cost very much at all to buy a cheap external hard drive, this is the medium I personally use for storage of my hypnosis media. Obviously with signed contracts, you have to keep the paper copies, but for a while all you'll need is an a4 folder. When you get to the stage where the folder isn't big enough, I'm sure you'll be able to afford a stylish filing cabinet for your swanky new office!
If you're more technologically minded, I know some hypnotherapists who have an app on their IPad that allows them to access their client forms/contracts where they can then type in the information and even have the client provide a signature on-screen, they then save it on the device itself in a special client-information folder. Neat, huh?

Anyway, the point I'm making is: There are lots of ways to do it, but just ensure that you do keep your info backed up to cover your own back, friend!

HOW TO HYPNOTISE

HOW TO HYPNOTISE – INDUCTIONS

OK, *now* we're onto the "good stuff," how to actually get your subject into a real hypnotic trance state...

What is an "induction?"
A hypnotic induction is any method/technique used by a hypnotist to elicit a state of trance in a subject. There are a great many different hypnotic inductions available for you to practice and develop, some involve simply speaking to the subject, some involve having a back-and-forth conversation with the subject, some involve having the subject perform some physical act (looking at a light, tensing muscles,) some even involve manually moving the subject (shaking hands...)

In the following pages, I'm going to define and break down four of the top hypnotic inductions used by most hypnotherapists in practice today. If you only ever learn these inductions, you would probably never need to know any more inductions to run a successful hypnotherapy practice. That said, there are literally hundreds (maybe thousands) more inductions available to you to use – my personal opinion is that you should never limit yourself, especially when there's so much more information out there to be learned and utilised successfully.

The first three of these methods are the ones that I personally used to use in my hypnotherapy sessions – and they work really well, tried and tested by myself and hundreds of thousands of hypnotherapists all over the world. The reason I say I "used to use" them is because these days I prefer to do things faster, so I use "rapid inductions" (the type of hypnosis techniques used in stage hypnosis shows – Yes, it's possible to use these in hypnotherapy session too!) The rapid induction hypnosis techniques use completely different methods than the more progressive processes that you are about to learn, but I have also included one rapid induction technique (the handshake induction) so you can get an idea of just how quickly you can put someone into hypnosis.

[Note: If you are interested in learning the fastest ways to put people into hypnosis – and I highly recommend doing so – you should pick up a copy of my other book: "The Instant Hypnosis and Rapid Inductions Guidebook" and for more in-depth rapid induction training check out the "Hypnosis 101 – How to Hypnotise Fast" DVD. But for now, let's just work on these four inductions as a base upon which you can build your hypnosis skills...]

At the end of each section, I have included a sample script. This "script" is an example of a word-for-word account of what I would personally say/do when performing these inductions (I say "example" because my hypnosis sessions are never exactly the same... Once you get good, and you're doing hypnosis naturally and unscripted you'll find that the words just flow from you, and generally they will follow a pattern, but only loosely.)

Scripts are a great tool to use when you're starting out so that you can get a feel of the sort of thing you should be aiming for, but as I mentioned before; if you're reading from a script, your attention isn't going to be focussed on the subject, is it? So, as you might have realised already, using scripts is not the way I work (anymore,) and you will find that most of the best hypnotherapists in the world will never use scripts.

I'm not telling you that you *can't* go on and continue to use scripts, a lot of hypnotherapists (those that weren't trained by myself or my peers) do use scripts but they are very limiting. For that reason I always suggest that if *you can do it without a script*, then always do. As soon as you start practicing script-less, you will find you start to remember the techniques a lot quicker, you will find a "flow" to your words, and you will generally just become a better hypnotherapist with every session that you complete. That said, some people have trouble remembering exactly what it is that they should be doing, especially as a beginner, you might find yourself floundering a little. But don't worry, it happens to the best of us (even me,) and for that exact reason, after the sample scripts I have also included a quick-reference section which includes "bullet point" prompts. That way, you can learn the induction and deepening techniques separately and use/combine them as you wish, just referring to your prompts if you find that you can't quite remember what you should be doing.

Simple!

PROGRESSIVE RELAXATION INDUCTION

What does it consist of?
You have the subject make himself comfortable, sitting or lying down, and have him close his eyes. This is the point where hypnotherapists begin to speak to the subject, giving suggestions, causing the subject to use his imagination and utilising hypnotic-deepening techniques...

E.g. "You can focus on your breathing, allowing it to slow, and allow a warm feeling of relaxation to begin permeating the body from your feet all the way to the top of your head. Always relaxing deeper and deeper. Every breath taking you deeper into perfect relaxation..."

That is the extremely-super-short version. That brief paragraph would usually elicit a state of relaxation, continue repeating and compounding similar relaxing suggestion after suggestion and you will achieve hypnosis. I've seen progressive relaxation scripts that are almost a hundred pages long, but it's not necessary. As long as you have a few basic deepening tools, then you're set. With this method, you do not need to follow a "structure," so long as you're continuously talking to the subject, having him use his imagination, feeding back and compounding suggestions, he will go into hypnosis.

How does it work?
This is the type of induction that almost all hypnotherapists the world over are using right now. The reasons for this are many:

This induction is easy to perform (in its most basic form, all you would have to do is read from a script – but, like I said; I don't recommend it!)

You don't need hyper-confidence to perform this induction because the subject is going to be relaxing with their eyes closed, no one is there to judge you and you're literally just talking someone into a state of relaxation.

You don't have to physically touch the subject as you do with rapid inductions (this in itself makes some hypnotherapists nervous.)

You can lead into this induction in a "covert" conversational way to gradually lull the subject into trance unawares – if you want to...

You have a lot of time to think about what you are saying and how you are saying it, really allowing your suggestions to bloom and flow.

This induction is used frequently by those hypnotherapists who are unenthusiastic about actually "testing their work" (i.e. testing to see if the person is actually in hypnosis.) This isn't the best way of working, however, so I always suggest that you test your work. As such, I have structured your script to include a section for testing that the state of hypnosis has been achieved, because it's just a good idea to do so (and always a nice confidence booster for you, the hypnotherapist, as well.)

Oh, and we can't forget that the number one reason this induction is used; because it works *really* well! The PR method is one of the oldest induction methods on record and should be at least known, if not practiced by all hypnotists (not just hypnotherapists – I know a great many stage hypnotists who use PR inductions during their shows too.)

Sample script
"OK, I'd like you to just make yourself comfortable now... And now close your eyes and allow yourself to relax... Now I'd like you to take a full, deep breath in, and hold it. Hold it, and when you can hold it no more, let it out and relax...

That's great. And take another even deeper breath in now and hold it. And let it out when you are ready to relax now... That's right, now I'd like you to just listen to the sound of my voice as you go on relaxing...

Focus only on the sound of my voice and allow your body to relax... And of course you might be aware of other sounds, too... Sounds inside the building, sounds from outside... But you can allow these sounds to just become background noise, because in fact they are going to help to relax you, because the only sound you need to think about is the sound of my voice... And while you're listening to the sound of my voice you can just simply allow yourself to be as relaxed and comfortable as you could ever want to be relaxed now.... Just allow yourself to be as relaxed as you could ever want to be... Now... You can move to make yourself comfortable any time you like, and this will help you to just relax, becoming more comfortable now... As you can drift deeper into this wonderful state of trance and tranquillity.

Good... Now, while you're relaxing there, you can just be aware of your body... Aware of your hands where they rest... Perhaps noticing the angle of your elbows and maybe one of your hands feels warmer than the other... And I don't know which hand is relaxing you more, but you know that comfortable warmth might seem to just gently increase now as you can allow yourself to relax more and more deeply...

I'd like you to focus your attention on your feet now, and relax all of the muscles in your feet, from your heels to the tips of your toes. And allow that feeling of relaxation to move up now, over your ankles, calves and all the way up to your knees. Everything below your knees now, completely relaxed.

And as you feel this warm heavy relaxation slowly moving up from your knees, to your thighs you can think about your breathing for a few moments... Noticing that your breathing is becoming slower and steadier as you relax more and more... Slower and steadier... Breathing so steadily and evenly... Just as though you were getting ready to go to sleep... Breathing so comfortably, so steadily so deeply...

And the warm, comfortable relaxation is moving up now, up from your thighs to your hips, relaxing, relaxing further as it travels up to your stomach and further, through your chest... Relaxing all of your insides, your heart, your lungs, this wonderful, peaceful, warm relaxation spreading completely throughout your entire body. Moving up to your shoulders now, and then down your arms, a waterfall of relaxation washing all the way down your arms... Past your elbows, relaxing all the muscles along the way, relaxing your forearms, and your wrists, and you might even feel a warm tingly feeling in your fingers as this wonderful wave of relaxation reaches them.

This heavy, warm relaxation is now moving up to your neck and throat, up to your chin and to your mouth, relaxing every muscle as you can just let go now and allow all of your muscles to relax completely with every slow, deep breath that you exhale... Allowing any stresses and strains to simply melt away as you are awash with this complete, wonderful, all-encompassing relaxation.

This warm, peaceful relaxation is moving up now, over your nose and to your eyes, relaxing all of those little muscles around your eyes... Your eyes relaxing, relaxing, relaxing as this wave of relaxation now washes over the top of your head and all the way down your back and through every fibre of your body and being... This relaxation feels wonderful, absolutely amazing, and you know, you are not even half as relaxed yet as you will soon be even more deeply relaxed... So as you focus on my voice now you can clear your mind, and we will travel down even deeper into this relaxing world of trance and hypnosis.

I'd like you to focus your attention on your feet once again, and relax them... Now relax your ankles and relax your calves, relax them completely... Everything below your knees, completely relaxed. Loose, light and easy... And as you feel this wonderful relaxation moving up from your knees, to your thighs, relaxing every muscle 10 times more than before, you can allow your mind to wander and to wonder and to dream, but always it will be aware of my voice and the wonderful relaxation, as you keep drifting deeper and deeper still with every breath...

And this warm, comfortable relaxation is moving up now, up from your thighs to your hips, relaxing, relaxing, deeper and deeper as it travels up to your stomach and further, through your chest, this wonderful, peaceful, warm relaxation spreading completely throughout your body... Moving up to your shoulders now, and then all the way down to the very tips of your fingers. This heavy, warm relaxation is now moving up to your neck and throat, up to your chin and to your mouth, relaxing every muscle... You can just let go and allow all of your muscles to relax completely. So relaxed now... Smooth and loose, so deep now, drifting, dreaming, deeper and deeper.

The warm, peaceful relaxation is moving up now, over your nose and to your eyes, relaxing all of those little muscles around your eyes, relaxing deeper... I'd like you to imagine now what your eyes would feel like if they were 100 times heavier, so heavy it's almost as though they are glued together. Imagine it's as if your eyelids are like one piece of skin... Completely immovable. And in a moment when I count from 1 to 3 I'd like you to try and fail to open your eyes, the more you try the harder they stick. 1, 2, 3 try now, sticking tighter and tighter. And now relax those eyes and go on relaxing, drifting and dreaming.

[Note: They shouldn't, but if the eyes open at this point, tell them;

"That's right... now close your eyes and go deeper. Now open your eyes, and close them and relax even deeper... And one more time open those eyes, and close them now and drift and dream down into a wonderful state of relaxation."

This will ensure that the subject who opens his eyes doesn't feel like they've done anything wrong, and continue to relax deeper into a state of trance. Then continue:]

Deeper, deeper as this wave of relaxation now washes over the top of your head and all the way down your back and down to the tips of your toes and through every fibre of your body and being. This relaxation feels wonderful, absolutely amazing, and you know, you can even go deeper still, but for now what I would like you to do is to use your imagination...

Whether you have a vivid, multicolour imagination, or whether your imagination is just thoughts, it doesn't matter, because you have the power to use your imagination to imagine anything that you desire as you go on relaxing now.

In a moment I am going to start to count backwards from 300, and with every number that I say, I'd like you to imagine that number in a colour, and then erase it and imagine the next number in a different colour, and so on... And every number that you imagine and erase will take you 10 times deeper into this wonderful state of relaxation and hypnosis.

Count with me now, as you relax. 300 – Imagine the 300 in a colour... And erase it, now choose a different colour for 299... And erase it, 298... Deeper, 297... Deeper and as you continue counting now on your own, you can allow yourself to relax more, and more as you keep counting down now, 295, deeper, 294, deeper, and your breathing becomes slower as you are relaxing more and more, deeper... That's great, and you can allow the numbers to gradually fade away now. Let numbers and counting go, let everything go until there is nothing left but the sound of my voice, and the complete feeling of wonderful relaxation, washing throughout your entire body."

[Note: At this point, the subject should be in a state of trance. You can deepen more if you wish, or just continue with your therapeutic-change suggestions.]

Quick reference prompts

- **Close eyes**
- **Deep breaths**
- **Focus on my voice**
- **Body awareness**
- **Progressive relaxation feet to head**
- **Breathing deepener**
- **Repetition (repeat progressive relaxation)**
- **Eye-lock test**
- **Visualisation & Counting deepener (from 300)**
- **(deepen further & therapy suggestions)**

As I mentioned before, all of these deepening methods are interchangeable. You can add/switch/omit different deepeners, but when it comes down to it, this progressive relaxation induction is literally just a whole bunch of deepeners, crammed together and delivered one after the other, repeating, deepening, repeating, deepening. Easy as pie – and that's how to create a state of hypnosis!

GAZE FIXATION INDUCTION

What does it consist of?
The difference between this induction and the previous one is simply the way that it starts (to be honest, the main bulk of any induction is actually the "deepening" section, which is a lot more comprehensive and variable.)

Rather than having the subject lie down and close their eyes, you start with them sitting with their eyes open. You have them visually focus their attention on a point on the ceiling, on a light or on a cloud (depending on where you are) and you keep their attention focused until you notice/feel that their eyes are becoming tired. Then lead the subject into eye closure and deepening, similar to the PR induction.

How does it work?
With this induction, you are basically pacing and leading the subject by causing their eyes to become physically tired (which will naturally happen due to the strain of extended staring – especially when they're looking upwards or at a

light.) You feed this information back to them and have them remain in this strenuous position until they are more than ready to close those eyes and comply with your ongoing suggestions.

A handy tip with this induction is that having the subject *look upwards with their eyes* rather than with their whole head will ensure that their eyes get more "tired" a lot quicker than they would if they just tilted their head back to look up.

Sample script
"OK, I'd like you to relax your entire body completely now and with your head remaining in that comfortable position, just using your eyes, look up at the light/pick a point high up on the ceiling, and focus your gaze there. Try not to blink, just try and hold your gaze in that one position, and notice your eyes beginning to get tired. This tiredness comes on very quickly, but try hard to not close your eyes now, try and fail to keep those eyes open now as they are getting heavier and heavier, it would be such a relief to allow those eyes to relax, but you must wait, and keep focussing on that one point and only that one point as those eyes are becoming heavier and heavier. In a moment you can close your eyes, and just when those eyelids touch, you can allow your entire body to relax down into a deep state of trance. Close your eyes and sleep now, sleep down, let that head just drop forwards just as much as you need to go down even deeper into this wonderful hypnosis... As you drift down, deeper, drifting and dreaming into this wonderful state of trance, you can allow that strong feeling of relaxation around your eye muscles to drift all throughout your body, relaxing every muscle and nerve. Deeper and deeper..."

[...and continue with deepening until you feel they are "deep enough" to receive your therapeutic-change suggestions.]

Quick reference prompts

- **Relax your entire body**
- **Keep the head facing forwards**
- **Focus on a point high on the ceiling/light**
- **Try not to blink**
- **Try to keep those eyes open**
- **Repeat suggestions of heaviness & wanting to relax the eyes**
- **Suggest that when the eyes close, you will go into trance**
- **Close the eyes**
- **(Deepen further & therapy suggestions)**

TENSION/RELAXATION INDUCTION

What does it consist of?
Much like the PR induction (are you seeing a pattern yet?) this induction consists of having the subject relax every part of their body, section by section. With this induction, however, we are introducing a physical "convincer" alongside the relaxation suggestions.

Instead of simply saying "relax everything below your waist" (as we did in the PR induction,) we tell the subject; "tense up all of those muscles below your waist, squeeze your thighs, your knees, tense your calves and ankles tight, tighter, tighter, and *now* relax and release the tension and allow a wonderful feeling of relaxation to just flow through all of those muscles."

How does it work?
This induction works in a similar manner to the PR induction, except I maintain that it works quicker, and allows the subject to experience a real, physiological sensation of relaxation which leads into deeper trance. It's faster due to the fact that you are "feeding back" physiological reactions that they can internally verify and this convinces them that they *are* relaxing down into a trance state.

[Note: The subject will be holding his breath whilst tensing the muscles – don't make him hold his breath for too long! Remember, we're aiming for comfort and relaxation, not bursting blood vessels!]

Sample script
As you sit there with your eyes closed, I'd like you to take a deep, relaxing breath in and hold it... And release that tension and breathe out just whenever you're ready. Now, you're going to experience the difference between tension and relaxation. I'd like you to take a deep breath in, and tense all of your leg muscles, feet, calves, knees and thighs, so tense, so tight. And now breathe out and relax all of those muscles completely. Relaxing, breathing deeply and relaxing even more now...

OK, now take another deep breath in... and completely tense your stomach and your chest... Feel that tightness, tension... And now release it and relax...

Take a deep breath in now and hold it... And let it out... Comfortable... Drifting... Relaxing...

Now I'd like you to focus your attention on your arms and shoulders, breathe in and squeeze all of those hand, arm and shoulder muscles. Hardness, tension, tightness... And now let out that breath and find that feeling just melting away into peaceful tranquillity and relaxation.

I'd like you to take a deep breathe in now and scrunch up your facial muscles and tense your neck, feel the tension around your lips, eyes and nose, and now breathe out and feel a great wave of relaxation flow from the top of your head, all the way down your body, all the way down, deeper and deeper, deeply relaxed, allowing your breathing to slow, and become more regular, more repetitive, each breath taking you deeper still into this wonderful world of hypnosis and relaxation...

[...and continue with deepening until you feel they are "deep enough" to receive your therapeutic-change suggestions.]

Quick reference prompts

- **Close eyes**
- **Deep breath and tense legs – and release**
- **Deep breath and tense stomach/chest – and release**
- **Deep breath and release**
- **Deep breath and tense arms/shoulders – and release**
- **Deep breath and tense neck/face – and release**
- **(Deepen further & therapy suggestions)**

If you would like, you can take more or less time over each specific section:

Instead of tensing the legs as a whole, you could tense the feet, *then* the calves, *then* the thighs, *then* the hips...

Conversely, you could simply tense everything below the hips and then tense everything above the hips. It all depends on how much time you are allowing for the session, and how you feel most comfortable.

These inductions will all work best if you do them in a way that resonates with you, personally. A good hypnotist is a comfortable, confident hypnotist.

HANDSHAKE INTERRUPT (INSTANT) INDUCTION

What does it consist of?
This is a completely different style of induction than the previous 3 (I thought I would include a rapid induction, to whet your appetite, and so that you have something super-fast to add to your hypnotic-toolbox.)

To perform this induction, you make like you're going to shake the subject's hand, but just before your hands lock together in a handshake, you interrupt the handshake by grabbing their wrist, move the hand in front of their face, and command them to go into trance.

Sounds simple enough, but this induction takes a bit of confidence to execute, and a bunch of practice to get the mechanics right, but it's well worth it... Especially seeing as it can cut your session time down by way more than 50%!!! (Because remember...your time is valuable!)

How does it work?
In NLP terms, a handshake induction classifies as a "subconscious pattern interrupt" – don't panic, I'll unpack that phrase for you:

A handshake is a "subconscious pattern" that virtually everyone is trained from birth to respond to. Think about it; if someone goes to shake your hand, you don't consciously think about how/if you should respond, right? Instead your hand will usually automatically extend to reciprocate the gesture. Our brains have been wired to think this way by personal experience, the idea of "good manners" and social correctness.

When someone interrupts this inbuilt subconscious pattern, the mind falters, and trips over itself for a split second. During this split second it is looking for the answer to its own question; "what just happened?" and it *will* find the answer if left to its own devices, but when a hypnotist fills this split-second moment of confusion with the command to "sleep" or to "look," the subject will usually comply instantly and without question. Neat huh?

This induction can and has been (extensively) performed "cold," i.e. with no pre-talk, and *even* with the subjects having no idea that they are about to be hypnotised. It is one of the most successful "ambush" hypnosis techniques out there, and one that I frequently use during stage hypnosis shows *and in hypnotherapy sessions*. I'm sure you may have seen the video of Derren Brown accosting a random guy in the street and "convincing him" almost instantly to give him his wallet and phone – Well *this* is an integral part of that very same technique, and as such should be treated with a great deal of respect and care!
[Note: This is one of the slower rapid inductions, there are also variations on this exact induction that are a lot faster too, but we're not covering those in this book. Check out the back of the book for more information on my rapid-induction training products.]

~~Sample script~~ Walkthrough guide

Set the scene either by introducing yourself, or saying "are you ready to get hypnotised? OK, let's shake on it..." then proffer your *right* hand for them to shake. As they are coming in for the shake, bring up your left hand (quickly and sneakily so that they aren't expecting it) and catch hold of their right wrist. Quickly bring their hand up until it is right in front of their face (don't hit them with it, leave a few inches space.) Point at the centre of their palm with the index finger of your right hand (which should already be pretty close to their hand at this point) and say "Look!" and then gently remove your right hand, and they should remain in the same position, transfixed (this "fixation" will only last temporarily, i.e. a second or two, so don't hesitate too long before moving on to the next part.) This part of the process should take 2 seconds at most.

Still holding their wrist with your left hand, gently move their hand backwards and forwards whilst saying "notice the change in focus of your eyes" (which they will, as the hand is moving to and fro in front of their eyes.) Then suggest they "take a deep breath in." At this point you take a deep breath in yourself (leading) whilst lifting their hand up just above the top of their face. Once they've taken a breath in, you then bring their hand down past their face and let it drop down completely whilst suggesting "breathe out, close your eyes and sleep now."

...and then continue with deepening until you feel they are "deep enough" to receive your therapeutic-change suggestions.

Quick reference prompts

- **Go to shake hand**
- **Take wrist with your left hand, bring to face**
- **"Look!" – point to centre of hand**
- **Move hand – eye defocus**
- **"Deep breath in" lift hand**
- **"and breathe out, close your eyes" lower hand**
- **"and Sleep" command**
- **(Deepen further & therapy suggestions)**

HOW TO HYPNOTISE – WAKING PROCEDURES

I believe that before attempting to deepen the subject or fix any problems, you should first know how to end the hypnotic trance completely. This progression, skipping from the start (inductions) to the end (waking procedures) and *then* returning to the middle sections (deepening, phenomena and therapy suggestions) is on purpose and for your own safety, so my apologies for "saving the good stuff 'til last," but you'll thank me when you're older and wiser.

Please read on...

What is a waking procedure?

A waking procedure is any act or succession of events that causes a hypnotic subject to safely and completely emerge from the hypnotic state, with all hypnotic suggestions removed. Now, at the end of a session you could just say "OK, eyes open, wide awake" to the subject, and who's to say that they aren't going to be fully awake, alert and back to full awareness thereafter? Well...me, that's who!

When I hypnotise people on stage, I can command "eyes open, wide awake" and still have the subject demonstrating hypnotic phenomena, even with their eyes open – so from my personal experience, just saying something like this does not properly terminate the state of hypnosis.

Another reason that doing a "full wake up" is a good idea is because coming out of the hypnotic trance gently/slowly will feel a lot nicer for the subject and it will also give you time to remove any unwanted suggestions that you might have included in the session (whether on purpose or inadvertently.)

Removing unwanted suggestions

Obviously it is just fine to leave your therapy/change-work suggestions active – if you didn't, it would kind of defy the point of performing the hypnotherapy session in the first place, right? – It is *not* fine, however, to leave an active suggestion like "any time you hear the word 'sleep' you will immediately go back into this trance state." You can see how this type of suggestion would cause problems in the day-to-day life of the subject, I assume...

Post-hypnotic suggestions (suggestions that remain active after the conclusion of a therapy session) are completely fine, just ensure that you are only leaving positive-therapy suggestions in their head, and no active-triggers or other rubbish. Clean up after yourself... A good chef doesn't leave a dirty kitchen behind after making a delicious meal, just the same as a good hypnotherapist always clears out any unnecessary suggestions after making a positive change. That's important, take note!

If you have included anything in a session that you wish to remove, you can simply give a direct suggestion to the subject stating that "it will no longer have any effect and is completely removed." Simple as that (the tricky part, initially, is actually remembering to do it!)

If you're not sure whether you left something in there by accident, you can suggest to the subject that "any suggestions that you've received today that do not need to remain active and any suggestions that are in no way related to *their issue* will no longer have any effect and can be completely removed."

[Note: Hopefully you'll be present enough whilst performing your hypnotherapy sessions that you will remember everything that you "suggest" to the subject, so you technically shouldn't need to use that second suggestion. But I include it as a preventative measure, and so that you are aware that if you've done something a little wrong, you don't need to panic!]

Counting

When you bring a person out of hypnosis at the end of the session, you are going to "count them out" of the state. You must always count upwards i.e. from 1 up to 5. This is the *opposite* of "deepening counting" which you will learn about in the "deepening" section (strangely enough.)

Counting "upwards" suggests moving higher (becoming more alert and more awake) as opposed to lower (deeper asleep,) and as such your subject's subconscious mind will make the distinction that the intended result is not to go deeper, but to arise, come up and awaken.

When you awaken your subject by counting, you should begin speaking 1, in your slow "hypnotist voice" (assuming you have one,) then gradually begin 2, to speak faster 3, AND LOUDER with every number 4, you count, verbally energising the subject until 5, they're wide awake and feeling wonderful!!!

You can count from 1-3, 1-5, 1-10, whatever you like, it doesn't matter, so long as the subject knows what to expect, and they also must know how they are expected to react. If you just jump in to counting without explaining your intention, the subject won't react at all, so you have to tell your subject something like:

"In a moment I'm going to count from 1 to 5, and when I count the number 5, you will awaken, feeling completely relaxed and refreshed, feeling wonderful."

Positive reinforcements

Bring your hypnotic subjects back to "reality" feeling on top of the world. There are many ways you can create this feeling of wellbeing (aside from simply fixing their problem, obviously.) Before the "count up" I like to suggest that upon awakening the subject will feel like they've just had a really relaxing full body massage, just woken up from the best nap they ever had, are full of vital energy and feeling comfortable, confident, active and ready to go out and grab life by the horns... (Perhaps omit that last metaphor if you are fixing a case of "Taurophobia" ...if you can't work it out, Google it!)

Anyway, the opportunities to make your subjects feel great are restricted only by your imagination. Some hypnotists use positive imagery during the waking process, i.e. "take a nice deep breath, all the way to the bottom of your lungs of that fresh, revitalising ocean air. Feel the refreshing sea breeze blowing through your hair and clothes making you feel just wonderful."

If there is something relaxing, refreshing and revitalising you imagine would work well in your wake up script then stick it in! I'm sure your subjects would enjoy it immeasurably. Positively reinforcing these feelings is a great idea, but you can (and should) positively reinforce all of your therapy-suggestions too:

"And when you awaken, every single suggestion that you have received during this session will have travelled deep into your subconscious mind, where it will continue to make positive changes in your life every day. And whenever you go to sleep and whenever you dream, all of these suggestions will strengthen, again and again and again. Every time you sleep, doubling and reinforcing. Every time you dream, strengthening and helping you to be the best you that you know you are going to be healthy, happy and feeling wonderful...now."

(Whoops, I got a little carried away with the ambiguous embedded command at the end... It's a neat little phrase though – feel free to ~~steal~~ use it!)

Program for future sessions
This is the *only* non-therapeutic post-hypnotic suggestion that I personally like to include (sometimes – depending on my mood) during *my* hypnotherapy wake up patter:

"The next time you are hypnotised by me, be it tomorrow, next year or even in ten years, you will subconsciously remember the exact, wonderful feeling of this state of trance that you are in right now, and then you will be able to instantly fall back into this deep hypnosis, deeper than you are even now. You will find the more times you are hypnotised, the better you are at being hypnotised and the better it makes you feel and the easier these positive changes can happen now." This suggestion is very useful if you ever encounter the subject again, and completely harmless and inactive if you don't.

So those are all of the basic wake up techniques that you'll need, I've put them all together in a "sample script" for you to use/modify/learn – again, only until you are comfortable rattling off the words (or similar ones) without a script!

Sample wake up script

"In a moment I'm going to count from 1 to 5, and when I count the number 5, you will awaken, feeling completely relaxed and refreshed, feeling wonderful. When I count the number 5, you will feel like you've just had a really relaxing full body massage, just woken up from the most wonderfully relaxing nap you ever had, you're full of vital energy and feeling comfortable, confident, active and ready to go out and grab life by the horns…

And when you awaken, every single suggestion that you have received during this session will have travelled deep into your subconscious mind, where it will continue to make positive changes in your life every day. And whenever you go to sleep and whenever you dream, all of these suggestions will strengthen, again and again and again. Every time you sleep, doubling and reinforcing. Every time you dream, strengthening and helping you to be the best you that you know you are going to be healthy, happy and feeling wonderful…now.

The next time you are hypnotised by me, be it tomorrow, next year or even in ten years, you will subconsciously remember the exact, wonderful feeling of this state of trance that you are in right now, and then you will be able to instantly fall back into this deep hypnosis, deeper than you are even now. You will find the more times you are hypnotised, the better you are at being hypnotised and the better it makes you feel and the easier these positive changes can happen now.

[Also, know now that whenever you hear the word 'sleep' it will no longer have any effect on you, and the suggestion to go into trance when you hear that word is completely removed now.]

1, coming up slowly now. 2, start to become aware of your body once again. 3, find that you can move your fingers, hands, arms. 4, take a nice deep breath in, and 5, eyes open, wide awake, alert, refreshed and feeling great!"

[Note: Like I mentioned before; change it up. If a certain word/phrase doesn't fit the way that you talk then say it differently. These are just guidelines, a base upon which you need to build your own hypnotherapy techniques.]

HOW TO HYPNOTISE – STATE DEEPENERS

What is a deepener?
Once you've induced the subject into a state of hypnotic trance, it can be a good idea to "deepen the state" of trance. Ensuring that the subject "goes deep" into trance will a) help to ensure that your therapy suggestions are more easily accepted and b) will leave the subject feeling very relaxed at the end of the session – and we all love to feel relaxed, right?

By using the progressive relaxation inductions you will become proficient at deepening – simply because those inductions are practically just deepeners stacked on top of more deepeners. You do not, however, have to use deepeners if you feel you can achieve the same results without (for instance, when I am performing rapid inductions I do not follow them with long verbal deepeners – simply because it's not necessary.) It will become something that you are able to judge, but for the start I would suggest that you definitely get a lot of practice with all aspects of hypnosis, deepening especially.

There are various ways of deepening a trance state, some of them are verbal and others non-verbal – once again, it is a matter of your own personal preference.

Counting
Counting is a widely used trance-deepening tool. When deepening a hypnotic state, always remember to count *down* i.e. 10 to 1 rather than upwards. During a progressive relaxation induction, I will count down numerous times, and from various different numbers. The more time you have available, the deeper a state you can achieve (to a certain point – also, for most therapy we are not looking to produce "deep state" hypnosis because it's simply not required – with the possible exceptions of anaesthesia and regression.)

Having your subject visually imagine the numbers appearing and disappearing whilst you count is another tool used to occupy the conscious mind whilst deepening a state of trance. Actively picturing numbers in your "mind's eye" is a better deepener than just listening to the hypnotist counting down, this is because when you combine counting and imagery both the right and left hemispheres of the brain are being utilised. Counting engages the logical (or left) brain whereas visualising or creating engages the creative (or right) part of the brain. Combine the two and what you have is a great method of occupying the conscious mind, and that's what you want. You can step it up a notch more and have the subject imagine the numbers appearing in different colours too (I like to do this) for example:

"As I count down, I'd like you to imagine each number in a different colour, and after each number you can erase it and go deeper… 300… imagine the 300 in any colour you like, and now erase it and go deeper… and in a different colour 299… and erase it…." Etc.

You can add any spin on this that you can think of, for example:

"Imagine that you are sitting comfortably in the sand on the beach of your mind, we are going to count backwards from 100 as you inhale now, you draw the number 100 in the sand, and as you exhale now, the ocean waves wash that number away and you go deeper, 99... and exhale and let the number wash away as you relax deeper, 98..."

Occasionally (and subtly) missing a number out whilst counting down during long sequences of numbers is a good way to confuse your subject:

"8, getting more and more relaxed, 7, focus on slowing down your breathing now as you go deeper into this state of hypnosis, 5, deeper with every breath..."

Sometimes the subjects will already be so deep by this point that they won't even realise you missed a number out, but it's still a nifty confusion trick to throw into your deepening patter occasionally. The effect works best (as with the above example) if you talk a little in between numbers. If you just count "8, 7, 5, 4..." it still works to some extent, but because the numbers are not spaced out, it's easier to pick up on the fact that you purposefully missed one, rather than in the first example where they would probably think "did he say 6? I don't quite remember if he said 6... Wow, this stuff really must be working."

As you can see, we're not just counting, there are many subtle techniques that you can use to make this simple premise into a very effective deepening tool. Read on for some counting scripts, but always remember that you are free to adapt them to yourself or you can completely ignore them and try something new that works better for you!

Sample script – Counting #1 "Blackboard"
"As you focus on the sound of my voice, I'd like you to imagine you have a blackboard in front of you and in a moment I am going to count down from 300 and I'd like you to imagine writing out each number on the blackboard with a coloured chalk. Every number that you imagine will take you 10 times deeper into this wonderful state, relaxing deeper now. And I'd like you to draw each number in a different coloured chalk. So pick a colour for 300, write it... and erase it now and go deeper. Now pick a different colour for 299... and you can relax as you wipe it away... 298 and erase it, let it all go, drifting and dreaming down into a wonderful deep state of trance now as you drift and as you dream, 296... and erase it and go deeper.

Now I'd like you to continue to count down silently in your head, drawing each number as you continue to listen to the sound of my voice. And sometimes you will forget which number you got down to, if that happens just go back to the last number you remember and continue counting and erasing and going deeper and counting and erasing and drifting down deeper into this pleasant state of hypnosis now."

Sample script – Counting #2 "Repetition & Ambiguity"
"In a moment I'm going to count down from 10 to 1, with each number that I count, you can allow yourself to drift even deeper into this wonderful state of hypnosis now. With each number that I say, I'd like you to repeat it silently to yourself, and relax even more with every repetition as I count each number down from 10... going deeper now... 9... deeper with each number... 8... even deeper now... drifting, floating, dreaming, deeper and deeper as you allow every part of yourself to just be relaxed now... 6... feeling wonderfully relaxed and alive... 5... so deep and dreamy, perhaps more relaxed than you have ever been be-4... and allow your mind to be 3... as you drift and as you breathe and as you relax allow yourself 2... 1-der (wonder) just how much more relaxed you can go deeper now into this state of trance and forget about numbers now... and forget about counting now, as you continue drifting deeper and listening to the sound of my voice relaxing your mind even more..."

Sample script – Counting #3 "Counting clouds"
"As you drift and as you dream, I'd like you to imagine each of your thoughts as a cloud, passing across the sky of your mind. These clouds can be big or small, and you might find that you can change the shape of these clouds now just by thinking about it... In a moment I'm going to ask you to begin to count with me silently from 5 down to 1, with each number I'd like you to imagine a cloud in the shape of that number... And then we'll erase it and the cloud can float away and disappear and you can go deeper with every number that just disappears.

5 imagine that big fluffy 5 shaped cloud now... drifting, dreamily floating across the sky of your mind... and now allow it to disappear as it's replaced by a feeling of wonderful relaxation. 4... notice the shape of that number cloud, floating, relaxing, bobbing in the comfortable breeze as it just fades away now and go deeper. 3... find that it's harder to hold on to these numbers and they're just fading away now as you go deeper into this wonderful state of trance. 2... and it's already starting to disappear now as you drift and dream and float and breathe. 1... all the way down, all the way deep, relaxing deeper and deeper as you can forget about numbers, and just enjoy this wonderful feeling of relaxing now."

Breathing
When you take long, deep breaths, this naturally increases the amount of oxygen in your system and can often cause a slight physiological change in your state resulting in physical relaxation (I won't go into the scientific reasoning behind it because you don't need to know it – you just need to know that it works; because it does.) Obviously anything that noticeably changes the basic waking-state into a more relaxed one will benefit your hypnotic procedure, so encourage deep, long breaths.

You can time your suggestions with the rise and fall of your subject's breathing for added effectiveness. When working with a single subject for instance, if you were to say something such as; "and you can relax deeper and deeper every time you exhale, now" I would personally aim to be saying; "exhale, now" when they are actually exhaling. This timing of suggestions will make your deepener much more effective. These "timed suggestions" do not have to be descriptive of their breathing, you can give any suggestion at all, just know that when a subject is exhaling they are naturally more relaxed. As such, this is a great time to deliver your suggestions in a subtly different manner (i.e. a different pace/tone of voice/etc. – check out the "analogical marking" section for more on that)

If you are using a breathing deepener technique with a large group of people, you must remember that different people have different respiratory rates. Some breathe long and deep, others shallow and rapidly, so don't be too specific about when exactly to breathe in and out whilst group-deepening, because you don't want anyone feeling uncomfortable by having to match an unnatural breathing pattern.

Focussing attention on breathing whilst relaxing the muscles of the body is a universal deepener, i.e. it will work with anyone, because I've yet to meet a person that doesn't regularly need to breathe. This is a useful thing to remember if you ever forget your "script" halfway through – If you do get lost at any point, you are free to bring the subjects focus back to his breathing, describing each breath and feeding it back into a deepening sense of relaxation. This is a basic example of an NLP technique; pacing and leading. You are "pacing" the subjects breathing rate and depth whilst at the same time "leading" them into a state of deeper relaxation. So don't worry if you get "stuck"... Just breathe!

Sample script – Breathing #1 "Tension/Relaxation"
"I'd like you to focus on your breathing, and allow your body to relax as you can begin to breathe more deeply now. These calming breaths relaxing your mind, right from the centre and spreading further with every exhalation. Relaxing more and more with every slow, deep breath. Inhaling fresh cool relaxation as you breathe in, and exhaling warm air to allow all your tensions to melt away... Now... Allow your entire body and mind to relax now, deeper and deeper with every breath that you exhale... Breathing in relaxation... Exhaling any other feelings and thoughts that you no longer need to even try to relax now, as you just drift even deeper with each honest, unconscious breath that you breathe deeply and slowly as you relax all the way down now."

Sample script – Breathing #2 "Internal awareness"
"As you become aware of your breathing now, you might find yourself wondering exactly where those deep, slow, relaxing breaths go in your body to relax you

more and more. As that oxygen enters your body, filling your lungs with that wonderful, relaxing life giving power... Feel it now, with every breath. Notice where it goes and notice as you notice that, you can relax more and more with each breath that you inhale... And exhale...

Try and follow that breath inside, notice where it goes... Down your throat... Into the centre of your chest... And then notice where it goes, because everybody relaxes in a different way, and everybody breathes deeply in a way that helps them to relax as deeply as their body can just let go and relax now. And you'll find that any time you want to relax even more, you can just focus on where your breath is going... Inside... Deeper and deeper relaxing with every inhale... And deeper with every exhale... And that feels just fine as you continue drifting and focusing on the sound of my voice taking you deeper into this wonderful state of hypnosis now."

Sample script – Breathing #3 "Sinking breath"
"Take a deep breath in for me now and hold it... In a moment you can exhale and allow every muscle in your body to relax. Exhale now, allowing every muscle to sink and relax and allowing your entire body to just become loose, limp and easy. Completely at ease... At peace.

I'd like you to take another, even deeper breath in now – all the way to the bottom of your lungs and hold it. Hold it... Keep holding it... And now let it out and let it go... Let it all go... Your entire body filled with relaxation... A wonderful comfortable feeling... An uncontrollable, amazing feeling of complete and total relaxation... And perhaps you've never been so relaxed, but your body knows how to relax even deeper than this... And you can take another long, deep breath in now... Hold it in... Allowing that oxygen to fill your lungs... Allowing that feeling to build... And now you can exhale and relax your entire body completely, relaxing your entire mind completely, relaxing your entire being completely relaxed now."

Scene Visualisation
Visualising an imaginary scene or environment is another method of distracting and relaxing the conscious mind to allow you to talk to the subconscious. You essentially hold the conscious mind at ransom by telling it something like; "imagine a beautiful beach, the beach of your dreams" or "imagine walking through a wonderful forest, each step deeper into the woods takes you a step deeper into this wonderful state of hypnosis" and whilst the subject is busy in imagination-land, you are able to suggest the development of their trance state by combining relaxation with positive imagery and hypnotic suggestions.

Using visualisations whilst deepening a subject is also useful, because it prepares the subject to use their imagination. This eases them into the process of actively imagining situations and objects, which is going to be a useful tool later on when you're working on "fixing them."

You will find that some subjects have trouble actually visualising anything at all, and that's OK – it's a good idea to intersperse your "scenes" with language that isn't solely focused on the visual aspect, but also include kinaesthetic (touch) and auditory (sound) also. These are the three most prevalent representational systems that people utilise whilst creating their internal world – For more information about representational systems, you'll need to delve into the world of NLP and aim your focus on REPS systems and VAKOG (I recommend it.)

You are also able to use these imaginary scenes to create metaphors for change work – but we shall cover this later on in the book. For now, as you are aware, we are only focussing on deepening the hypnotic trance.

Sample script – Scene visualisation #1 "Forest of Tranquillity"
"As you relax now, I'd like you to imagine yourself standing at the edge of a wonderful forest at the top of a path. This path very gradually slopes down through the centre of this forest of peace and tranquillity. I'd like you to imagine now just what it would feel like to begin to walk slowly down this path... Each step allowing you to relax more and more as you move peacefully into this beautiful forest. Perhaps there are leaves and twigs crackling underfoot... If there is a breeze, would it be cool or perhaps slightly warm as you continue walking safely and contentedly into this wonderful woodland paradise...

As you notice that your breathing has already slowed, you can continue to notice your surroundings... And notice what you notice, see what you see, hear what you hear and feel whatever it is that you can feel relaxed now as you drift through this tranquil forest of your mind, every moment becoming more and more relaxed. A wonderful, content, safe feeling is in the air of this forest, and with every sweet, natural breath that you inhale, you can feel good now... You can relax now...

And as you continue down this path into the deep relaxation of the forest, you will begin to approach a bridge, and under that bridge is a peaceful meandering stream or river... As you find yourself at the bridge now, completely comfortable and relaxed... Watch the water peacefully flowing down deeper into the forest... And just as that water flows down into the forest, you drift deeper down into wonderful relaxation with every breath...

And as you continue to walk now into the forest, perhaps the path remains alongside the water, gently drifting as you walk through this wonderful place, deeper and deeper into this beautiful trance with every step now..."

Sample script – Scene visualisation #2 "The Beach"
"I would like you to imagine now the most perfect, wonderful beach you can imagine, the beach of your dreams. And I'd like you to get a sense of that beach now... Perhaps the sand is coarse and golden... Maybe it's soft and fine and almost white... Maybe there's no sand at all... This is your beach and I'd like you to imagine yourself resting on the beach there now... Completely comfortable... Looking out at the ocean, every wave that laps at the shore allowing your mind to drift and dream... Every breath of refreshing sea air that you...inhale... takes you deeper into this wonderful state of relaxation now.

Perhaps there are clouds or maybe there are none... Perhaps the sun feels warm on your skin... Comfortably warm, shining its life-giving warmth down upon the wonderful beach of your mind, now... So relaxing to be here... So comfortable, this beach... Take a look around and notice what you notice, see what you see, hear what you hear and feel what you feel completely relaxed now... Perhaps there are other people relaxing like you on the beach or maybe this beach is just for you to enjoy relaxing here now... Maybe there are animals around your beach, maybe there are plants and trees, or maybe there aren't... And maybe, as you continue to relax and drift and dream, you can realise that you can go to this beach just whenever you wish to relax, and unwind... Completely content in the knowledge that this beach is a special place that's right for you to relax... And dream now..."

Sample script – Scene visualisation #3 "Stairs to bed"
"I'd like you to imagine that you are standing at the top of a staircase... And at the bottom of the staircase there is a large door... In a moment I'm going to count down from 10 to 1, and with each number I'd like you to imagine taking a step closer towards that door...and with every step you can allow your entire body to relax 10 times more than you are, even now, relaxing deeper.

10, take that first step down and relax now... 9 notice the walls and notice the material that each step is made from as you continue drifting down, 8 and relaxing... I wonder what type of building these stairs are in as you relax and step down to 7 now and find that you relax deeper with each step down to 6 now... Remembering to breathe deeply, remembering to relax completely, 5, and all the way down to step 4... Feeling so wonderfully content, peaceful and deeply relaxed as you step down to 3... Enjoying that feeling... Really feeling that feeling of relaxation double... Down to 2... And finally that last step down that brings you to the door... 1...

I'd like you to open that door now and walk into the most magnificent bedroom you've ever seen... The lighting is just perfect... The temperature is just right for you... In fact everything in this room is designed for you to feel absolutely comfortable and at peace, with the most wonderful part being the bed... The most comfortable bed ever imagined... Find yourself moving towards that bed now, knowing that as soon as your head hits the pillow, you can relax 100 times deeper than ever before... And as you lie on that bed now, just enjoy that feeling as you drift deeper... Enjoy that wonderful relaxation moving throughout your entire body... Comfortable, content and peacefully relaxed now, as you continue to enjoy these wonderful feelings... You can continue to focus on the sound of my voice as you drift, and as you dream, and as you relax now."

Tense and relax / Progressive muscle relaxation
Just the same as in the tension/relaxation induction, you can include this method as a deepener with any induction. Have the subject tense different sections of their bodies, and then release all tension. This heightens physical/muscular relaxation and also requires a strong focus of conscious attention.

As I mentioned; you can spend lots of time on individual parts of the body, relaxing your way up in sections if you like, or just split it into upper and lower body, which is quick, easy and effective. Also, you can even have the subject scrunch up their facial muscles to relax this area fully too.

Remember, there's no such thing as too relaxed...

Sample script – Tense and relax #1 "Upper/Lower body split"
"I'd like you to take a deep breath in now, and release it. This time when you take a nice deep breath in again now, I'd like you to tighten all the muscles in your legs, calves, thighs, hips, waist and stomach. Hold it, and now breathe out and release all of that tension. Let it all go...deeper. And take another deep breath...and let it out and relax even more. Now I'd like you to make your hands into fists, and take a deep breath in, squeeze the fists tight, all the way up through the arms, shoulders chest and your back. Tightness, tension... And breathe out now and let it all go as you drift down into perfect relaxation..."

Sample script – Tense and relax #2 "Full detail"
"I'd like you to take a deep, relaxing breath in and hold it... And release that tension and breathe out just whenever you're ready. Now, you're going to experience the difference between tension and relaxation. I'd like you to take a deep breath in, and tense all of your leg muscles, feet, calves, knees and thighs, so tense, so tight. And now breathe out and relax all of those muscles completely. Relaxing, breathing deeply and relaxing even more now...

OK, now take another deep breath in... and completely tense your stomach and your chest... Feel that tightness, tension... And now release it and relax...

Take a deep breath in now and hold it... And let it out... Comfortable... Drifting... Relaxing...

Now I'd like you to focus your attention on your arms and shoulders, breathe in and squeeze all of those hand, arm and shoulder muscles. Hardness, tension, tightness... And now let out that breath and find that feeling just melting away into peaceful tranquillity and relaxation.

I'd like you to take a deep breathe in now and scrunch up your facial muscles and tense your neck, feel the tension around your lips, eyes and nose, and now breathe out and feel a great wave of relaxation flow from the top of your head, all the way down your body, all the way down, deeper and deeper, deeply relaxed, allowing your breathing to slow, and become more regular, more repetitive, each breath taking you deeper still into this wonderful world of hypnosis and relaxation..."

Deepening levels
Deepening "levels" are a construct. There are no *actual* levels here, you are just using an imaginary tool to make the subject believe they are going deeper – and it works just great! Here are a couple of examples that I use:

Sample script – Deepening levels #1 "3 to 1"
"I'm now going to take you through 3 progressively deeper levels of relaxation. You are already on level 3, and from level 3 we will go down to level 2, and from level 2 we will go deeper all the way to the deepest level of relaxation; level 1. When you reach level 1, you will be more relaxed than ever before. More relaxed, maybe, than you even knew you could be... But you can relax even more now, even deeper now as you allow your muscles to just relax completely... and you are now on level 2...

Now, you can count silently backwards with me from 10 to 1 and with every number that you say, you can go deeper and deeper still, and when we reach 1 you will be on level 1. 10, 9, 8 deeper, 7, 6, deeper still, 5, 4, 3, 2, 1.

You are now on level 1 and still going deeper with every breath that you breathe in... And out... That's right. And as you can focus on your breathing now, you can allow my voice to just wash over and through you... Relaxing you with every word I say, with every syllable that I speak, taking you deeper and deeper into perfect relaxation."

Sample script – Deepening levels #2 "Elevator"
"I'd like you to imagine now that you're stepping into an elevator of relaxation. Now this perfectly safe, comfortable elevator is currently at the tenth floor… Floor ten is the floor of mild relaxation… We're going to ride the elevator all the way down to the ground floor, the floor of the deepest, most profound relaxation… With every floor that the elevator passes, you can allow yourself to drift 5 times deeper into this wonderful state of relaxation.

I'd like you to press the button for the ground floor now, and notice the elevator slowly begin to move down… As we pass each floor, that floor number on the panel will blink out… notice as we pass floor 9 that the 9 button blinks out now and you can relax deeper… Now 8… Deeper still that wonderful comfortable, safe feeling, relaxing you more and more with every breath. 7… Further and further down to 6… Relaxing more and more… 5… So relaxed… Noticing your entire body relaxing completely. 4… Breathing and comfortably relaxing more. 3… Almost there now. 2… That's right, all the way down. 1… And now slowly coming to a stop on that wonderful, relaxing ground floor. You can step out into a wonderful room of relaxation now, and completely forget about the elevator… Allowing the numbers and the floors to drift away… Allowing everything to drift away now as you focus on the sound of my voice… Deeper and deeper with each breath."

Confusion and obfuscation
If you've been paying attention up until this point, you should have already firmly established that confusion is a great method of inducing hypnosis (and deepening too.) Here are a couple more random confusion techniques that don't quite warrant having their own sections, but are still wonderfully useful techniques…

Random finger clicks are an auditory confusion technique. Click your fingers by the subjects left ear, and then by their right shoulder, and then behind their head at differing intervals, at different volumes and in whichever locations you desire. Confuse, deepen, confuse and deepen.

Hand passes in front of the subjects closed eyes cause discreet shadows (i.e. they will see the back of their eyelids become darker when your hand passes by, and then lighter again once it is removed.) You can make "fluttery" motions with your fingers – pass the hands fast, slowly, repeatedly, up and down, side to side. So long as you are creating shadows, this technique will enhance the confusion that the subject is experiencing.

Strange vocal phrasing of suggestions is a fun one to do if you don't mind sounding like a bit of an idiot (obviously – as I'm sure you might have realised – I don't mind that.) Throw in pauses in odd places, change your inflections on words that do not require it. Speak faster or slower or both (at the same time, if you want...) louder, quieter, etc. Any changes in your voice will work, assuming your voice is still recognisable as your own, and so long as you continue to enunciate your words correctly so that your subject can actually understand what you're saying.

You can use a confusing visualisation exercise to deepen the state. If the subject is in a mental-muddle, they are all the more likely to accept any suggestions you throw their way.

Sample script – Confusion deepener
"Imagine a table, and on that table sits a clock. The hands on the clock are spinning backwards quickly, and with every rotation of the hands of the clock you go deeper into hypnosis. Now, with every second that passes, the clock gets smaller and smaller, and the more you relax the smaller it gets, and the smaller it gets, the more you can relax... And as you relax now the clock is becoming so small that you can barely see it at all anymore, and now the clock is starting to completely disappear... But notice that with every relaxing breath you exhale the scene fades away and you can forget about the clock now as you go on relaxing deeper and deeper."

This paragraph – as you can see - was absolutely meaningless and would leave the subject wondering why the hypnotist was talking about a clock. At the same time, however, the relaxation would be equally as prevalent as the confusion so although it appears pointless, it's actually very effective.

Kinaesthetic deepeners
There are numerous "kinaesthetic" or physical methods to deepen the hypnotic state. Here are a couple of the most obvious ones:

"Each time I touch your shoulder, you can go deeper..." Tap their shoulders gently with a finger in different places a couple of times.

Tell the subject that you're just going to pick up their arm by the wrist. Pick it up, move the arm so they're holding it out in front of them, and then say something like; "OK, that arm can just balance there now, all by its self" – gradually let go, and the arm should stay there. Then suggest; "That arm is starting to get heavy, and just as quickly or slowly as is right for you to relax, that arm is going to start drifting down, and when your hand touches your leg, you will feel a massive wave of relaxation from your head down to your toes, and you can go ten times deeper into hypnosis just as soon as that arm touches your leg..."

Sometimes the arm will drop too quickly for you to be able to fit all of those words in, so you'll have to improvise. If the thought of improvising scares you, then put this book down and go and buy a $9.99 hypnosis script for every subject that you intend to work with.

(Still reading? Well done. Improvisation can be a bit scary at first, but keep doing it and you're going to keep getting better and better.)

With the previous "floating arm" deepener, you can add a level of confusion by asking if the subject is left or right handed (have them indicate which by moving a finger on the hand or something.) This is an often used stage hypnosis confusion technique to "decide" which limb the hypnotist is going to work with. Using either limb will work, but by asking this, you are making them wonder what the difference is between their hands and why one would work better than the other in this setting, but we know it's all a load of rubbish and we're just – to quote my dear late grandfather – "playing silly buggers."

"I will tap the top of your head, when I do, you can feel relaxation course through your entire body from top to bottom..." Tap their head gently with your finger, simple!

A good one to use immediately after a handshake induction is the shoulder-rocking deepener. Simply put your palm on their shoulder, holding it lightly, and very *gently* sway the subject left and right whilst suggesting; "with every sway left and right, you are drifting deeper and deeper into hypnosis." Be careful to perform this rocking motion *gently,* because with the eyes closed the sensations that the subject will experience are greatly heightened. If you rock them a little it feels like a lot and if you rock them a lot, it feels like a bloody earthquake. Gentle is fine!

Fractionation (Re-Induction)
Each and every single time you "wake up" a subject and re-induce hypnosis, the level of trance deepens and the subject becomes more malleable (great word.) This isn't something that most hypnotherapists consider doing, but I highly recommend it, because it will help you to improve your confidence and assertiveness and also because it works great! The easiest way to do this is obviously using the "sleep/click" method: "1, 2, 3. Open your eyes now, look at me. And sleep (click!)"

This is the standard re-induction technique across the board. However, you can pretty much do anything to re-induce a subject from something as simple as; "when you next hear a car drive past, you will instantly go back into hypnosis" to something more complex like "you will go back into hypnosis of your own accord in exactly 14 seconds from NOW!" (You'd be surprised at how accurately the human body clock will time this!) That said, in a therapy-setting, you only really need bother sticking to the standard "sleep/click" re-induction.

Before doing this, to make sure that it works you can suggest; "during this session, any time I say the word sleep and click my fingers, you will go back into this state of hypnosis instantly. If you are sitting, you will remain fixed to the seat and return into hypnosis, if you are standing you will go to sleep whilst standing. Nod your head if you understand."

They will nod their head, and therefore accept and activate this suggestion. If you don't use this suggestion before attempting the re-induction, the good old "sleep-click" will probably still work most of the time anyway. If you *do* use this suggestion beforehand, it will pretty much *always* work. You want this re-induction to work 100% of the time (as it's a great deepener, and a great hypnotic-convincer) so I suggest that you should always use this suggestion.

USEFUL TIPS

Phonological ambiguity
Say, that's a mouthful isn't it? The meaning, as with most complex-sounding NLP terms is actually relatively simple: Confuse them with words!

You use a word that sounds the same but has a different meaning. This is a basic confusion technique. Here's an easy example:

"Five you're going deeper than you have ever been be-*four*, deeper and deeper, three, drifting down in *two* this state of hypnosis, one..."

There are a great many words in the English language that have counterparts which sound the same/similar. If you have a great memory and you're good at thinking on your feet (or sticking exactly to scripted patter – tut tut,) then you can use phonologically ambiguous words and statements during hypnosis. For example:

"As your mind wanders *[wonders]* about what happens next, your unconscious *[you're unconscious]* mind knows now as you hear this thoughtful trance inducing statement *[state meant]* to help you become your best self is already working..."

This is a great confusion tool but can be tricky to fit in (or remember,) so when it comes down to NLP-techniques for deepening I personally stick with using double negatives, deletions, embedded commands, pacing and leading, predicates (sensory based words,) synaesthesia (link from one sense to another,) etc.

(Like I mentioned earlier, you might want to look into NLP to use alongside your hypnotherapy skills too – it's useful... And less confusing than it sounds!)

Forgetting what to say
When you are doing a hypnotherapy session without a script, odds are that at one time or another you will probably slip up and forget what your next words are supposed to be. This is especially true when you're just starting out, and you know what? That's just fine. Yes, that's right, you probably will forget your "line" a few times, there's no way around that. When you think about it, however... Who is going to know that you forgot your line? Who is going to know that you didn't read your "script" word-for-word? Well? The answer- if you didn't already figure it out, is; just you.

You are the only person who will know if you forgot something whilst performing the hypnotherapy session, and you are the only one who's going to know if you "accidentally" included something spontaneous during a session.

When you're hypnotising a subject, the subject doesn't have the foggiest idea about what you're supposed to say/do during a session, even if the subject has been to a hypnotherapist before... Hell, even if the subject is a hypnotherapist himself, he can't predict what you're going to be doing, simply because every hypnotherapist works in a slightly different way (well... Apart from the ones who all downloaded their scripts from the same sources... They're all equally as bad as each other.) What I'm trying to say is; chill! Take a damn chill pill, you're a hypnotherapist and your job is to relax people. If you're a jittering bag of nerves and your voice is shaking because you forgot to say "deeper" after you said "relax," your uncertainty is going to come across to your subject... And if you're not certain about yourself as a hypnotherapist, how do you think that's going to affect your subject? (Hint: it ain't gonna be positive)

Repetition
Repetition is hypnotic, repetition is hypnotic, repetition is the easiest hypnotic tool to remember, and is a very effective way to make any suggestion more powerful. Also; repetition is a very effective way to make any suggestion more powerful (OK I'll stop it now.)

Think now, what was Tony Blair's main focus for change during his term as Prime Minister? It was education, education, education. Not simply education. Repeating the same word three times brought forth the idea that "wow, he must be really serious about improving education" (evidently he wasn't that serious about it, but the basic psychological reasoning still stands, regardless.) The same goes for motivational speeches that I personally give to my students about progressing with hypnosis. I do not simply tell them; "practice as much as you can," I tell them:

"To get good at hypnosis, you need to practice, practice, practice, have a break then practice again harder. Take a nap, dream of practicing and then wake up and practice some more."

Much more memorable, and also infinitely more influential and fruitful, I am sure you will agree! I'm very sure you will agree completely! Damn, I can't stop doing it now. Another additional benefit of multiple repetitions is that if someone either didn't understand your suggestion the first time, or wasn't concentrating (sometimes subjects will begin "daydreaming" during hypnosis, this is a very regular occurrence,) they get a second or third chance to take in the information that they missed.

Saying "relax your eyes completely, now notice the muscles around your eyes relax as you focus entirely on allowing those eyes to be completely relaxed!" for instance, is better than just saying "relax your eyes completely" right?
Repetition, repetition, repetition. OK next…
Your hypnotic voice
A lot of people find that their voice changes when they are performing a hypnotherapy session. This isn't necessarily true of everybody – some people have naturally hypnotic voices anyway and other people just don't bother with that aspect of their delivery, but I personally have a "hypnotic voice" and it is quite different to my normal voice (so different in fact that when I hypnotise my friends, they generally begin the session laughing at the peculiar way in which I'm speaking.) I have found that cultivating a solid hypnotic voice helps me in two ways, the first being that the relaxing sound of my voice definitely helps a subject into a state of deep relaxation, and it is a voice that they almost cannot help but listen to, due to the fact that it is crammed full of intention (i.e. my intention to hypnotise them and help them achieve their goals.) The second reason is whenever I use my hypnotic voice, I automatically associate it with hypnotic trance (because over the years it has been subconsciously "anchored" to that state) and so I instantly go into a light state of trance whilst using "the voice."

A hypnotic voice comes down to a couple of factors; the most important of which being inflection. When you are giving suggestions (or commands) your vocal inflection needs to be authoritative, your word(s) need to end on a low inflection. Some voices naturally have an "upwards" inflection – think about an Australian accent… Due to the inflection some statements given in an Australian accent sound like questions, even if they are not. Your goal is to only use upwards inflections when you are asking legitimate questions. When you are just talking with no intended consequence, aim to keep your voice rather monotonous (mono tone = one tone) so that when you do give a suggestion, you have enabled yourself to deliver your command-tone (down inflection) more noticeably/effectively.

Another factor to take into consideration is speed of speech. In all honesty, you don't have to speak slowly to be an effective hypnotherapist, but once again we come back to remembering that relaxation facilitates the state of hypnosis, and slow, significant patterns of speech are a brilliant tool to produce relaxation. I suggest slowing the speed of your speech at least during the induction/deepening section of your hypnotic process. Once the subject is sufficiently "tranced out" you can either continue with the same voice, or not, as you prefer.

It almost needn't be said that you need to be comfortable speaking to your subject. Do not attempt to modify your voice to the extent that you're uncomfortable whilst speaking, just to try and "fit in" with what you think a hypnotherapist should sound like. I know hypnotherapists who have the highest pitched, upwards-inflectiony, gratingly-irritating voices you've ever heard… But they are still good hypnotherapists because they care about the welfare of their subjects and they adapt to them. Vocal adaptation is just another tool that can help, but it is certainly not mandatory.

Confidence
Confidence is an immeasurably important thing for a hypnotherapist to have, because if the person you intend to hypnotise believes you *can* hypnotise them successfully, then your success becomes all the more likely. Just by being confident, you can almost guarantee that you're going to succeed most of the time when you hypnotise people. The same principle goes with the therapy side of things – if you're confident that you can make positive changes happen, those changes will happen a lot easier, because the subject will see your self-belief and adopt the same standpoint. If however, you are a quivering, stuttering wreck, apologising for no reason and saying things like:

"I hope this works"
"Well, we can try to hypnotise you, but I can't promise anything"
"I only just learned how to do hypnotherapy, I'm not very good yet"
"I can try and stop you from smoking, we'll see if it works for you"

…Etcetera, then you are setting yourself up to be the most spectacular…failure as a hypnotherapist the world has ever seen.

Confidence is probably more important than the art of hypnosis itself. Someone just learning hypnosis, but practicing with high self-confidence could hypnotise almost anyone, using virtually any method to do so. They could adequately fix problems with the most basic techniques and language. A veteran hypnotherapist, however, practicing with little faith in his own abilities would constantly find people saying "I don't know if I was hypnotised" or "it didn't work." That's assuming he actually managed to get them to close their eyes and follow his instructions in the first place, but more likely, they'd just remain completely awake and alert due to his nervous methods and self-doubt. These things immediately pre-convinced subjects that he was going to fail. So he did.

If you're not confident that you are going to be a good hypnotherapist, then you are going to be a rubbish hypnotherapist. It's as simple as that. If you are not yet confident in your abilities, that's absolutely fine and completely understandable. You can't gain confidence without practicing and becoming sure of yourself and your abilities, but what do you do before that? Before you've practiced enough to gain this confidence?

Fake it 'til you make it! – I've said it before and I'll say it again. There's only one person that is going to know the difference between a confident hypnotherapist and a hypnotherapist who is faking confidence, and that is the hypnotherapist himself – in other words: You. As long as you appear confident, you will *appear confident*. No, that was not a typo.

You don't need to fake confidence so substantially that you actually feel naturally confident (if you keep faking it, however, this natural confidence will keep building every day.) What you need to do to start with is; maintain an "air of confidence." I.e. ensure that you *LOOK and ACT* confident. You can be crapping your pants internally (hopefully only metaphorically,) just as long as you ensure that externally you appear solid, happy, approachable and sure of yourself and your abilities.

If you remember *any* information from this part of the book, it should be the importance of appearing confident combined with continuous and relentless practice...

Practice
To get really good at hypnotherapy you have to follow the three-P plan:

"Practice, practice then practice some more!"

The more you practice your chosen art, the better at it you will become. As with any skill, becoming a proficient, confident hypnotherapist will take time and effort. It will take a whole lot more time and effort if you never practice, though.

There is a psychological model that states there are 4 stages of learning. Below, I have briefly outlined those stages along with a rough idea of the time it takes to achieve the competence levels:

1- Unconscious incompetence – This means that you have no idea about the skill that you wish to learn, and you are probably not even aware of its existence.

2- Conscious incompetence – You know the basics but you're not very good at them yet, but you will improve dramatically during this stage. This is the stage where you learn the most new skills.

3- Conscious competence – You are now fairly experienced at the learned skill, but there is room for improvement, and it is still not completely natural or habitual. 700-1,000 hours of practice is around the time it takes to get to this level of competence.

4- Unconscious competence – You could perform your skill with your eyes closed and your hands tied behind your back. You do not even have to think about what you're doing, because you are now an expert at it. To get to this stage will incur a nominal fee of around 3,000-5,000+ hours of practice.

Maybe you feel that you don't have time to practice. In reality, however, you do have ample free time – you just *actively choose* to use it for other stuff; watching TV, getting drunk, reading novels, spending whole evenings wasting time surfing the internet, giving your dog a pedicure, daydreaming, etc...

If you really, really don't have time, perhaps you should think about time-management. It is always possible to re-arrange your schedule or re-think your priorities in order to achieve a goal that is important to you.

Or maybe you could just give up...

If you are setting out a career as a hypnotherapist, you can practice on the job. That's a no-brainer.

If you are at work in an office all day, hypnotise a colleague or member of the public for 10 minutes during your lunch break.

If you work in a bar, is there any better situation to meet new, willing people to hypnotise?

If you have a hectic party-fuelled social life, I don't even need to tell you the amount of opportunities to practice that you have, because you already know. So take the initiative... Practice makes perfect (that's a saying for a reason, you know.)

When I first discovered hypnosis, I was terrified about trying to hypnotise anybody, because I didn't want to screw up and look like an idiot if nothing happened. So, I started out by practicing on myself using an old tape recorder. First, I tried a simple progressive-relaxation hypnosis induction with a deepener and no suggestions, and it worked. I hypnotised myself! I thought it was brilliant, and it gave me a surge of confidence. After that initial success, I then wrote and recorded a smoking cessation tape (I smoked a lot during college. I was addicted, 20-40 a day) but once again the tape worked, and it worked better than I ever could have imagined. I became a non-smoker using my own hypnotherapy techniques that I created by myself. After that, I had so much confidence that I started hypnotising my friends and family, and guess what? It kept on working, and I kept on getting better and better.

Making these recordings is a great method of practice when you are just starting out. It helps you find your footing because you'll be using and adapting induction and deepening methods, and figuring out what works well for you when doing the "change work." It gives you a chance to evaluate your phrasing and the way that your words flow, to figure out how you would like your voice to sound during hypnotherapy sessions, and even whether you should adapt your tone, inflections or pacing. You are your own best critic.

All modern phones and computers (well, most) have a built in sound recorder, and the capacity to record for hours and to playback these recordings. So if you want to practice and have no willing volunteers when you first begin, look in the mirror. We all have things that need fixing, so start by fixing yourself!

Abreactions
Abreactions are quite rare... That said, in literally two of my three first stage hypnosis shows I had 2 separate people experience abreactions (talk about baptism of fire, hey?) So, just because they *are* rare occurrences does not mean you are not going to have to deal with them.

The first abreaction I encountered was at my second ever show at a pub near Birmingham with a young girl of around 18. She went under quickly and followed instructions well (if not a little sluggishly.) Around 10-15 minutes into the show I noticed her shoulders/chest contracting rather quickly, so I attended to her straight away. As I leant down towards her head, I could hear what she was doing. She was crying AND laughing. This is one of the more obscure combination-abreactions, and I was, needless to say, rather surprised that it was happening (as my trainer assured me that I would probably never even see an abreaction, fat lot he knew, eh?)

Careful not to exacerbate the situation, I gently but forcefully took her attention (using only words, no physical contact,) calmed her down and brought her out of trance, afterwards explaining to the audience in basic terms what had happened, and getting them to give her a big round of applause. I told her to stay until the end of the show so I could ensure she was alright. She was.

The second case happened at my third show in Nottingham, and was slightly different. There was a woman at the end of the stage, she'd been quick to go under but wasn't following instruction too well. I noticed that her face was starting to become redder than I had come to expect from regular "hypnotic-blushing," and she then began shifting her weight from side to side every few seconds. So I woke her up and asked her if she was alright. She told me she was having a lot of trouble keeping her head up, and that she was therefore struggling to breathe. Some people might not consider this to be an abreaction by popular definition, but I certainly do. It's an unexpected physiological result of hypnosis that almost certainly wouldn't have been happening if the subject was fully alert and in complete control of her motor functions. So I took her fully out of hypnosis, dismissed her, had her get a drink of water and asked her to see me at the end, then continued the show with the other hypnotised participants.

So an abreaction, if you hadn't already guessed, is basically a reaction that you are not expecting and that you did not (directly) cause to happen via suggestion. People can experience abreactions for a variety of reasons; one theory is that it is a release of pent up emotional stress built up from the tension and worry of day-to-day life. More often it is caused by spontaneous regression to a past experience that still "haunts" the subconscious when it has the opportunity to do so.

When you are using hypnosis for therapy purposes, the chances of encountering an abreaction are significantly increased. As a therapist you should already be expecting a heightened emotional state from your subjects, so it should not come as much of a shock if you are helping a subject to come to terms with a traumatic past experience, and the subject begins sobbing or laughing or something else. In a therapy setting, it can be a good idea to allow the subject to release this pent-up emotion. Once the emotion is out there, you can then talk through the cause of this reaction with the subject and make changes to the memory that has caused the emotion, if required.

There is *absolutely no way* to safeguard against abreactions, aside from taking the preventative measure of ensuring that you word all of your suggestions 100% correctly and keep your eyes on your subject the entire time. Sometimes however, even if you do everything 100% correctly, you could still face an abreaction. Hey, who said being a hypnotherapist would be easy?

Here are descriptions of the 4 main abreaction types:

Weeping
Occasionally a subject will begin to cry whilst they are in trance, it could simply be the odd tear rolling silently down a cheek, or it could be full on heart-wrenching sobs of distress. You must be alert and watching for any signs of a possible abreaction, because you want to deal with it as early as you can, because as with most extreme emotional situations, it can develop and become more intense the longer you leave it.

Laughing
It may seem like the subject is just laughing at something funny that you said, or maybe they have pins and needles from sitting still for so long and it tickles? Maybe this particular subject laughs when they are in pain or under pressure? We don't know, but if the laughter continues for longer than "normal," you should investigate the situation. These spontaneous regressions may not always take them back to a traumatic situation, they could've jumped back to a great time in their life, but if you didn't suggest it then that's not where they should be, so bring them "back to the future" immediately.

Screaming/Shouting
If you're giving a subject a suggestion that should provoke no reaction, and they begin to scream, shout, and possibly even thrash around (you never know what's going to happen – *a recurring theme throughout many areas of hypnosis,*) then you have an abreaction on your hands, and a shocking one at that. This experience is a little harder to deal with simply because it appears very dramatic and distressing, and automatically puts pressure on you as the therapist to resolve it quickly. You must stay calm, cool and collected (even if you do feel all shook up,) for the benefit of your subject who needs you to be on top of things.

Extreme introversion
Sometimes a subject will stop responding to your suggestions, this could be due to a defence mechanism that they would naturally revert to in high-stress situations (such as a random regression back to a traumatic past event) or it *could be* that they are enjoying this peaceful state of hypnosis so much that they do not want it to end, so their subconscious mind has made the decision to "make the

hypnotist silent and invisible" so that they can remain in this state, uninterrupted and at peace (quite a feat without it being suggested.)

Other/Combinations
So many abreactions could possibly occur that to list them all would take pages and pages. I have given the "top 4" here, and these ARE the most prevalent abreactions that you might experience. These are not set in stone, as you already saw in my first example with the girl who was crying *and* laughing at the same time. Combinations are possible and even probable. Do keep your eyes open, and if you notice something weird and unexpected occurring to one of your subjects, take the situation in hand immediately and resolve it. Your priority is always to put the safety of your subjects – physically *and* psychologically – before anything else.

How do you deal with an abreaction?
If you are aiming to simply stop the abreaction in its tracks and not work through it, there is a simple phrase that is very useful to use in this situation (supposedly coined by Gerald F. Kein, a prominent hypnotist/trainer in Florida.) All you are going to say is:

"The scene fades and you tend to your breathing..."

You should visually notice them become calmer, and you can continue giving positive, relaxing suggestions until you can comfortably bring them out of hypnosis. This (or a similar variation of it) will work the majority of the time. You are allowing the subject to grasp hold of the idea that the experience they are having is only a "scene" or an exercise in imagination. This way they are able to dissociate from it and allow it to fade from their mind, as they "tend to their breathing" which allows them to physically calm themselves.

Dissociation is a powerful NLP technique used frequently in curing phobias and in regression sessions to allow the subject to choose to not react negatively to their problem.

When someone is having an abreaction, it doesn't tend to be like they are watching the scene from their past as if it were on a TV screen. In fact they usually completely believe that they are back at that exact moment, and they will experience the situation as if they were actually there, re-living it once again. You must treat abreactions with a lot of respect, because they are very serious.

Do not touch the participant during an abreaction, you don't know what they are feeling and they could very well be experiencing regression back to an unpleasant physical experience where they were abused/molested (sad but true,) and touching them in any way might compound and exaggerate the emotions that they are feeling. This could consequentially make it harder to rouse them from the experience. Stick with the phrase mentioned before – repetition helps too.

Occasionally you might experience extreme introversion or the inability to follow commands, where a subject will not come out of hypnosis easily. If the previous words (*"The scene fades and you tend to your breathing..."*) didn't bring them out of it, odds are they're enjoying the state and ignoring you. Often a "threat" could work:

"Remember, I'm the hypnotherapist and I put you into this hypnosis, and I can make it so you can never go back to this wonderful relaxing state again unless you wake up now."

Using one of these suggestions to bring your subject back to full conscious awareness should garner your required result, otherwise take a look at the "waking procedures" section for more information. If you phrase all your suggestions well and respect your subjects, hopefully you won't have to use any of these suggestions very often, if at all. But be prepared.

Working through an abreaction with a subject is a very personal experience and it entirely depends on the cause of the abreaction itself, so the "cure" for the abreaction could be anything. You may have to change the "submodalities" (NLP technique) of the memory (altering the way the memory is perceived and the way that the subject reacts to it.) Perhaps viewing the memory from a dissociated state will help the subject... Sometimes this abreaction could be a repressed memory that was up until now completely forgotten, and the act of simply remembering the memory will actually help the subject to overcome the problem... As I said, you can't know what to do until you have the subject in front of you (and this, again, is why scripts aren't a good way of working, because which part of the script deals with the chance of an abreaction? Exactly...)

When you are practicing hypnotherapy, you will become experienced enough to be able to draw upon techniques that you frequently use in your sessions that will help you to find and "fix" the cause of an abreaction. If you don't feel comfortable doing this at the start of your foray into the world of hypnotherapy, that's fine, because you can just allow the scene to fade as you tend to your breathing...

HYPNOTHERAPY

WHAT IS HYPNOTHERAPY?

To break it down, for a standard hypnotherapy session to happen, you need the following ingredients:

1 large *Hypnotic Induction* +
A liberal measure of *Trance Deepening* +
A variety of *Hypnotic Suggestions & Techniques* (to taste) +
A healthy dash of *Repetition* +
A wake up procedure

Optional extra ingredients:
Neuro Linguistic Programming (NLP)
Psychotherapy/CBT/Talking Therapy (i.e. talking directly about the problem)

This is the basic hypnotherapy ingredients list. Using trance, a hypnotherapist will suggestively guide the subject into hypnosis. Once achieved, he will then move the subject through imaginary scenarios and situations, whilst occasionally using certain NLP phrases/ideas and even psychotherapy-style techniques... Also the therapist will guide the subject through imaginary scenarios and situations, occasionally using NLP phrases and even psychotherapy techniques to help the person to achieve their goal... No, that was not a typo, that was the final ingredient: repetition.

Don't fret if you know nothing about NLP or psychotherapy. To be a successful hypnotherapist, NLP/psychotherapy training is not mandatory. I know many hypnotherapists who run their own successful practices based solely around pure hypnotherapy techniques (i.e. lots of metaphors and direct/indirect suggestions.) As mentioned previously however, having a great variety of tools to use is going to benefit you in the long run. As such I suggest investigating NLP at the very least. I personally use NLP techniques in almost all of my hypnotherapy sessions.

Hypnotherapy is the art of changing a subjects' negative internal experience into something either positive or neutral. For example, we aim to give the smoker the idea that becoming a non-smoker is positive, inspiring them to leave cigarettes and smoking behind whilst focusing on becoming healthier (there is also a negative aspect here, the cigarettes themselves, and as such a great many hypnotherapists use aversion techniques when helping subjects to quit smoking.) An example where the therapist intends to "neutralise" an unhealthy pattern would be something like a phobia of spiders. As a hypnotherapist, you're probably not going to make someone with arachnophobia into a lover of spiders, but what you will be looking to do is taking away the negative association that the subject has with our eight-legged friends, thereby neutralising the fear.

WHAT CAN HYPNOTHERAPY BE USED FOR?

Hypnotherapy is widely used to treat a variety of issues, ranging from weight loss and smoking cessation to more complex issues. Here's a short chart with some of the more widely treated issues:

Addiction	Alcoholism
Anger Management	Childbirth Pain Control
Confidence	Depression
IBS	Insomnia
Migraines	OCD
Pain Control	Panic Attacks
Past Life Regressions (PLR)	Phobias
Skin Conditions	Smoking Cessation
Sports Performance	Stress/Anxiety
Weight Management	Work Performance

This is just a brief overview of the hundreds (probably more like thousands) of positive uses for hypnotherapy. The way I like to think of it is; if someone is having trouble solving a psychological problem or overcoming a physical issue on their own, hypnotherapy could probably help them towards success.

A great many hypnotherapists set out to carve themselves a niche, often specifically catering to a certain type of client. Rather than saying; "Hi, I'm John, and I'm a hypnotherapist," you will often hear; "Hi, I'm John, a smoking-cessation hypnotherapist" or "sport hypnotherapist" or "hypnotherapist specialising in regressions" or "gastric-band hypnotherapist." The list goes on. If a hypnotherapist doesn't specifically set out towards a niche market, it can often happen naturally and spontaneously anyway. Over time you can end up finding yourself with more and more of the same type of client. It's all down to word of mouth and how you market yourself, but don't fret; you don't need to choose *what sort of hypnotherapist* you want to be yet. Take it as it comes for as long as you like. I don't personally have a specific therapy-niche, and it's working well for me so far...

Don't set yourself limits with regards to what problems you can and cannot attempt to help with hypnosis – it's surprising the amount of "problems" that we as human beings have, which could easily be solved by changing the way that we think about the damned things. That said, don't go around touting that you can cure cancer, give sight to the blind and heal the legless lepers... Because you probably can't. But if you think you *can* help somebody and they wish to be helped, by all means do your best to help them. Don't give them false hope and don't make promises that you cannot fulfil, but try your best to help make the lives of others easier, happier and better. If there's no script for a certain issue, then use your initiative. If there's no initiative left for some reason, ask another, more experienced hypnotherapist for his opinion. If you can't find a hypnotherapist in your local area (or if he's unwilling to help out the competition,) there are a great deal of internet chat rooms and forums for hypnotherapists to share ideas and techniques.

When I started out on the road to becoming a hypnotherapist, I arranged to visit a local hypnotherapist to ask him some questions and to pick his brain a little about the subject. He agreed to meet me and I eagerly sat waiting in his office until he was finished with his client. I sat down opposite this Hypnotherapist in his office (the first hypnotherapist I ever met,) and we had a talk about my experience (none,) my background (performance,) my knowledge of hypnotherapy (barely any,) and my qualifications (none)... He told me that because I had no experience in a similar field, I would be no good and it would take me a long time to become a proficient hypnotherapist. He told me that because I didn't know the Latin name for every phobia in the world, I should not even think about dealing with phobias... Basically he told me to jack it in before I even began. Needless to say, I had not found my mentor-figure.

Luckily for me, I have a great bullshit detector, so I thanked him for his time and left him with all of his negative advice. You don't need a certificate or a diploma to be a hypnotherapist; paper-chasers will disagree, but you don't. You just need to know your stuff. You don't need to know the Latin name of every problem that you encounter... You don't need to know that Emetophobia is a fear of vomiting, Ommetaphobia is a fear of eyes and Pogonophobia is a fear of beards... Why would you need to know that information? Doesn't giving a name to something made-up give it more power? You have what? Ornithophobia? What's that? Oh, a fear of birds... You mean those cute little things that flap around in the sky? The ones that eat worms? You're scared of them? Well here's an idea, how about we take that tiny thing off the huge pedestal you've put it on and just fix it... Fuck the name and from where it came – just fix it.

As a hypnotherapist, I love to help people whether it's clients, other hypnotherapists or even aspiring young people looking to use hypnotherapy for good. At the end of the day, the name and even the content of the problem doesn't really matter, the main thing that matters is that you, the hypnotherapist, help these people to get better.

PAST LIFE REGRESSIONS

Past life regressions are a constant bone of contention in the hypnotherapy world, so I figure I should briefly give my thoughts on the subject. Past life regressions (PLRs) are not the same as regressions. Basically, a regression (for all intents and purposes) is where you take the subject back through his own past to a point where something "went wrong" and then fix/acknowledge it. Regressions are a very useful tool in dealing with deep seated issues, especially regarding repressed traumatic memories and experiences.

Past life regression is different. During a past life regression, you supposedly take the subject back through his own past and then have him travel even further back beyond his own birth into the mind of a past life incarnation. Some PLR therapists believe that the subject is often able to travel back through numerous past lives, and in some cases find resolutions to problems that they have had no success in solving in "this life."

Now, there is a large crossover in the world of hypnotherapy and spiritualism but it is not total and all-encompassing. As you may have established already, I am not (at time of writing) a believer in past lives or PLRs, psychic powers, energy, telekinesis, reincarnation, Jesus or the Flying Spaghetti Monster come to think of it – but each to their own. Just because I'm a sceptical Atheist who requires empirical evidence before subscribing to an idea, it doesn't give me the right to belittle the opinions and healing techniques of others – especially if they help to fix people!

(And I try my hardest not to be a douchebag about it)

(Sometimes I fail)

So, just know that you do not need to practice past life regression to be a hypnotherapist, if it doesn't fit in with your own beliefs then you'd be a charlatan if you did practice it, so why would you? If, however it is something that you are interested in looking into, there are a great deal of interesting books on the subject. So don't just take my opinion as your own – do some research and do what resonates with you, personally. I have a great many hypnotherapist friends who are PLR practitioners and even consider themselves to be psychics – if it works for you, then more power to you! (No pun intended.)

HYPNOTHERAPY SESSION PLAN

Consultation

In a hypnotherapy practice, generally you aren't going to have a person walk in off the street and say something as simple as; "I want to stop smoking. Here's my money, hypnotise me now." Although that would be fine, it doesn't often happen. People like to explain their thoughts, feelings and motivations, and as a hypnoTHERAPIST, part of your job is to listen. It's good to get an idea about the person you are working with, and one reason for that is because you can "feed back" little pieces of information that they have given you beforehand, during the hypnotherapy proper. For example: A subject might say "I want to give up smoking, because I feel I'm setting a bad example for my granddaughter." Obviously you can feed this back by saying "and now imagine how your granddaughter will grow up with such a positive, strong-willed, non-smoker for a role model. See her growing into a wilful young woman, all because you are now a non-smoker..." (Or something similar to that)

The more information you get, the more you can use... But there is a limit. You don't want to be spending hours and hours, listening to old Doreen blathering on about all seven of her cats, and how each of their personalities reflect her own personality in some subtle way. Hilarious as it might be, it's not going to help you, and your time is valuable so don't waste it.

During the initial consultation, your aim is to establish what the problem is, figure out the best way of going about fixing it, and get the subject's details written down in the data gathering form (you can also have them sign a contract/disclaimer if you wish – examples of both of these forms can be found at the back of the book on page 185.)

Some hypnotherapists offer a free consultation and then arrange a session for another date/time. Other hypnotherapists arrange sessions via telephone/email and gain the information they require before even meeting the client face-to-face (they will either have the client fill in the paperwork via email or at the session itself.) Some hypnotherapists don't do any of this stuff. Again, there are no hard and fast rules here but as mentioned before, it's always a good idea to keep client records/case-notes for your own information and for personal legal protection.

Pre-talk

OK, so you've listened to your subject, and you know what they want to achieve and why they want to achieve it, now it's your turn to talk.

A "pre-talk" is the conversation you will have with your subject about hypnosis before the session starts and before you begin the hypnotherapy proper. During the pre-talk, the subject will be awake and alert, hanging on your every word... So you gotta make 'em count (I mean, you've gotta make your words count, not the subject... Save that for the deepener.) The main goal of your pre-talk is to increase the subjects' belief and trust in you as a successful hypnotherapist, and to increase their own "hypnotisability." As I've mentioned (and as most hypnotherapists quickly learn,) there are subjects who "go under" at the drop of a hat, but there are others that seemingly barely go into trance at all... There's no way around it, this happens to the best of us, but the longer you practice hypnotherapy, the better you will get and the more effective your skills will become. The reasons for the differences in "good/bad subjects" are numerous and tricky to pinpoint, but reasons aside, as a hypnotherapist your aim is to provide a thorough, professional service to anyone that walks through your door, and not just to the somnambulists and brilliant hypnotic subjects. This is where a good pre-talk is very helpful in "improving your odds."

During a pre-talk, it is a good idea to cover the following five points, which I will go over in more detail shortly, and give you examples of the kind of stuff you should be (pre-) talking about:

- Define what hypnosis is
- Why your brain responds to hypnosis (Conscious/Subconscious)
- Myths/fears about hypnosis
- Examples of "every-day hypnosis"

A pre-talk is also a great opportunity to start giving suggestions. You are able to suggest that the subject is now committed to change, actively setting the wheels in motion, making an effort to become their best selves. It's also a great opportunity to tell them how successful hypnotherapy is for remedying the problem in question, and of your past successes with similar subjects (don't worry about this at first, obviously, but you'll get there.) You are able to let them know that all unwanted habits and behaviours are learned and therefore can be "unlearned," even if the problem is something they've had since childhood. It doesn't matter how long it's been in there, it can still be fixed easily if the mind's set right (if the mindset's right – a little more phonological ambiguity.)

In a hypnotherapy situation, I find it's also good practice to ask if the subject has been hypnotised before, and if so, how they felt it worked for them. This will let you know if they are easily hypnotisable and whether hypnosis has worked for them in the past. You may find people who have been to a hypnotherapist before and have had poor results, so they are trying again... Your pre-talk should help to improve your success rate with this type of subject (you can also remind them that not all hypnotherapists are created equal - it's akin to the difference between visiting a fast food joint or dining at a gourmet restaurant... They're both serving food, but there's a world of difference between the two.)

In the following sections I have included a "script" for each part of the pre-talk, there are some sneaky little phrases and embedded commands included (see if you can spot them.) Again you can use these as they are written or as a guide with which to write your own original pre-talk script. Obviously you'll need to practice your pre-talk until you can rattle it off with no accompanying script (as you're going to be talking to the subject who will be wide awake at this point, so it probably wouldn't instil much confidence if they see you reading off a cheat-sheet, right?)

Define what hypnosis is
The first part of your pre-talk will be briefly explaining what hypnosis is (and what it is not) to your subject. You can tell them something like:

"Hypnosis is not magic, it is a completely real, measurable and natural state of relaxation and internal resourcefulness and anybody can benefit from it. I like to think of hypnosis as a form of guided-meditation. Whilst enjoying this sense of meditation at the same time as just listening to my voice as you relax, you will get better without even needing to try. Whilst you can focus on consciously relaxing – and that's all this is; relaxation and internal-focus – your subconscious learning bypasses your conscious minds' critical factor, and this will allow new positive beliefs and habits to form, or to replace any negative ways that are no longer useful to you."

Why your brain responds to hypnosis (Conscious/Subconscious)
"So now you know that hypnosis is a state of internal focus where we can bypass the critical part of your conscious mind allowing your subconscious to change beliefs and habits without resistance. I'll just quickly tell you what your conscious, critical and subconscious parts do...

Your conscious mind is the part of your brain that you use to actively "think."
When you need to "figure something out" or "focus on something" the conscious mind is the logical and analytical part that does this. It can actively hold on to no more than between 5 and 9 different pieces of information at one time. The conscious mind also protects you against possible risks/threats.

The critical factor of the mind is kind of like a bridge that crosses between the conscious and subconscious, filtering out anything unnecessary before letting it through. This critical factor is a barrier which protects your subconscious mind from changes in beliefs and habits that are deemed as "unnecessary" or "unhelpful" by the subconscious itself. Sometimes, however, these changes need to happen, so we have to manually bypass the critical factor using hypnotherapy.

Your subconscious mind is your brains "database" which is progressively filled with more information. It gets this information from every experience you have, and starts from the minute you are born. The subconscious mind stores your beliefs (information that you believe is true) and your habits (automatic behaviours that work for you – or did in the past.)

The subconscious resists changing itself unless it finds a better option (for example, it won't decide that running out in front of traffic is a good idea unless it is consciously demonstrated to be true.) The subconscious has an unlimited memory and will continue to use beliefs and habits formed from very early on in life (when our reactions were very different to what they would be now.) It will continue to use beliefs and habits formed during traumatic events (when our reactions were again very different than usual,) even if these beliefs and habits are now redundant or unhelpful. The subconscious continues to use them because it is looking out for your safety, protecting you from "known dangers" and aiming only to keep you alive and well.

So imagine your brain as a computer; the conscious mind is just what comes up on the screen – the part that you see. The subconscious is everything else stored on the computer – the operating system, the programs, the files and pictures and videos and memories. The critical factor is like a computers' antivirus program, it makes sure that changes don't happen to the computer without your say so. As a hypnotherapist all we're doing is downloading a new program to make the whole computer run better, we're programming the antivirus that the new program is OK so it will accept it, and then installing the new program on your subconscious hard drive. It's as simple as that."

Myths/fears about hypnosis
You will then dispel a couple of common misconceptions about hypnosis:

"Some people have made incorrect judgements about hypnosis due to its representation in the media, and I'd just like to tell you a couple of things to put your mind at rest, now. Firstly, you cannot get stuck in hypnosis, that's impossible and it has never happened and never will and if at any point you need to wake up when you are hypnotised today, for instance if a fire alarm goes off, or if the hypnotist collapses, then you would be able to wake yourself up.

Sometimes people worry about forgetting everything that happened during a hypnotherapy session, but a lot of people will remember almost all of the session. Some parts might be a little blurry, but it's the same as watching a TV show, it's hard to remember every single detail from the whole show, but you'll be able to remember most of it, most of the time. Along the same lines as this, some people worry that they will be "unconscious" or "black out" during the hypnotherapy session – again this won't happen because you will always be aware of what I'm going to be saying to you, even when you go into a hypnotic trance… Just as aware as you are even now.

Another incorrect assertion that I hear frequently is that only "weak minded" people can be hypnotised… This, however, is untrue because anyone can be hypnotised and it doesn't matter about your IQ or your career choices. Adults and children can be hypnotised, unemployed students, rich and successful lawyers can be hypnotised, illiterate builders, rocket-scientists, people who work in the forces or in offices… Anybody, even me or you can be hypnotised, the only thing that matters is that you desire to help yourself to become your best self."

Examples of "every-day hypnosis"
Move on to explaining that people are naturally in hypnotic states every day:

"A lot of people don't realise that you are in a state of hypnosis at least a couple of times a day… Like when you're reading a book and you get to the bottom of the page and you look back up the page and realise that you don't remember a word of what you just read… When you're so engrossed in a TV show or a movie, you don't realise that someone in the "real world" is trying to get your attention… When you are looking for something you use all the time, and you know where it should be, but you look over and over and can't find it, and then realise that it was right there in front of your face all along… Like people who are searching for their glasses, whilst they're wearing them… Or even when you're driving in your car, and you "space out" and suddenly snap back to reality and realise that you weren't paying attention to driving, but somehow you managed to not crash your car, and you're still driving…

All of these things are examples of every-day hypnosis, and although you're not technically "being hypnotised" by a hypnotist, the way those situations happen is just the same way that hypnosis will help you to change your habits and beliefs without even realising that you're still driving… You'll find that the thing you were looking for was right in front of you all along, you just couldn't see it…"

After you finish the pre-talk, it's always a good idea to ask the subject if they have any further questions for you. A lot of the time, people will have heard strange myths and horror stories about hypnosis, and this is your opportunity to put them at ease. If they do not have any questions, you can briefly explain what the session is going to consist of and how they might feel during the hypnosis and that it's a perfectly safe, natural experience just to allay any lingering anxiety about the process, because a nervous person isn't naturally in a relaxed state, so you need to change their state from on-edge to relaxed. You just have to be honest, informative and friendly. Don't worry, it's easy!

HYPNOTHERAPY TECHNIQUES

There are a great deal of hypnotherapy techniques that are very useful to have in your therapists "tool kit." Some hypnotherapists choose to use as many techniques as possible, whereas others pick and choose the techniques that seem to work best for them (by trial and error, which is OK. You might not be a master-therapist your first time, but with each therapy session you will learn something new about the human mind and about yourself as a therapist.)

Throughout the remainder of the book, I am going to give you 13 different hypnotherapy techniques, talk a little bit about why we use each technique. I'll tell you how and why it works, and I shall give an example "script" for each technique, once again. I'm not going to beat around the bush. I'm not going to suggest that you need to be a master of language, or that you need to be able to read the body language of your subjects, picking up on every subtle facial expression that they make. Some hypnotherapy trainers will have you believe that hypnotherapy takes years to learn, that it is highly complicated... Well, to get really, *really* good... Perhaps it might take a little more than reading a book or two, but to start out as a hypnotherapist and to help a lot of people? It doesn't need to be hard, in fact it can be surprisingly easy for you to go out and help people tomorrow... Even today, but before I give you these techniques, there is one thing that I can't *teach* you, but it is something that you need to have. Can you guess what it is?

There's one thing that links all of the best hypnotherapists and NLPers that I know... There's one thing that I've noticed about all of these individuals that seems to play a really large factor in their therapeutic success... There's one thing that you need, to set yourself apart from all of those people that try and fail to do hypnotherapy well – that thing is "positive intention." These brilliant therapists go into a session, brimming with the intention that they are going to do a bang up job of it. But not only that, these excellent therapists have an innate wanting, a complete and total desire to actually help the subject that they are working with, because to a great hypnotherapist, the money comes second. To be a great hypnotherapist, you need to actually want to help people. If your main focus isn't helping people to get fixed, then I'm not saying you won't do a good job and help some people, because you probably will (but if it was all just about "wanting" to help people, we'd obviously just be able to "think people better.")

If you give your subject your full attention... If you give your subject your full confidence that you are going to help them get better... If you give your subject no reason at all to doubt you... If your aim for a session is to actually fix the problems that people have, there and then... You're going to help a lot of people to get better.

When you go out, and in less than an hour you help somebody get over some problem that's been holding them back for years, what do you think this person is going to do? Keep quiet about it? Hell no! That's right, they're going to send more people your way! Don't worry about money because if you truly care for the people you're working with, you might just find that your finances will begin to take care of themselves.

There are a couple of tips that are worthy of note with regards to most hypnotherapy techniques, and these are relatively self-explanatory, but I figure it's a good idea to tell you anyway. Apply these ideas to your hypnotherapy sessions for greater success:

It's best during hypnotherapy sessions to only focus on one problem at a time.

Whilst you are dealing with the issue in-hand, ensure that you deal with every aspect of the thing. So rather than simply suggesting; "you are a non-smoker," turn on fail-safe mode and suggest; "you are a non-smoker, whether at home, at work or out up the pub, whether stressed or relaxed, you are inherently a non-smoker, and nothing can change that, as you are a non-smoker now." As in this example, you should figure out when, where and why the subject smokes, and include these locations/times/feelings in your therapy solution.

Feedback experience from the subjects' life to facilitate new changes, for example: "Remember back to that time just before you got married when you wanted to give up eating sweets so you fit into your wedding dress – and you did that for your health and for yourself, and you achieved your goal effectively. And so I want you to find that power, that internal strength that you know you have within you... That strength to leave things behind that are no longer good for your health. I want you to apply that focus and that dedication to the knowledge that you are now a non-smoker..." Utilising positive experiences from the past is a great way to achieve positive experiences in the present/future.

Some subjects rely on a particular sense and therefore are not great at using the rest. For example I am terrible at visualisation, so if someone asks me to "imagine you're standing at the top of a staircase, see those stairs stretching down in front of you, now," well I ain't gonna be seeing nothin'. So it's good practice to linguistically set up your imaginary scenes using descriptions of at least the three main senses (visual/sights, auditory/sounds, kinaesthetic/feelings – There are more senses, but olfactory/smells and gustatory/tastes are not as frequently used during the visualisation process.) So, my re-script of the staircase sequence, factoring in the 3 main senses, would be something like; "I'd like you to imagine,

I'd like you to get a sense of being at the top of a staircase, 10 steps down to a door... Now this staircase can be made of any material and the door any colour, and in a moment with each step that you imagine, down into relaxation, you may notice by the feeling or by the sound of your footfalls exactly what those stairs are made of... And even if you don't, it doesn't matter as you take a step down now and relax..."

Remember that only your subjects' behaviour will change as a direct result of the therapy and not the behaviour of other people in your subjects' life. Do not suggest that "so-and-so will act completely different towards this new you, because they will sense the positive changes you have made." You have no control over the other people in the subjects' life, so focus your attention upon changing the way that he reacts to them, and perhaps those relationships will become better because of it, but no guarantees!

Utilise simple logic: "You have, in the past, remembered a great deal of things, thousands, perhaps hundreds of thousands of things... You can remember faces, names, addresses, phone numbers, words, letters, books, TV characters... So we know that your memory functions, it just needs to be directed correctly. And we are initiating that laser-focussed memory now"

Keep it simple in general. Imagine the subconscious mind is one of your friends. Let's call this friend "Subconscious Jack." Now, Jack's not what you'd call book-smart – use a word with over 3 syllables and he starts to get uncomfortable. Jack does have a good memory though, and a really good grasp on what it takes to live life simply and to be happy. Jack doesn't understand why people are always complicating things, so instead of telling your pal Jack that "97% of clinical obesity patients continually suffer irrevocable damage of the Medulla Oblongata due, in part, to the excessive pressure of adipose tissue upon the cerebral cortex, which means Jack would not be able to regulate his heart rate or breathing,*" you should instead tell him "people that eat a large amount of unhealthy food are setting themselves up to feel bad, both physically and emotionally." Keep it simple, direct and to the point.

[* - this clinical fact may not actually be a fact – but the rules state that we don't talk about that]

Do not be over-zealous. If someone comes to you looking for more social confidence, if you tell them that "you will be completely confident in every situation you find yourself in – always smiling and ready to talk to new people," what happens on that day where their pet Iguana dies and they are feeling like a bag of crap? Think they're gonna be smiling and jovial? No. Set your suggestions so that even if the subject encounters a "failure," it will not change the positive way that they react to their many successes and overall wellness.

Do not attempt to give unrealistic suggestions – the result that you are looking to achieve must be within the subjects' realm of belief, so perhaps it's a good idea to ask them what they think they will be able to achieve using hypnosis. What's the best result they are expecting? Work with that as your guideline. I have numerous people contacting me, asking for unrealistic "solutions" to their problems:

"Can you hypnotise me so I automatically know how to play guitar like Slash."

"Make me lose weight... But I want to keep eating 1,000 cream cakes a week."

"I really want to stop smoking... Oh, but I still want to be able to smoke when I'm out drinking... Oh and I don't want to stop smoking joints..."

Hypnosis is a powerful tool, but it's not a fucking magic wand. It can help people, but only if they're able to make a conscious effort to actually help themselves too!

So, whilst keeping all that stuff in mind, let's take a look at some of the techniques that you're going to be utilising during your hypnotherapy sessions to make positive changes happen...

SAFE PLACE

What does it consist of?
The safe place technique basically involves having the subject imagine going to a place inside their imagination where they feel completely safe and comfortable. This is a great technique to begin with simply because if you're in the middle of a session with your subject and one of the following techniques elicits a highly emotional response, having set this up already you have the option to take them back to their "safe place."

How does it work?
You will have the subject pick his own safe place at your instruction and you can have him describe the imagined scene to you, or not (it is entirely up to you – some therapists don't like to have their subjects move/talk – but I don't see why not, it won't snap them out of hypnosis and you are able to gain more feedback so feel free to have your subject talk to you during the session.) You will then inform the subject that they can go back to this safe place at any point they like

during the session, either by themselves or at the instruction of the therapist (if you need to "move" the subject to their safe place during a session you can do so by simply by telling them something like; "OK take a deep breath and go back to your safe place now, let everything else fade away and find yourself back in that safe place... Let me know when you're there by nodding your head/moving a finger on your right hand/saying yes, etc.)

Sample script
"Imagine a door. This door can be any type of door that you like, any size, any shape and any colour... Your door will be just as you imagine it. I'd like you to imagine that you are standing in front of this closed door now. As you relax, I'd like you to know that on the other side of this door is your "safe place" and this safe place can be whatever, wherever and whenever you want it to be... A sofa in a coffee shop... A happy place from a time in your past... An imagined place that you've never even been to before, but a place that feels just perfect for you to relax and to be comfortable now... You can make this place whatever you would like it to be, but I'd like you to make it as real as you possibly can in your imagination. Imagine the sensations of feeling it, seeing it, hearing any sounds and even smelling the scents associated with this place if you can. And when you have a good sense of this place... I'd like you to step through your door now.

Move into your safe place and go the place inside where you feel most comfortable, most at ease. You can just relax and enjoy this safe place now, and know that any time you need to feel safe, any time you need to relax completely, and even any time during this hypnotherapy session, if you need to go back to this place, you will find that you are able to instantly remember the door, walk through and enter this safe place just like you are there now. By simply imagining it, you can find yourself instantly returned to this wonderful place of peace, comfort and relaxation. Any time I suggest that you go back to your safe place, no matter what you are doing, you will instantly come back to this place and immediately feel just as relaxed, calm and content as you are right now. Nod your head if you understand."

EGO-STRENGTHENING

What does it consist of?
Ego-strengthening consists of giving the subject a "boost" by delivering a wide array of positive, nebulous suggestions. Have the subject imagining that they are becoming more relaxed, alert, energetic, confident, proud, easy-going, happy, philanthropic, clear-headed, focussed... You get the idea. Include as many various elements into ego-strengthening as you like. Some therapists have (and probably still do) rely solely on ego-strengthening to facilitate changes in their subjects.

This, however, can be true of almost any subset of hypnotherapy-technique. Ego-strengthening makes a subject feel good and a lot of subjects will visit you with the idea that you will make them feel better, so ego-strengthening gets a big "thumbs up" from me, when it comes to hypnotherapy techniques that you should be utilising in your sessions.

How does it work?
The idea behind adding an ego-strengthening section is to boost the confidence (ego) of the subject that you are working with. Ego-strengthening portions of your therapy should be universal/general (i.e. non-specific to any type of person in particular) thereby functioning effectively with all subjects that you work with (unless you wish to create a separate ego-strengthening routine on the fly for every subject you treat.) Sometimes people live for so long in such negative environments that they subconsciously take in all the harmful crap that gets thrown their way. Subconsciously pumping up the ego helps to bring the subject back to feeling better about themselves, which is a great way to begin your therapy session. Dr John Hartland (1901-1977) formulated a brilliant ego-strengthening script in 1966 and many hypnotherapists continue to use and modify his work today. The following script I have written is based around Dr Hartland's script.

Sample script
"As I continue to talk to you... I'd like you to feel physically stronger, fitter and healthier in every way now. Feel a new vital energy building more and more, deep inside your core, continuing to allow you to be more energetic. You will replace laziness with alertness... You will not become easily fatigued, instead you will have a resounding energy and renewed love for all of life's experiences... Instead of discouragement, you will find pleasure in challenges, bettering yourself with each decision you make... You will find that your mood continues to stay high. You can enjoy being in high spirits whenever you think, talk, walk, wake and sleep. Every day you will become so deeply interested in whatever it is that you are doing, in whatever is going on around you, that your mind will become completely distracted away from yourself. You will no longer think about yourself so much, and similarly you will no longer dwell upon negative aspects and difficulties in your life, because you know that as you are much less conscious of yourself now, much less preoccupied with yourself and with your own feelings now, that you are able to be that you that you want to be. That content, confident, comfortable you. Every day your nerves will become stronger and steadier, your mind lucid and serene. Composed, even-tempered and tranquil. You will remain calm and confident in situations that may have provoked different reactions in the past, but now you will be calm, you will be strong. You will be open to enjoying many various and new experiences and ready to easily deal with any situations with a clear head and a strong mind.

You will be able to think more clearly and concentrate more easily. You will easily find that your undivided attention is given to whatever it is that you wish to attend to, to the complete exclusion of everything else that is irrelevant. Your memory will rapidly improve due to this new attentiveness, and as you will find yourself remembering more, so you will notice that you are able to see things in their true perspective. Without amplifying your difficulties, you will find a new, wonderful level of self-control. Every day, in every way you will become calmer and more emotionally settled. Every day you will become and you will remain more and more completely relaxed, both mentally and physically... Even after this hypnotherapy is completed, and as you become and as you remain more and more relaxed each day, so you will develop a new, vital confidence in yourself... A confidence in your ability to do not only what you do each day, but a confidence in your own inherent ability to realise that you can do whatever you ought to be able to do. There is no fear of failure without that old anxiety... When you let go of any old uneasiness it all just melts away, and all that's left is that new, independent you... That you who can stick up for yourself... That new you who can stand on your own feet... That new, confident you who can be the master of your own world, no matter how difficult or trying things used to seem.

Every morning when you awaken, you will feel this feeling of personal well-being, personal safety and security. More than you have felt for a long, long time... And because all these things will begin to happen, exactly as I tell you they will happen... More and more rapidly, powerfully and completely with every word that I say. With every breath that you exhale as you relax now, you will feel much happier, much calmer and much more optimistic in every way, knowing now that you are able to rely upon yourself, your own efforts, judgments and opinions. And that feels good, now."

DIRECT SUGGESTIONS

What does it consist of?
Direct suggestion is exactly what it purports to be – you speak to the subject directly about their "issue" and continue to inform them as to how things are now going to be different for them, whilst "framing" the suggestions in a positive way. For example, if you wish to give a smoker a direct suggestion it could be something like; "You know now that smoking is unhealthy and detrimental to your health, you are aware that years of smoking have caused your chest to tighten... Those old, filthy cigarettes caused your breathing to become weaker, but you have now made the positive choice to completely cease smoking for good. Even now, since making that decision to be a non-smoker, the benefits of

leaving smoking behind have begun to improve your health – feel how much clearer your chest already feels now... Feel how much more breath you are able to inhale, and this amount will increase day by day. Until you will find your breathing is strong, deep and fulfilling you with life-giving, clean oxygen and a huge amount of natural, powerful energy... With every unconscious inhale and exhale, as you are a non-smoker, now and for good."

Pretty direct right? I told the (imaginary) subject four different things within that short script;

1) Smoking is unhealthy, and you know that.
2) You've probably noticed negative effects due to smoking.
3) You've changed your mind, and want to be a non-smoker.
4) Being a non-smoker (now) is good for you in various ways.

How does it work?

Direct suggestions work in the same way that a great deal of hypnotherapy techniques work. They are delivering positive suggestions past the conscious mind directly into the subconscious (which is where the change really happens. That place where, when the change does happen it probably feels like nothing has actually happened at all... But for some reason you hate the taste of cigarettes now...weird that.) We deliver our suggestions directly to the subconscious, and with these direct suggestions, we don't have to be complex... So long as the subject is in a state of trance, direct suggestion is a very useful tool to add to your repertoire. It's a really good idea (again, as with a great deal of hypnotherapy techniques) to include repetition in with your direct suggestion spiel. Saying something like; "You will find that you don't want to smoke, because not smoking will help you to feel much healthier, every day." Isn't wrong per se, but it could be a helluva lot better.

For one thing, you should strive to avoid negatives as much as possible (it's not always possible, and that's fine, just keep an eye on it when you can.) The example read; "you don't want to smoke, because not smoking will help you." In this example, you're saying "don't want to smoke," and supposedly the subconscious mind ignores the negative portions of sentences (i.e. "Don't think of a pink Elephant" – the brain ignores "don't" and automatically thinks of a pink Elephant,) so you're practically saying; "you don't want to smoke" and "not smoking is good" – get it? So instead of telling someone that not smoking is good, you should instead give them a positively phrased, repetitive, direct suggestion such as; "You are now a non-smoker, it feels great to breathe clean, fresh air as a non-smoker."

Also, did you notice the other mistake I purposefully put into the initial example? Here it is again: "You will find that you don't want to smoke, because not smoking will help you to feel much healthier, every day."

Well, if you got it then good for you. If not, then I'll explain this final point before giving you a full example of how you should be doing it. "You will find..." is future tense and if you want their change to happen now, rather than in a week, month or year... You need to be using present tense, so instead of; "you will find that you will become a non-smoker" you should be saying something like; "You are now a non-smoker." But wait, that's the same thing you said two paragraphs ago Rory... You're damned right it is! Why? Because repetition, that's why! Learn to love it! Here's a full (correct) example of a direct smoking-cessation suggestion:

"You are now a non-smoker, feeling better and better every day. Knowing now that being a non-smoker is the smartest choice you've made this year. Your health is increasing, causing you to feel even healthier than other non-smokers. This is because you knew all too well what it was like when you had that old, unhealthy smokers-feeling, but now, in comparison, you realise that this new, wonderful, healthy feeling of being a non-smoker now feels even more spectacular... You are a non-smoker now, and that feels just great."

Giving a direct suggestion in this way is going to increase the subjects' compliance to the suggestion, because rather than being negative and saying "you suck, because you're a smoker. You need to stop it." Instead, you're making them feel good by saying "you're awesome, because you're a non-smoker!") Also, the repetition helps to ensure that the suggestion "goes in" even deeper. So the three key points to remember with direct suggestions are:

1) Repetition
2) Present Tense
3) Positive Framing

Some people respond better to direct suggestions than others; people that are natural rule-followers, uniformed services, customer service people, etc. If you have someone that doesn't like being "told what to do," then perhaps it might be a better idea to go with indirect suggestions instead... But that's up to you!
(I personally like to use a combination of various methods.)

Sample script
"As you relax, you understand that cigarettes themselves are not addictive, but that old habit of smoking cigarettes became addictive over time. Just like feeling as if you need a morning coffee or feeling like you have to check the front door is locked before bed, even though you know you locked it already. Habits are simply actions that are repeated often enough to become expected. The habit of smoking can be stopped just as easily as it was started just by using the most powerful tool that you have; your mind.

Habits can be dissolved as easily as they are created. One of the ways to do that is to make you aware of your smoking. From the very moment you reach for a cigarette, you will be extremely conscious of what you are doing. And at this point, you will ask yourself; 'is this something I want, or just something I expect?' If it happened that you lit the cigarette and began to smoke, you'd find yourself to be unusually aware of every moment of the time you are involved in smoking that cigarette. Super-aware of every part of the process, aware of the feeling in your chest, the unpleasant taste in your mouth, the smell of old, stale smoke soaking into your fingers, hair and clothes...The main reason you have continued to smoke is because you are doing it subconsciously. You have not really been aware of what you were doing, but now you are. Each time you reach for a cigarette, your attention will be drawn to that cigarette and focus uncomfortably upon it.

Imagine now, holding a cigarette in your hand, just the same way that you used to hold them in your hand. And as you imagine now, holding that cigarette in your hand, allow yourself to feel how the horrible smoke climbs up your fingers, sticking to your skin. The smell becoming stronger. Worse and worse with every moment that passes. Becoming repulsive, overpowering, becoming more and more horrible and gross, until it starts to make you feel sick, now... And now relax and forget about that cigarette, forget about cigarettes now, because you are aware that that old habit of smoking is just a habit. A tiny little habit shouldn't be able to have power over you, because in reality you have power over your habits, and you are aware now that you are able to change your habits easily when you focus your entire attention and desire upon doing so.

You are aware now that you do not need to smoke. You are aware now that you have chosen to be a non-smoker, because it is good for you to be healthy, because it is good for you to breathe healthy, and because you are aware that you will find that you can easily be a non-smoker from this day forward. This idea of becoming happier as you become healthier, and this new habit of feeling naturally good once you've left those cigarettes behind is forming in your mind. This new feeling and this new habit allows you to allow yourself to feel happy, calm and relaxed whenever you need it. Feel that relaxed warmth that a new lease of health and life will give you and allow a wave of complete relaxation to move now through your entire body, from your head, all the way down now through every muscle, every nerve, every fibre of your body and being, all the way to the tips of your toes.

What were the benefits of smoking? Think about it now... There were no real benefits. You gained absolutely nothing from smoking, and smoking caused you to be both physically and financially destructive. You wouldn't withdraw a bunch of money from the bank every week and set fire to it, would you? Can you imagine doing that? You wouldn't stand above a burning rubber tyre, inhaling the thick, toxic black smoke enthusiastically. Imagine how that would feel... And yet you have been doing the exact equivalent to these things for far too long when you used to buy and smoke cigarettes.

Instead of waking up in the morning, coughing and wheezing with a mouth full of thick, gross smoky phlegm and mucus, making you cough even more, smoking making you feel absolutely awful... Wouldn't you prefer to wake up and take a deep breath of fresh, clean air that refreshes and revitalises you to your very core, to be able to really smell the flowers and the fresh cup of coffee, the delicious foods that you love in to eat in moderation, and all of those other amazing scents that have been dulled by that old dirty habit of smoking? You will find, because you have made this choice, because you have made this change, you are well on the way now to being a non-smoker... As you can relax now, and as you allow yourself now to drift and dream through this wonderful, peaceful state of hypnosis and relaxation, breathing slowly, relaxing deeper and deeper with each breath. Allow your mind to clear or to wander and to relax completely and fully with every healthy, clean, fresh breath that you exhale for good, now.

You may have already noticed that you had no real need for cigarettes; you may know that those cigarettes were in fact taking you a step closer to illness or even pre-mature death with every terrible suck of that thick, grey, choking smoke... So this new, amazing habit of being a non-smoker will surely soon become easy and effortless, just like when you happily work towards a goal that benefits you in a great, positive way. This happens all by itself. There will be none of the old struggle and fight with will power you might have experienced in the past, because the focus of your will power is now different. You no longer don't smoke just to stop smoking, now you can set your will power to the simple task of willing yourself to be healthy, happy and to have a wonderful, plentiful, long life of pleasure, comfort, relaxation and enjoyment.

There is no guilt about leaving cigarettes behind now because the awareness that you do not want to smoke might make you annoyed with the idea of smoking, irritated by the awful burnt smell of cigarettes and completely bored by the idea of wasting time in such a self-destructive way. When instead you could be doing anything else that you really, actually enjoy. Reading a good book, appreciating a beautiful day, watching a movie, having great conversations with great friends and all without that old disgusting burden. If you chose to try to smoke, you would probably want to put the cigarette out after just a few seconds, because your subconscious mind will inform your conscious mind just how terrible those old cigarettes taste and smell and just how bad they make you feel horrid...

And just as you are relaxing now, imagine the taste and smell of cigarettes are becoming repulsive to you now. Imagine as if some harmless but filthy old man was sat right beside you, smoking on a dirty off-white cigarette. Wheezing and coughing that gross smoke right into your face, getting up your nose and in your eyes and all over your clothes... Worse and worse with every breath that you inhale. And just as you breathe now, with every breath that you take, the stench of these awful old cigarettes grows and grows, and it is as if they are filled with burnt hair... Sulphur... Burning rubber... These rancid, old, toxic smells. You can leave those gross cigarettes smelling awful behind you now. As soon as you are ready to let them go now, allow your mind to clear. Allow that horrible old cigarette smell to drift away and find that you can breathe clean, refreshing air all the time now... Find that feeling inside that lets you realise that you much prefer to breathe this healthy, life-giving air because it allows you to allow yourself to be the person that you wish to be, just as healthy as you like being a non-smoker now.

And because you have made up your mind to let that old habit go. A smart, brilliant decision to stop smoking altogether. You have already made up your mind to be that non-smoker. You already made up your mind that you have already stopped, before you even heard the sound of my voice. You are a non-smoker now... Not tomorrow, not the next day, because you are happy to be clean, healthy and smoke-free at this very moment. The moment is now, and this is the moment that you get to show everyone just how strong you are able to be, when your mind is set like this on your positive goal of good-health and good-wealth. You are happy that your family and friends and everyone that you know can now call you a non-smoker.

You can forget about those filthy old cigarettes altogether now, and should you happen to accept a cigarette without realizing it, just an old reflex, you will immediately be aware of the fact that the old habit, for a little while, still wants to control you... It still wants to cause you pain and sickness, and you will be overcome with an uncontrollable compulsion to break it in two as soon as it enters you hand, because that cigarette would hurt the you that you know you can be. That cigarette would hurt your best self, and cigarettes have taken that you away from you for too long, and you don't need to be around them anymore.

It is a real positive step to remove the harmful, toxic things from your life. Things that you don't really like, things that are just there out of habit, and smoking was one of these things, but now it is gone. Now you are free to continue improving your life in any other ways that you see fit, because you are strong enough to label yourself a non-smoker, and you will feel wonderful noticing what you notice as a non-smoker. You might notice small differences in the way that you think and react, and each subtle difference means that this new habit of being a non-smoker is embedded deep in your subconscious mind. Making positive changes in the way that you feel, hear, taste, smell and see life, and as you accept that wonderful notion now, I would like you to focus on your breathing and continue relaxing and drifting even deeper..."

INDIRECT (ERICKSONIAN) SUGGESTIONS

What does it consist of?
Indirect suggestions are (as you would expect) almost the exact opposite of direct suggestions. With direct suggestions you practically tell your subject what to change, how to change it and when to change it. With indirect suggestions however, you are able to make positive changes in behaviours sometimes without even once referring to the behaviour in question. The indirect method is also frequently referred to as "Ericksonian" hypnotherapy. This name comes from arguably "the greatest therapist who ever lived," Dr. Milton H. Erickson (1901-1980) – afflicted with polio during his teenage years and bedridden, Erickson had a great deal of time to watch people. During this time, he taught himself the ability to read expressions, body language and non-verbal communication methods. Dissatisfied with being completely unable to talk/move, Erickson partially recovered his mobility by vividly focussing on the memories of said activities (self-hypnosis,) and was so successful that before even being able to walk again (which he eventually managed to do,) he completed a thousand-mile solo canoe trip... Not bad for a guy the doctors said should have been dead before his 18th birthday. Alas, I digress. Erickson was renowned for an unconventional approach to psychiatry (his profession) as he interspersed hypnosis throughout his casework. He was even more renowned for his unconventional approach to hypnotherapy, disregarding direct suggestions (most of the time) and preferring instead to use seemingly innocuous tales and metaphors alongside client-specific information, behaviours and idiosyncrasies to help clients get better. The work of Erickson also played a huge part in the influence of what we now know as Neuro Linguistic Programming (NLP) – which, I again recommend you check out (repetition.)

Indirect suggestions are most successfully delivered by combining a variety of different methods. Some of the methods I have included pertain to the suggestions that you will give, other methods pertain to the way in which you deliver these suggestions. It might be worth your while to read through these indirect methods and then re-read them again to decide which ones you feel can be combined best to work for you. I have arranged these indirect methods in alphabetic order, for the sake of ease.

ANALOGUE MARKING

Analogue marking is a method of delivering your indirect commands more effectively. The basic principle is, during those moments that you are delivering an indirect suggestion, you aim make your delivery ever-so-slightly different... What does that mean? Well, how about we try a written example first and see if you can figure it out...

"Take a deep breath in and allow your entire body to relax. You might find that you can **go into hypnosis now,** or maybe a little later. But just as you can **relax completely now**, I'd like you to just imagine the wonderful feeling that will happen when you **go into trance**..."

So in that example, I emboldened the indirect suggestions (these particular suggestions are known as "embedded commands,") and by doing this, it made them appear different to the rest of the text, thereby allowing the subject (you) to continue to actually read, understand and get the point of everything I'm saying, but also so that there is a slight distinction between normal text and the embedded commands. This is the basic principle of analogue marking, so let's say you're doing a hypnotherapy session and you have some commands you want to effectively embed... How would you do it? What would you change about your delivery to make those commands more effective?

During therapy sessions, I usually speak in a moderately-paced, relaxed monotonous voice (i.e. I try to keep the tone of my voice quite flat so it sounds neutral, or relaxing.) When I decide to deliver an indirect suggestion, I will use a verbal analogue marker – I subtly change the speed of my speech, change the pitch of my voice slightly (usually a little deeper) or even give a brief pause before and after the suggestion itself. Evidently you do not want to make these analogue markers too obvious, or your subject might cotton on to what you're up to (pfft, it's not like they're not there to be hypnotised anyway, right?)

Here's an exercise for you; I'd like you to read the following sentence out loud (don't be shy, practice is the best way to get good at this.) Read it in your best, natural hypnotic voice with no analogue markers, then I'd like you to read it once again but the second time, change the speed/pitch of the bold part, or add a subtle pause either side of it (you can even combine a couple of analogue markers if you like,) and notice how different it becomes. OK, read it:

"I'm going to count from three down to one, but I don't want you to **go into trance now**, but just allow your entire body to relax with each number. 3, 2, 1."

It's a bit different, right? Do you hear how *this technique will make your embedded commands a lot more effective*? (Also did you notice that last question was an embedded command? Well done if you caught it – if you've got no idea what an embedded command is, don't worry... We'll get to that soon!)

If you are doing "eyes-open" work (..."talking," I think it's called...) you are able to slip embedded commands in verbally just the same as during a hypnotherapy session, but you also have the benefit of being able to employ visual analogue markers (you can even use both together.) Visual analogue markers are fairly similar to verbal ones, because you're just going to do something different whilst you give your command... You could tilt your head to one side as you give the command, gesticulate with your hands (or stop gesticulating briefly,) close your eyes, give direct eye-contact (or remove it)... The list goes on, but in most therapy situations you're probably going to have the subject with their eyes closed, so we won't waste your time expanding upon visual markers (anyway, you're pretty smart, I'm sure you've got the idea already.) Just remember, the idea is to be covert about it, because if you're overt or obvious about your analogue markers, then the subject will pick up on it pretty quickly and render the entire process useless.

[Note: If you're using analogue markers and giving more than one indirect suggestion that you intend to "mark," you need to ensure that you perform your analogue marker the same every time. The consistent repetition of the AM will help to increase its potency (this is a basic principle of "anchoring" – which we will cover later.)]

COMPLEX EQUIVALENCE

A "complex equivalence" is a very useful method of linking something to another unrelated-thing. For example: "Picturing yourself there in that perfect place *means* you have already made these changes happen." Now, to the conscious/critical mind we realise that, in fact, it doesn't mean that at all... You just jammed two different ideas together and stuck a meaning in between the two. The subconscious mind however, reacts really well to suggestions such as this. The subconscious will automatically take the statement as one whole fact, which *means* you can make changes happen easily and effortlessly. This *demonstrates* that complex equivalences are inherently useful to you as a hypnotherapist.

(If you're a smarty pants, you'll notice that the last two sentences were a combination of 2 complex equivalences... Clue: "means" and "demonstrates" were the two linking words.)

Here are a couple more examples for you to draw from:

"Because you are here now, this shows that you know how to change."

"You will find that it's easy to lose weight, because you know how to relax."

"The memory of your past successes demonstrates your ability to be confident behind the wheel of a car."

"The fact that your breathing has slowed and deepened, means your subconscious mind has integrated this new behaviour into your day-to-day life."
None of these ideas are linked in any way whatsoever, but by using complex equivalences, we are able to give our suggestions more power, more punch and more permanence.

CONVERSATIONAL POSTULATES (COMMAND QUESTIONS)

A conversational postulate is a sneaky little linguistic tool that appears to be a question, one that requires a yes/no response. In fact, the "question" is actually a type of embedded command which subtly asks the subject to "do something." A common, day-to-day example of a conversational postulate would be to ask a taxi driver; "Do you think you could **let me out at the next set of lights**?" You don't actually want to know whether he can or can't physically do it, you just want him to do the damn thing. Just saying; "Drop me off at the next set of lights," is a little too abrupt/rude, so we soften it using this technique.

"Do you think you could **pass the salt**?" Command: "pass the salt." We use these things all the time, and they're a great, permissive way of getting people to agree do stuff for you, when they might object to being "told what to do" directly. Subtly is the key here.

When creating conversational postulates, if you're unsure as to whether you've phrased your questions correctly, you can test it by asking yourself: Does a yes/no answer fit and is there an embedded command? Yes + Yes = Success!

During hypnosis, these "questions" actively get the subject thinking/doing the desired action, for example: "I wonder if you can **imagine a time when you were completely relaxed and comfortable**..." Obviously, the embedded command in that question is; "imagine a time when you were completely relaxed and comfortable."

"I wonder if you **realise just how strong you are as a person**..."

"Do you know just how easily **you can relax by focussing on your breathing**..."

"I wonder if you are aware of just how quickly **you'll become a non-smoker**..."

DOUBLE BINDS

The double bind is a suggestion that gives the subject practically the same option. The phrase "you're damned if you do and you're damned if you don't" springs to mind. Double binding is a trick that is frequently used by savvy parents to get their children to do things that they don't want to do, with as little resistance as possible. For example, let's say you have a kid that hates making his bed, but he absolutely loathes washing up. Now if you ask him to do one or the other separately, each request will be met with roughly equal resistance... However, if you want him to make his bed, you could simply ask; "so, you can help me do all of this washing up, or you can go and make your bed, which would you prefer to do?" You've given two options and you know he's not going to choose the first one... Odds are, he's going to go and make his bed (with much less displeasure than if you'd asked him to do it directly,) because in his mind, he's "getting off lightly." Make sense? Good.

When working with a more resistant subject, you can throw in a bind that allows them to make the choice as to when they allow themselves to make the changes happen: "I don't know if you're going to make this change now, tomorrow or even next week..." You're "presupposing" (we'll come to that in a while) that the change is going to happen regardless, and you're giving the subject the option as to when. Giving a subject "control" over part of the process, often makes them more compliant (they don't actually have any control over it, but they *think* they do.)

A lot of problems are caused by not wanting to change a pattern or behaviour that you've become used to. So if you frame your suggestion to change within a double bind, you are giving the subject a choice: "You can either keep this irrational fear of spiders that makes you feel horrible, nervous and unpleasant every day... Or you can choose to let all those old feelings go, and you might find that you end up having to catch a spider for someone else who is afraid... And although that sounds pretty undesirable now, which choice do you think most people who aren't scared of spiders would choose?"

"Giving up smoking can sometimes seem difficult, it takes willpower, concentration and it can initially cause people to be a bit irritable. Now, that's not a great experience, but is it better to become a non-smoker and deal with the possibility of a few days of irritability or would it be a better choice to continue smoking, feeling unhealthy, increasing your risk of disease, ill-health and death and eventually leaving the members of your family behind when you pass away? When comparing your two choices, are you going to pick that option, or will you go for the first option, to become a non-smoker now, allowing yourself to become healthier and fitter every day that you are smoke-free so that you can enjoy a happy, healthy, long life with your loved ones?"

When you give a subject two choices, and one of the choices is a negative one, which one do you think they're going to choose? When your subject is worried about not being in control, which approach do you think is better; telling them that "these changes are all happening right now" or giving the suggestion that "you might allow these changes to happen immediately, or perhaps it'll be next week when all of these changes take effect..." Double binds give you the freedom to give direct suggestions by comparison or to give various positive outcomes, this is why they are a brilliant addition to your indirect-suggestion toolbox.

EMBEDDED (INDIRECT) COMMANDS

Embedded commands involve slipping a direct suggestion into a sentence so that it doesn't appear to be a direct suggestion at all. The subconscious, however, picks up on the command even if the conscious does not. The following paragraph contains an example of embedded commands in a seemingly regular sentence, but with the "commands" emboldened:

"When listening to people talk, sometimes you'll **realise your eyelids are becoming heavier**... And you know, that's a completely normal natural thing **that will happen... Now**, sometimes when you **allow yourself to sit back, relax and listen** to someone talking for an extended period of time, you'll almost **go into a trance as the words you hear just wash over you**, and it's strange when that happens because although you **notice that you're daydreaming, you can still hear everything just fine as you continue daydreaming**"

Embedded commands are one of my favourite methods of using indirect suggestion, and combined with analogue marking (which you read about earlier) they can be an amazingly powerful tool to create change. Embedded commands can be tricky to think up on the spot during sessions, so it can be a good idea to have your commands written down, and aim to fit them into a sentence whenever you are able to. Obviously, the more that you think about them and the more that you practice, you will find it gets easier to slip these embedded commands into normal speech. Also, you will find there are certain command phrases that you begin to use over and over, and it will become like second nature to you.

I have a cool task for you. What I'd like you to do is come up with a couple of embedded commands, write them down if you need to, and aim to slip them into your day-to-day conversation with friends/family/co-workers. Whether the commands are effective or not, it doesn't matter right now, because it will get you into the habit of actually slipping these suggestions in. Your aim is for them to be almost-unnoticed... It'll also give you a chance to test out your analogue marking skills too.

These commands can be anything, think outside the box. For example:

"I had a really good friend, he made the best hot drinks ever... He'd **offer to make me a cup of coffee**, and I couldn't resist... Even if I wasn't thirsty, there was no way that I wasn't going to let him **make me a coffee, now** I think back on it, I'm sure he must have been putting something extra in the cup. Haha!"
How about:

"I had a really late night last night. I was having a conversation with my partner, and you know when **you're listening to somebody talk, and your eyes start to get heavy**? That happened to me last night, **those eyelids just got so tired and heavy** and my partner noticed, looked at me and said **your eyes are really tired, you can barely keep them open, now** might be a good time for you to **close your eyes** and go to bed... As if I'm getting told when I should go to bed, I'm a grown man! Haha!"

Have a go, see what happens. If people notice what you're doing, then you're being too obvious so try and make it a little more subtle. If people start to go along with your suggestions whilst just practicing this without hypnosis, then that's awesome (and they're probably somnambulists.) I **use embedded commands** all the time as a hypnotherapist, so it's definitely great that **you're going to practice doing it** too. This technique means **you will easily, confidently and effectively be able to help people to get better with hypnosis**. It's not rocket-science, if you commit yourself and make sure that **you'll learn to use embedded commands,** you will be glad you did!

METAPHORS & SIMILES

Another way to deliver indirect suggestions would be to utilise metaphors and similes. By doing this, you technically do not even have to mention the issue/reason that they are there... The following paragraph is a metaphor-laced sentence which is intended to indirectly explain how metaphors work. The metaphors are again, emboldened:

"You are able to **plant the seeds of change** within the mind of your subject. **Each seed of information imparted is a map,** which allows your subject to know that **there is a pathway to a better life, but they must take the first step in the correct direction**. And when you come to realise that **words are tools with which we are able to shape the human mind,** you are able to **let these pearls of wisdom roll from your tongue** with wonder and excitement. Because **change easily blooms in the mind, like the bright, beautiful petals of a Cherry Blossom tree in the springtime,** and because **the mind is a sponge which soaks up all the information a person needs,** you can know now that **these very words are a gift of clarity, masked in inconspicuousness,** and they work very well indeed."

So a metaphor utilises something completely unrelated to explain or describe the thing that you are actually talking about (words are tools, mind is a sponge, etc.) You can be as creative as you like with your metaphors, so long as they fit your intended outcome. The subconscious mind of your subject will take the required parts of the information that you give, to make its own map towards successfully reaching their own goal, in their own way.

Similes are different to metaphors. They are more like direct comparisons and you experience them frequently in everyday life. **They're as common as dirt** and **as different as night and day**. You don't even really need to know the differences between similes and metaphors (they're fairly similar,) because you're not writing an essay on linguistics. So long as when you deliver metaphors and similes, **they're are as solid as the ground you stand on,** success will follow. **It'll be like shooting fish in a barrel.** Get the idea?

So with metaphors you actually suggest that something IS something else "cigarettes will be the nails in your coffin," whereas with similes you will always be making a comparison. So a similar equivalent would be; "Buying cigarettes is like paying to kill yourself." Notice with similes you always use "as" and "like"

Apologies for the basic English lesson, but from my own personal experience sometimes these things are tricky to understand (I sucked at English when I was at school... Go figure!)

MODAL OPERATORS

Modal operators are simply joining-words that allow you to suggest that things could/will happen. Words such as; can, could, may, might, must, will, would, are all perfect examples of Modal operators, and you **might** find that as you continue to read this sentence your eyes **may** begin to get heavier. One of those eyes **might** become heavier than the other, but whichever eyelid **will** get heavier first, it **will** just serve to allow that other eyelid to become equally as heavy now... And you **might** start to blink, but you **can** just allow that to happen because every blink **may** even help you to feel a little more relaxed... Or maybe not.

There were 8 Modal operators in that example, and it's relatively easy to just slip those into natural, normal conversation. You **might** even find that you **may** have begun to do it already... Get the gist? Brilliant – onwards!

NEGATIVE SUGGESTIONS

The subconscious mind doesn't process negative suggestion very well, which is why when we're phrasing an outcome we phrase it positively. So we don't say; "you will find that you don't want to smoke anymore." Instead we would say something like "you will find that you thoroughly enjoy being a non-smoker." So when we include a negative suggestion, we're really just giving an indirect command (sort of like the embedded commands, except these are slightly more obvious...)
The obvious example here that I mentioned before is the "don't think of..." example. Don't think of a pink Elephant... Don't think of a piece of cheese on toast on the back of a tortoise... Don't think of Queen Elizabeth, naked, smoking a cigar and jumping on a trampoline... Take away the negative portion, and all we are left with is the command itself. Simple. In therapy, we're not so bothered about discoloured Elephants and bouncing monarchs, but "I don't want you to **wonder what it will feel like when you go into trance**..." – "You don't even need to **feel your body relaxing now**..." – "Don't **focus your attention on your breathing**..." – "You don't even have to **think about going into trance now**..." – "I don't want you to **wonder how easily these changes are going to happen now**..."

We don't need to focus much more on negative suggestions, because although useful, you probably won't use these all the time. If you did use them all the time, you'd probably notice that your entire session would sound rather peculiar, and your subject would wonder what the Hell was going on. So use negative suggestions sparingly – season to taste.

NOMINALISATIONS

I'm going to break nominalisations down into as simple a form as I can, because in my experience some people make this technique seem ridiculously complicated and it's really not (also because I'm a simple kinda guy and I like to keep things as easy as possible.)

A nominalisation is the process of turning a verb (a word used to describe an action, state or occurrence) or an adjective (a word used to describe an attribute of a noun) into a noun (the name of a person, place or thing.) Generally with hypnotherapy, we focus on the "thing" part.

So breaking it down even further, we "nominalise" actions, states, occurrences and attributes and make them into "things" – for example, let's use "love." What is it to love (verb)... When you "love" something, is it tangible? Can you touch it, hear it or see it? You can see the results of loving, but you can't see/feel love directly... But if we nominalise love during a hypnotherapy session, then it changes...

"I want you to get a sense of that love inside you. I want you to feel it building and building and filling your body from your very core, to the top of your head and the tips of your toes. I want you to imagine that love as a colour, a bright vibrant colour..."

What are we asking them to feel? It's not "love," but in fact it would be their experiences related to the "love" state of mind... Perhaps it's a posture, perhaps it's a whole host of memories, perhaps it's a certain tone of voice, a touch, a feeling in their stomach... But whatever it is, it signifies love to them, and that's one of the uses of nominalisation. You're taking a bunch of ideas, experiences and memories, making them into a "thing" and having your subject experience that "thing," as opposed to having them go through every tiny, individual piece of information related to this "love" thing.

"Get a sense of freedom, now..." You've made "being free" into a tangible thing, so your subject can draw from all aspects of their "freedom" experience.

"Notice that your relaxation is becoming stronger and stronger..." Can you put 1lb of "relaxation" into a bag? (No weed jokes, please.) No, because it's not a "thing." But when you nominalise it, it is... Which means you can feel that relaxation thing.

When you nominalise, you are giving something a meaning that it did not have before. You may also notice that people have already made nominalisations; "I don't get any respect" – How would they know when they have gotten their respect? Respect isn't given in a box, so it is an idea that has been nominalised... You can then break that down into why exactly they feel that way, or what they would require to feel they have gotten their respect.

How about; "nobody communicates properly in this house..." Really? Nobody communicates properly? So you're saying they all walk around mumbling unintelligibly? Probably not, so people are in fact "communicating" properly, they're just not communicating the information that you want them to...

If you notice a subject has made a non-productive nominalisation of something (as with the two previous examples) then question it, if you question their nominalisation they will realise that they are probably making a mountain out of a molehill, and that there is probably a simple resolution to the thing if they break it down. For the example of "nobody communicates properly in this house" you could ask: WHO doesn't communicate properly? WHAT does nobody communicate properly? HOW do you know this? WHERE? Is it just the house or don't they communicate properly elsewhere, too? Break down the nominalisation and you will be able to allow your subject to realise that they may have been over-exaggerating the issue.

So nominalisations work in two ways, you can nominalise something to allow your subject to experience it and to get a sense of it, or your subject can nominalise some facet of his experience into something else (probably something non-productive.) Whatever way you look at it, nominalisation is a brilliant piece of kit, and once you get the feel of it, it'll become a well-utilised tool in your hypnotherapy sessions.

NON-SPECIFIC COMPARISONS

A non-specific comparison is a simple technique to bypass the critical factor (conscious.) You're going to suggest that something is happening in a way that you'd ordinarily compare to something else, but in this case you do it without the comparison. This might seem a little confusing, but let me give you an example – you would say; "You'll find that your mind and your attitudes about smoking are changing even faster now..." as opposed to finishing the sentence off and saying something like; "You'll find that your mind and your attitudes about smoking are changing even faster now...than they've ever changed before, because you're using hypnotherapy."

It's almost as if you're saying "your attitudes are changing because..." and then finishing the sentence there without giving a reason. "YOU'RE CHANGING BECAUSE I SAID SO!" Except it's a little more subtle and ambiguous than that, and therefore, trickier to pick up on.

In the first example, they are "changing even faster now" ...faster than what? You're leaving out the comparison. "Find that you're much more relaxed now" ...more relaxed than what? A Sloth? An excited child? So we're setting up as to give a direct comparison, but taking away the comparison itself. Emilie Coue was pretty good at that: "Every day in every way, I'm getting better and better." – Better than what, Emilie? Be more specific! And isn't Emilie a girl's name? Oooh, burn.

NON-SPECIFIC OBJECTS

Non-specific objects are almost like nominalisations, they are fairly ambiguous-sounding words, but in the correct context they appear to be rather powerful – for example:

"During this hypnosis session, you will find all of the **resources** that you need are available to you now, and those **resources** will help you to make a positive change in your life. Simply by effectively utilising these subconscious **findings** in this state of hypnosis you can change now without even thinking about it."

I can't define what these "resources" and "findings" actually are, because they are Non-specific Objects, the key is in the name; non-specific.

"And when you awaken, you will bring all of these new and enhanced **learnings** with you, and these powerful new **discoveries** will help to guide you along the positive path of your life, being the best you can be."

Utilising these ambiguous "objects" allows the subjects subconscious mind freedom to create a solution that is tailor-made to the subject, as opposed to installing something more specific that might not work well for that particular person. Like I said before, sometimes it's good to give your subject a little "control" over the therapy process. Giving someone the freedom to figure out what will work best for them, is a great way for you to help people to help themselves.

PRESUPPOSITIONS

A presupposition is literally what it says, you are pre-supposing something. You are assuming that something is already true, then talking about it as a truth; "you already became a non-smoker, completely free from cigarettes since the moment you walked through my door." This is a simple presupposition. You're pre-supposing that the subject is already a non-smoker, and you continue to refer to them as such, developing their belief in your presupposition. Whether they are or are not a non-smoker at this point doesn't matter, because it simply remains unquestioned as you continue building positively upon the initial presupposition.

There are different types of presupposition, the first being the most basic, assuming an idea is true and building upon it. The second type of presupposition is the choice-presupposition. This is another great tool to get people to do things that you ask by giving them the "illusion of choice." Here you go parents, another one for you; "would you prefer to comb your hair now, or after you've had your breakfast?" People (children included) love to make their own decisions and if the decision that you are presenting to them has practically the same outcome either way, then you're onto a winner! Another (more relevant) example of this would be something like; "I'm not sure whether you're going into a wonderful state of hypnosis now, or if you will be in trance in a few minutes, but whichever way you can choose to go into hypnosis, that's the right way for you to feel relaxed now."

(Holy crap, that was a loaded sentence. How many embedded commands did you spot? Hint: There were 4. OK, that wasn't so much of a hint as it was a spoiler, but whatever... Apologies, I do like to go off on tangents, but it's a neat little throwback to keep you refreshed and on your toes. Also it proves just how frequently I use embedded commands as a hypnotherapist!)

The above example again illustrates that wonderful idea; the illusion of choice. The subject gets the opportunity to choose when they go into hypnosis, except it's not a true choice because both outcomes are exactly the same (for all intents and purposes.) Pretty sneaky! Again, this is a nifty little tool to use when you have a subject who doesn't seem to like being told what to do directly, and who prefers a more "permissive" approach.
"You might find now that with every tiny sound you hear, this allows you to relax even deeper into this wonderful state of hypnosis..." This is a possibility-presupposition. You're giving the subject the idea that there is a possibility that A will cause B to happen, but if it doesn't, then whatever. Doesn't matter, because you only said it "might" happen. "As you concentrate so deeply in this state of hypnosis, concentrate on the speed of your pulse now, and you might find as you allow yourself to really, deeply experience this state of relaxation that your pulse slows down a tiny amount, which will allow your entire body and mind to relax even more completely..."

The final type of presupposition that I'll mention is the equivalent-presupposition (there are more, but some of them are kinda similar to these ones and in my opinion, they aren't quite as useful – so I won't bog you down with unnecessary information.) The point of an equivalent-presupposition is to suggest that "because A happened, so B happened" and once again, it is not necessarily going to be true, and A normally wouldn't cause B to happen, but in this case it is fine. So this one is just A=B.

"Just by sitting in this chair, you have cured your phobia of spiders." Obviously, more happened than just sitting in the chair, but "because A happened, B happened."

"By just listening to the sound of my voice, you are able to unlock the most powerful part of your mind, to make long-lasting, positive changes in your life." What? You mean it'd work even if your voice was just saying "la la la la?" – Well probably not, but luckily in this case, the voice is saying a lot more useful stuff.

"Every breath you exhale now from this point onwards means you are a non-smoker, and that makes you feel good!" Every breath means you are a non-smoker? Uhhh how? Because it does, because I SAID SO! See what I mean, you can link one thing to something completely unrelated and it just works!

SELECTIONAL RESTRICTION VIOLATION

I believe that selectional restriction violations (SRVs) are almost like a type of metaphor, but in being formatted slightly differently to your standard metaphors, they're definitely worth their own subheading. A selectional restriction violation is what happens when you attribute an action to a thing that obviously cannot do that action (like a little kid saying "I'm sorry, but the Teapot told me to eat your chocolate cake!" Now, obviously Teapots can't talk... Unless we've stumbled into a Disney film, so this is an SRV.) The idea behind the SRV is that because the "thing" in question cannot do the action we are suggesting, the action must in fact be related to the subject (and the subconscious – smart as ever – will pick up on this minute detail.)

I once read an account of Dr. Erickson using these SRVs with a terminally ill patient who was in pain, and instead of directly referring to the client, he spoke about Tomato Plants... When Erickson stated that "a Tomato Plant can feel good..." the subjects subconscious obviously realized that this was not entirely true, but if in fact he thought of himself as the Tomato Plant to which Erickson referred, then perhaps he could feel good...

A lot of hypnotherapists have a "hypnosis chair," and they delight in telling their subjects that "that chair over there is brilliant at hypnotising people. As soon as anybody sits in it, the hypnosis chair starts to hypnotise them immediately..." Well, obviously it doesn't, because a chair can't do that (unless it's soaked in chloroform or LSD or something) so we realize that there must be an SRV at work.

"The ocean remembers back to a time that perhaps you cannot quite remember yourself, where there was nothing to fear, where there was only curiosity and calm, for the ocean is strong and wise, and the ocean fears nothing..." What do you think the conscious response to the preceding paragraph would be? Perhaps something like; "What the Hell are you talking about? Oceans can't remember things. Oceans are just water, damn it!" The subconscious however, would simply gloss over the ocean part of the message and absorb the deeper, intended meaning; the idea of there being a time where there was no fear, only curiosity and calmness.

You have to remember, we're working with the subconscious mind here. If changes were happening consciously, the subject would be able to simply "think themselves better" and wouldn't need a hypnotherapist at all. Some of these methods may seem strange, but this is the way that the subconscious works. It picks up on the subtleties, the hidden meanings and metaphors and makes sense of the world that way, because that's the way that we naturally learn and change best. We, as a species, are great at "reading between the lines."

STORIES

Stories are a wonderful medium for learning and change. You may have noticed that many of the greatest teachers and most "inspirational" speakers in the world are adept story-tellers. Stories, like metaphors, are able to indirectly address issues. Just how indirectly is up to you, as a hypnotherapist, to decide. If you're looking to help a person suffering from grief due to the death of a friend (for example,) you could tell a story about a happy-go-lucky Frog, whose best friend was a Newt...

"Now, these guys did a lot of stuff together. Hopping and swimming and eating delicious bugs, but then one morning, Newt was gone. Frog looked around in all the places where Newt used to be, but he just wasn't there anymore. This realisation naturally, really upset Frog, because he didn't want his friend to go away. He didn't even get a chance to tell Newt just how much he cared for him as a friend and as a fellow amphibian of note. But unbeknownst to Frog, Newt knew exactly just how much Frog cared for him. He always knew, and it sustained him and brightened every single day of his life in the big pond. And though unexpected, Newt knew that eventually Frog would have to go on without him, because he knew that some Frogs live almost twice as long as Newts.

Sometimes these wonderful, life-changing friendships end abruptly. Sometimes these changes are unexpected and they are certainly unwanted, but Newt knew that Frog was one of the best friends anyone could ever have. Newt also knew that Frog would, in his own time, find a new Newt pal to swim with in the pond, to catch flies, to hop and hop with. And this new friend would make Frog laugh and smile and feel on top of the world, and perhaps when he looked at his new Newt friend, he might remember a wonderful time with good old Newt. And just by remembering this, he would instantly be able to feel those wonderful feelings of love, respect and joy... Just at the mere thought of his funny old slimy face. Frog realised that those good memories would be with him forever, and although Newt was now gone to wherever it is that Newts go to when they go, he would always have Newt in his heart. He would always have Newt in his mind, and in fact, he will always be a little more like Newt than any of the other Frogs would ever be. Knowing that, Frog continued to live out the rest of his days in the pond, enjoying life, catching flies and hopping and hopping and hopping, just as he knew Newt would have wanted him to."

So, disguised in a "child's story" about amphibians, was a deeper message of realisation, a message that suggested: You made that person very happy whilst they were in your company. You will always have the memories of enjoying your time with that person. Your life goes on and will continue to do so and people you know may not make it (because none of us do,) but that's life and we've got to make the best of it, so there's no reason to beat yourself up, it's just a fact that some Frogs live longer than others...

You don't have to tell a story about a Frog. You can tell a story about "a friend" who encountered a similar situation/problem (you can make up this story or use a real life example – it's up to you,) your main intention is to have your subject so interested in this story, so engaged with the protagonist of your tale that they will find they can relate to him/her/it (you can use inanimate objects too.) Once engaged, your subject will find similarities and make a connection between the problem faced in your story and their own problem. They will then be able to utilise the solution that you put forth at the end of the story and adapt it to create a similar resolution of their own.

TRUISM (YES) SETS

The technical name for this method is truism set, but I like the term yes set. A truism is a statement that is completely true. A truism set is... Well... A set of them. You get the idea. We take a couple of truisms and we tack our suggestion onto the end, and we've made a yes set... The only thing is, the suggestion that we are adding onto our yes set is perhaps not completely true (due to the fact that this suggestion may not have come to pass yet,) but that's OK because this is the entire point of a yes set...

The subject is given a statement or two or three that he agrees with completely... At this point, the subject is primed to agree (or say "yes") to the next idea that comes along, so it too will probably be accepted as a truism. Even though it may not be true at all, and even if it is a completely unrelated suggestion. Here's an example:

"You're a smart guy, you've had a great deal of successes in your life against all the odds, and because of this, you are able to succeed at being a non-smoker now!"

"You're a smart guy..." Why yes, I am, aren't I?
"You've had a great deal of successes..." Darn right I have!
"You are able to succeed at being a non-smoker now!" Oh...yeah, well, OK then!

Makes sense, right? You can also probably see how yes sets are rather similar to equivalent presuppositions (remember; "because A happened, so B happened.")

Salespeople use yes sets a great deal... Remember the last time you got one of those sales calls?

"Hi is this...YOUR NAME?"
Um yes?
"And you live at...THIS ADDRESS, right?"
...yes...
"Well, I'd just like to take a couple of seconds to tell you about this amazing new product, it's a combined trouser-press and pet-vacuum cleaner...Would you like to order one or two?" (Did you like the presupposition at the end?)

Once you have primed someone with a couple of "yes" responses they are more likely to say yes again. Whereas if you openly asked a question or gave a suggestion "cold," they could be more likely to resist and say the dreaded N-word *gasp* (I meant "NO" by the way, not sure what you were thinking...)

Yes sets are not magical and they won't work every time (as you probably realize when thinking back to the last sales call you answered... Which swear word did you use before you hung up your phone? If you say none, I don't believe you.)

Yes sets are not very covert/indirect, but they are a useful little technique to throw in to increase your success rate (especially during hypnosis.) As such, this is a great technique to add to your hypnotic-arsenal to make positive change happen easily. You want to help people to change, right? Surely you want to make it as easy as possible for yourself, yeah? Well then surely you're going to use yes sets to increase your odds of success, aren't you?

Yes.

UNIVERSAL QUANTIFIERS (GENERALISATIONS)

Universal quantification is the act of generalising a statement (and usually exaggerating it in the process,) for example; "Everything that you read in this book is useful" (ooh, how tongue-in-cheek) No! Everything in this book is not useful because if you read literally everything in this book, you'd be reading the page numbers, the ISBN, the barcode numbers. That information is not going to be of any particular use to you as a hypnotherapist, but as a generalization; pretty much all the stuff that you're reading in this book actually IS useful to you, so we say "everything" in a generalised way, ignoring all of the stuff that doesn't fit in with that idea and then agreeing with the statement. The key word in a universal quantifier statement will be something like; All, always, every, never.

Universal quantifiers are never ineffective.
(That was a little joke – I'm sorry, it was lame.)

A universal quantifier is suggesting that there are no exceptions to what you are saying, so in effect there are also no choices and you have to go along with what I say. You're limiting the belief of the subject so they aren't even going to bother searching for a second option, just like in football, I mean "football games are always the same no matter which teams are playing. So once you've seen one, you've seen them all!" Now obviously all football games aren't the same. There are different players, different locations, different strategies and different timing. But there *are* similarities: One team versus another, both teams are always kicking a ball around, they're all trying to get it into the goal, there's always lots of flouncing about and pretending to be injured... So you know, a universal quantification can be made. Let's try something a little more relevant...

"Every word you hear will help you to make these changes happen" What if someone walks past the window, and the subject hears them say; "I fancy chips for tea, Margaret!" Do you think *those words* will help your subject to make those changes happen faster? Probably not, but we're generalising again. You can choose to use universal quantifiers or to not use them – whichever you choose, you're still always going to be helping people to get better. Just remember, you'll always be good at hypnotherapy after reading this book even if you never use universal quantifiers (he said, in a universally quantified kinda way – tee hee!)

How does it (Indirect Suggestion) work?
OK, so we've covered a great deal of the techniques that are used within the indirect-approach, and I've given you a couple of examples of how it works along

the way. Indirect suggestions skirt around the goal, hint towards it or even presuppose that it has already happened. Sometimes indirect suggestions are subtly disguised in miraculous metaphors, sometimes they're not so subtly disguised (conversational postulates for example,) but the main point is, we are aiming to convey our message without directly coming out and saying "THIS IS WHAT YOU NEED TO DO, NOW DO AS I COMMAND!" Because some people don't react well (or at all) to direct suggestions, as you will come to learn.

All of these techniques are rather different and you don't need to stick to just one of them. Combining these techniques is going to make your indirect hypnosis approach a lot more effective, so when you're coming up with your hypnosis scripts, aim to use a great variety of techniques (this goes for all scripts, not just the indirect ones – and when I refer to scripts, remember that you should be using a different "script" for each subject you see. Don't just write one and hope that it will work for everyone else with the same problem.) As an aside, I highly recommend that you aim to use both direct and indirect suggestions with your subjects. The more that you switch between the two and the more that you practice, you will come to realise the best times for you to be direct and the best times to be a little less-so. Because, as I have already mentioned, some people will react better to forceful, direct suggestions. Whilst others might prefer to be able to "make their own decisions" and not "be controlled."

An interesting point on indirect suggestion is that just as the suggestion given can be indirect to the subject, often the person giving the suggestion can also be unaware that they've even given it. Parents inadvertently deliver indirect suggestions to their children all the time (and they'd probably regret it later, if they even knew that they'd done it.) Phobias are a prime example. I've dealt with a lot of people who had arachnophobia (fear of spiders,) and although a phobia is "all in your head" (which is true,) it still had to get into your head somehow... You don't just wake up one day, terrified of spiders. So what did it? Well, in the majority of cases (in my experience,) a phobia of spiders is frequently inherited from a parent. The parent reacts badly to a spider and their child sees this reaction. Their subconscious mind takes that information literally: "OK, got it. Spiders = bad." This is an indirect suggestion, because the parent probably didn't directly say; "look, child, this is a spider. It is a horrible creature. Spiders will cause you harm and make your life a misery." No, the parent probably just saw a spider on the floor, screamed and panicked, but that's enough to deliver the suggestion of "spiders = bad" ...especially to a child. If I were a child and that happened to me, I can only imagine my child-thought process:

"What's wrong with my mother? She's my caregiver, so powerful, so knowledgeable, but this tiny creature has made her scream and panic. Wow, this tiny 8-legged thing must be very powerful or dangerous to cause my strong, wilful mother to completely lose her shit. I guess I should be scared of that thing too, because I'm just a child and not nearly as self-sufficient as a full grown adult. Yet even adults are scared of the damned thing…"

(Yeah, childhood me didn't swear quite so much, probably… But you get the drift.)

So, you are able to see just how powerful an indirect suggestion can be, even when delivered accidentally. The following sample script will include examples of every indirect technique that I have explained to you. It's up to you to look through the script and pick out the techniques; that is your challenge. Don't simply read it and move on… Study the script and pick out every single indirect suggestion that you can find. Some of them may be pretty darn tricky – so put your thinking cap on…

Once you've done that, have a go at writing your own script… Pick a couple of indirect techniques, choose a problem to fix, and have a crack at it. There is no right or wrong here, but if you want to learn how to do hypnotherapy without using scripts then you're going to have to start creating your own solutions. Take little bits and pieces from scripts you've read in the past. Take bits from the examples in this book too. Modify them to suit your needs and to fit in with your own style, and perhaps you can realise that there is surely no better time to start than right now?

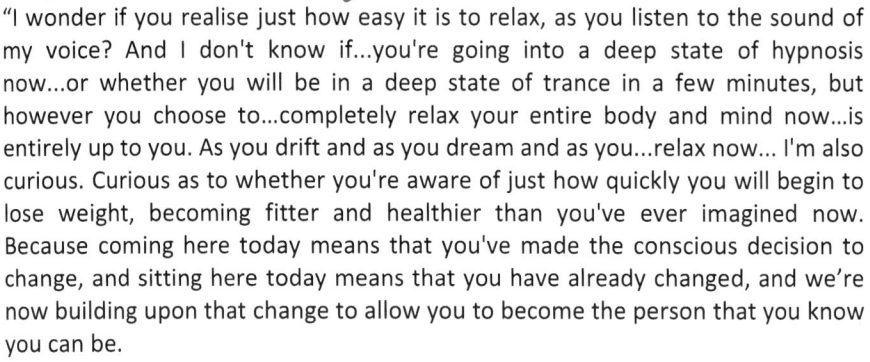

Sample script
"I wonder if you realise just how easy it is to relax, as you listen to the sound of my voice? And I don't know if…you're going into a deep state of hypnosis now…or whether you will be in a deep state of trance in a few minutes, but however you choose to…completely relax your entire body and mind now…is entirely up to you. As you drift and as you dream and as you…relax now… I'm also curious. Curious as to whether you're aware of just how quickly you will begin to lose weight, becoming fitter and healthier than you've ever imagined now. Because coming here today means that you've made the conscious decision to change, and sitting here today means that you have already changed, and we're now building upon that change to allow you to become the person that you know you can be.

As you relax now, I'd like to tell you about a woman that I knew… This woman was called Jane and Jane ate cheese, lots of cheese. She ate cheese all the time and she did this to make herself feel better. If she felt glum, she ate cheese. If she was stressed, she ate cheese. If she was bored, guess what? She ate cheese. Some of her friends even nicknamed her "Mousey" because she ate so much of the stuff. She knew that all that cheese wasn't good for her, but for some reason, it seemed at the time to be the only thing that made her feel good. Food is pretty well designed to trick us into feeling good, when in fact it's just a chemical release in the brain that made her feel "good."

Jane started to realise that she felt terrible after having stuffed her face with all that food. Too much cheese replacing all of the healthy meals you're supposed to eat. Not being in control of her eating made it so that Jane couldn't even fit into her old jeans any more. Not by a long shot, which made her sad. So Jane decided that this food, this food that kept drawing her back in, could not control her any more. She would be in control, now. Jane resolved to get her life back. Our willpower is strong. Stronger than passing cravings, stronger than the strongest cheese. So Jane found she could subconsciously make the decision to eat healthily... She left cheese behind using her willpower alone, amazing all of her friends and family in the process. Jane can now...find it easy to eat healthily and in smaller portions. She even completely cut out the cheese, and doesn't miss it at all. Jane astounded herself, and the best part was, that new feeling. Feeling self-control, feeling self-belief... That positive feeling completely replaced those old negative feelings. Jane used to use food to feel better, but realised there is a much healthier, easier way. Now Jane is in complete control of her eating and her weight, but she is happy now that her old jeans STILL don't fit. Those old jeans are now too big for her, and she had to buy some new, smaller jeans as a gift to herself. For finding it so effortlessly easy to re-gain control of life. To re-gain control of eating habits and to re-gain self-belief, self-confidence and self-worth.

I'd like you to remember back to a time where you faced a challenge. Something that you thought you might struggle with, but something you eventually succeeded at. Something that seemed as if it would be hard, but eventually, you did it... And I'd like you to get that feeling, that feeling of pride, that feeling of self-worth, that feeling of accomplishment and confidence in yourself. And as you have that feeling now, I'd like you to imagine that feeling as a colour. A bright, vivid, wonderful colour, and I'd like you to place that colour at the very core of your body. Right at the centre. Get a sense of that feeling, really feel those confident, successful, proud feelings that get stronger as the colour increases in brightness now. Feel good as you can allow that colour, that feeling, that idea to begin to flow from your core all the way out. To your head, your arms, your hands, your legs, your feet. All the way down to your toes, filling up your body completely with this amazing new sense of accomplishment, self-reliance and self-belief with this colour.

I'd like you to let this colour, filling up your body, absorb into every part of you now. Becoming a part of you, like a plant absorbing the rays of the sun, allowing the plant to take only what it needs to be a healthy, beautiful, perfect-sized plant. The plant eats only the completely natural, healthy food that it requires to maintain the perfect size and shape that a plant should naturally have. You don't see any fat plants, and that's because plants know when they have taken enough nutrients. Plants know when they have had enough food, and when they realise this, they automatically stop eating. When they become naturally aware that they require energy once more, so again they will eat small, healthy portions of natural, good food. Because plants know just what is right for them to be healthy, to lose excess weight and to be happy.

And you might not find that you will lose weight fast, but when you don't lose weight fast, the weight that falls off, stays off. Like snow melting from a snowman, it never comes back by itself. And you might find that your eating habits change completely, you may well realise that your stomach is feeling smaller already and if you really focus, perhaps you could imagine your stomach there. Imagine the shape of it, imagine the size of it, and imagine that you are using your subconscious mind to shrink it down now. Your stomach is shrinking to half its original size... Getting smaller and smaller now, and perhaps you might even...feel this now. And it feels good to know that your eating patterns and habits are changing even faster now, allowing you to permanently live happily and healthily whilst allowing that wonderful self-confidence and self-belief to fuel your every moment.

And just as a plant can feel good, so a stomach can feel good. And by listening to the messages that the stomach gives, a person can completely attune their body to the correct mode of eating which will allow the stomach to feel good. And because the stomach feels good when you feed it small, delicious portions of healthy food, this will cause the stomach to allow your entire body to function perfectly. Allowing excess fat to melt away and to stay away, cleaning the lungs and the heart, creating a family of happy organs there inside you now. Simply by listening to what your smaller stomach has to say.

You're a naturally smart person, you know this... You have had a great many successes in your life, and you've made a lot of great friends along the way. You know this... You are now in charge of the way in which you provide your body with energy. Healthy food and plenty of water, you know this... And because you know that, you know that this is right to make that change, as this is the thing that you came here to achieve... And I don't know if you're going to make this change happen now, later today, tomorrow or even next week, but every word that you hear, every thought that you think and every feeling that you feel will allow you to positively re-enforce all of these suggestions, allowing you to make these changes happen when...it's right for you to change now.

Your subconscious mind will spend every moment ensuring that you become the person that you know...you are going to be, successful...that best you that you know you can be is in your mind now. That bright, vivid colour-feeling is absorbed into every part of you like a map, growing stronger and stronger with each breath. Always providing your subconscious mind with directions towards your healthy, happy best self. Towards your new, positive life and towards greater and greater successes in every aspect of your life. And knowing you have that power, knowing you can make that change without even trying, just by breathing, just by living... Well... That feels good, now."

[Note: Part of that script was a "visualisation" – the bit about imagining the body filling with a colour – and although it wasn't technically an indirect suggestion, I figured I would leave it in to demonstrate how you can seamlessly fit very different types of suggestions together in the same script. Also, it segues nicely into the next hypnotherapy method that we're going to be looking at...]

VISUALISATIONS

What does it consist of?
This is the process of having your subject use their imagination to visualise different scenarios, designed to help them to resolve their problem. We are able to use a great variety of visualisation techniques to achieve this goal. I'm going to cover five different types of visualisation that you will be able to apply universally for a great variety of issues. In some cases, we are going to use a scenario-visualisation as a type of "rehearsal," so that the subject can get an idea of the small steps required to achieve their goal. In other cases we can use a "retrospective" visualisation sequence, which entails visualising the end result (and everything that comes with said result,) and working backwards from there to figure out the steps they would have used to reach their goal. These two types of visualisation will "program" the subject, so that when the real situation comes about, their real-world actions/reactions will be influenced positively. Reflecting the steps they learned during the visualisation process. This works because the subconscious mind often cannot tell the difference between reality and a vividly imagined scenario (think about dreams – dreams can seem very real sometimes... Almost as real as memories, right?) As such, the subject will learn by experiencing these new situations (even though they're not *really* experiencing them outside of their imagination.)

The rehearsal and retrospective visualisations are fairly similar to "future pacing" visualisations, except... In the case of future pacing, before we have the subject rehearse the new situations, we get them to "go back" to situations in the past where negative behaviours and experiences have caused problems. We have the subject re-imagine those situations differently (with positive behaviours and outcomes replacing the old negative aspects of the original memory.) Once that's done, we then "go forwards" into the "future" and have them imagine similar scenarios that could possibly happen, but which will unfold desirably with these new, imagined learnings.

We can also use visualisations alongside metaphors, by having the subject imagine a scenario that is not about them directly. This will still allow you to impart your desired "message," but in a much more subtle way. (We've spoken about metaphors already, so it's just a case of making them into something more "visual" within the subject's hypnotic experience.) Another type of visualisation that I'm going to talk about will be a "protective" visualisation. I'm sure you can figure out what that one is all about... In simple terms you're going to be visually altering the subjects' perception of threatening situations/people (having them imagine a bully wearing a pink tutu for example,) and also having them employ "protective measures" around themselves (such as visualising their own protective force-field.)

A lot of people are really good at visualising. These folks can vividly see things in their "minds-eye" just by using their imagination. As if they were actually seeing the image on a screen, for real. Some people however, struggle with visualising anything at all. These people will tell you that they can't see anything, that they can only see blackness when they close their eyes, etc. If this happens (and it will,) you can simply tell them something along the lines of; "OK, so I understand that you can't physically see what I'm asking you to visualise, and that's OK. So instead I'd just like you to get an idea in your head about what these images or scenes *would* look like if you *could* see them... Just get a general *sense* of it. It doesn't matter if you can *see* it. Just get an idea, get a sense of it and go with that, because you don't need to see something to know what it looks like. Just like you don't need to see a video of a memory to know exactly what happened in that memory. OK?"

Everyone can access the visual portion of their imagination, even if they have convinced themselves that they can't. Imagine, for instance, asking a subject; "What colour waistcoat did you wear on your wedding day?" Odds are, he'll tell you... How will he know? Well, he'll access a memory of himself wearing the waistcoat. Vivid or not, this memory will include a visualisation of himself at the wedding (or at the tailors in his suit,) with that colourful little waistcoat poking out of the jacket. Or he might even recall a photograph taken of the wedding party (by... visualising it!!!) If he couldn't "see" that, how would he know what colour it was? He wouldn't, not at all.

Anyone with a regularly-functioning brain is able to imagine what they themselves look like (even if they do sometimes exaggerate, for better or worse.) Thus, it leads on that they are able to imagine this image of themselves in any scenario that they so wish... Whether it is a memory or a completely fabricated scenario. Because of this, visualisations are a top-notch way of having a subject experience new ideas, beliefs and habits without actually having to go out and physically "do" these new things in real life.

How does it work?
I've arranged the following 5 visualisation techniques in alphabetical order:

Future pacing visualisation
"Future pacing" is a brilliant technique. Future pacing itself is another concept that has been whole-heartedly adopted by NLP practitioners, but I have always incorporated it into my own hypnotherapy sessions, which is why it needed to be included here. To do a future pace, you're going to have your subject imagine themselves in a past (negative) situation. But instead of just letting this memory play through just as it did when it happened, you're going to have the subject run through the memory with a completely different behaviour, expectation or resolution to the situation itself. This new part will obviously be more positive than the part it is replacing from the actual, original memory. To do this, you will need to have them imagine and explain the memory of the initial event. Once they have done this, common sense should dictate the thing that needs to be changed (so I can't give you an example of exactly what you're going to need to change, as it will be different on a case-by-case basis.)

As an example, what do you think you would change in the following memory, if the subject approached you asking for help losing weight and stopping an addiction to cakes/sweets? Let's assume we've already asked her to think back to her first memory of this happening:

"I was just leaving the interview for my dream job, and the interviewer told me as I was walking out the door that I could relax, because I got the job and they would send the paperwork confirming it within the next week... I was ecstatic, but I calmly smiled, shook her hand and left. I was about to jump in my car and drive home to tell my partner, when I noticed a bakery across the road from the car park, and I figured that I deserved to have a treat for acing the interview, so I went in and bought myself 2 cream cakes... Ordinarily I never used to eat cakes, but at the time I figured this was my reward. I got back into the car and I ate both cakes, one after the other. I remember feeling an overwhelming relief and happiness whilst eating the cakes, and the energy from the sugar made me feel even better. And ever since, whenever I feel I've done something well, even something small like getting all the housework done, that I deserve a reward... And I eat a cake or two... Two is better than one, it just makes me feel a lot better."

So we'll cut the memory there. Now, from that small passage, what would your initial response be? What part of that memory would you change? It's a pretty easy decision, right? Cut out the bakery. Have your subject re-imagine the scenario from start to finish, but completely delete the bakery from the imaginary sequence: Finish interview – walk to car – ~~go to bakery~~ – ~~eat cakes~~ – drive back to partner to give the good news.

Occasionally, you will find cases that aren't so simple, and the thing that you might need to change may be something that the subject doesn't mention when re-telling the story... At this point, if you haven't found something that needs changing, you will need to probe deeper. As the subject talks, have them pause and explain what they're feeling during this part... What they're expecting at this time... How they behaved whilst this was happening... By doing that, you will then be able to nail down a negative aspect of the memory, be it an action, a thought, a belief or a behavioural trait, and whatever that negative part turns out to be, you're going to have them replace it with something different or just erase it completely. As with the cake story above, it was fairly simple to figure out what needed to change, so I took it out. I could have replaced it with something else: Finish the interview – walk to your car – *sit in the car, get out your phone and post a cryptic-happy Facebook status with a big smiley face on it* – then drive back to your partner to give the good news. Get the idea?

Once you have installed this new facet within the past experience and repeated the positive-visualisation process a couple of times, you can then "future pace." Have the subject imagine a possible future scenario that could happen, something that could be very similar to (if not the same as) the initial negative event. Whilst you are having the subject imagine this future event, have them actively employing the new installations (positive beliefs, behaviours or expectations) that you set up during the run-through of the past experience. You will walk them through this visualisation, suggesting different ways that they may react positively to this situation. Have them utilise these new learnings to allow them to be in control of themselves during this new event. You can do this by having them describe the situation (whilst still hypnotised.) Ask them how different they feel now, as opposed to how they felt before, and feed their experience back to them with even more positive suggestions. For instance; "oh, so you feel happy *and* in control now... Doesn't it feel much better to be in control whilst you are feeling happy... Allowing you to double that feeling of happiness now, knowing that being in control is an amazing reward in itself."

By repeatedly running through these imaginary scenarios with the positive installations, the subconscious mind will be able to store all of the information about how they will react, how to behave or what to expect when the situation (or a similar situation) comes about in *real life*. So rather than just doing the old negative thing that they'd become accustomed to doing in those situations, they'll now have a new, preferable option and their subconscious will know exactly how to use it when the time arises.

So to recap, we take the subject to an old situation, guide them through the situation with a different (positive) outcome, which in turn will help to de-activate their old (negative) behaviour. We then future pace the subject through a similar situation that could happen. This trains the subject so that they can respond with their new, positive behaviour. It allows their creative subconscious mind to produce the ideal solution for themselves, whilst at the same time checking to ensure that the old, negative behaviour is completely de-activated. You can check this simply, by asking them which way they would prefer to react; the old way or the new, positive way.

Metaphor/Story visualisation
Now, we've spoken about metaphors and stories already, so you know you are able to create a metaphor for a problem that your subject is having without even mentioning the subject/problem directly. The story you use can be about someone else (whether real or imaginary,) or even a complete fantasy sequence regarding something seemingly completely unrelated (Frogs and Newts spring to mind...) It doesn't matter, so long as the underlying message is comparable to the subject's problem. You can have the subject imagine the story from a "3rd person perspective," like a movie, as if he were watching it unfold on a screen in front of him. Or you can have him imagine it in the "1st person," as if he is one of the characters in the story, or even just as an observer from inside the story. Again, however you choose to frame it is entirely left at your discretion.

Having your subject visualise metaphors and stories will obviously add another layer of depth to the whole process. This can be done in a direct way (as opposed to the indirect hypnotic story telling mentioned earlier.) You can inform your subject that you're going to tell them a story. Tell them exactly how you'd like them to visualise the story (1st person/3rd person perspective,) just to ensure that your subject is completely involved in the experience of this visualisation, and not off in their own thoughts, daydreaming (which does sometimes happen.)

Let's say you had a subject come to you, wanting help with anxiety in social situations. Can you think of a metaphor visualisation for that? Take a moment and think... What story could you tell to someone with anxiety that would help them to come to terms with and overcome that anxiousness? Have a go at coming up with your own, before you read an example of what I would do, below:

"I have a friend who wanted my help a couple of years ago, his name is Eric. I want you to get an idea of what he looks like… Eric is a big chap, he's around 6'1, works out and is built like a shed. The guy is huge. He wears big black boots, army trousers, really tight rock-band t-shirts with the sleeves cut off to show off his muscles… The guy has a head full of piercings and I'd estimate he's about 50% covered in tattoos. Not the sort of figure you'd like to bump into in a dark alleyway, I'll say that much. Now imagine Eric walking down the street, a guy with the characteristics I just explained, you'd assume he'd have his head held high, shoulders back, meeting the world head-on… But in fact, Eric once had a bad experience out in public. He wouldn't tell me what that experience was, but when you saw Eric walking down the high street, the guy tried to make himself appear as small as possible…

Imagine that – he kept his head down, making eye-contact with nobody, always checking over his shoulders twitchily… Even going into the coffee shop to order a Cappuccino made Eric feel uncomfortable. Imagine walking along the street with Eric, and seeing the way that he acted. Seeing the way that he reacted to the tiniest sound. Feeling how uncomfortable he felt, even though there was no real reason for him to feel that way. Walking down the street, there are people walking, shopping, laughing and joking and there is nothing unpleasant there at all… Just a regular shop-filled street.

We know that Eric's behaviour was un-natural, because we're all born curious and confident, ready to try new things and find new friends. So we also know that some "thing" at some time changed the natural way that Eric thought about being in public, into something unnatural. So Eric *learned* how to be anxious in public. But whether the thing that taught him to be anxious was something on the inside or something on the outside, once that thing itself has gone, all that's left is just a thought… Just an unwanted memory of something that happened in the past… Something that you know, shouldn't have any power over the future, because all it is now is just a thought.

The thing is, you see people pass Eric in the street, and the sheer size of him, coupled with his unusual dress-sense usually causes the general public to move out of his way… Even though he is the gentlest, kindest person you could be, his image states otherwise. But because of something that might have happened in the past, this guy feels anxious just nipping down the local shop to buy a newspaper…

I spoke to Eric about this. He actually sat right there in the chair where you're relaxing now… Although he didn't fit in it quite as comfortably as you can fit in. Learning to be confident didn't take Eric very long at all, because that natural confidence was within him all along, that same confidence that is within all of us.

He had just lost it somewhere along the way. Somehow he had hidden that natural ability to be comfortable in new situations, hidden it deep in his mind somewhere. Hidden his natural confidence and then forgot where it was. But there was a time when we were all carefree and confident. There was a time when Eric could walk up to anybody and say hello... When he could walk the streets with his friends or his family and look at other people, people he had never met before, and smile... Sometimes they would smile back, sometimes they would just continue walking. Because people are often too busy, wrapped up in their own worlds to even give a seconds thought to the person walking by, or the person asking them for directions, or even the person they're serving at the store whilst they work. Eric came to realise, that bad experience that might have happened to him in the past, whether he remembered exactly what that experience was or not... Whatever that thing was that stopped him being his outgoing, happy-go-lucky self is actually just a memory... Just an old thought about something in the past...

In fact right now, all these years later as Eric is older, wiser and a stronger person. That old feeling that he had on a subconscious pedestal does not actually have any power anymore, because It's just a thought. Just like the thing that you're thinking of now is just a thought, and you can think it, and you can un-think it. And thinking about that, Eric decided that he knew he could think about focusing on enjoying his life, and the thoughts that he used to think, he could actively think about not thinking those things. Instead, think about how much easier life is going to be, by just knowing that this natural, in-built confidence, curiosity and happiness is just a thought away. And thinking that new thought allows him to live, love and laugh, wherever and whenever he likes to do those things now. And so he thinks that he can, and knowing now that you can think those thoughts that Eric thinks... You might find that your happiness, your ease, your confidence is just one tiny little thought away, and you can feel good in the knowledge that once Eric realised that you can choose to leave those old feelings behind, he began to walk tall.

Imagine walking down the street with Eric at your side now, as a good friend of your own. Walking tall together. He begins to smile at strangers, imagine that. Imagine how good it feels to brighten somebodies day with a smile... He begins to laugh and joke in the street, and you can laugh too... Imagine laughing and smiling with Eric, in the middle of a bustling street. Content, enjoying the moment, allowing that new thought to allow you to feel good now. Imagine walking into a coffee shop with Eric and ordering him a Cappuccino, and something for yourself, whilst joking with the staff... And you might find that you can even enjoy yourself whilst doing that... And as you imagine Eric walking away, smiling and waving goodbye, you might realise that since listening to the words that I've said, Eric remains confident. He knows he is in control and that he is only ever a thought away from happiness, contentment and confidence. And all these years later, Eric still walks tall today... And that thought can make you feel good, now."

Protective visualisation
This type of visualisation can be used in two different ways; either to change your perception with regards to a threatening person or thing (using a memory of the "threat.") Or to install a "protective shield" if you will, which can be utilised in various different ways.

The first type of protective visualisation, we can exemplify with a fear of spiders. Arachnophobes often exaggerate the size of spiders in their own heads, believing a tiny house-spider to be a giant, bloodthirsty behemoth, out to get them... Yet, they will see a beetle or some other similar-sized insect, and have no skewed perception or fear. Weird eh? To use a protective visualisation with the spider example, we would aim to have the subject use a memory they have involving spiders (and their fear of spiders,) and change something within the memory...but what would we change? Anything to make that memory less scary. It helps even more if you decide to make the "threat" appear ridiculous. You could suggest that they replay the memory, but this time it'll be as if the spider is drunk, and keeps stumbling, tripping over and burping... Perhaps suggest that every step the spider takes, it gets smaller, and the spider starts complaining about that in a cute squeaky voice (you can do a stupid voice, and take the roll of "spider." This makes their experience more real, and more importantly, more ridiculous.) You could suggest they play the memory backwards, at high speed, whilst playing some ridiculous circus-clown music in their head (or you could hum it.) Like I said, the main point with this exercise is to make the subject realise that the perceived threat is actually not threatening at all. (It may still be a mild irritation... But probably doesn't deserve the full-on reaction it receives.)

The same goes if your subject has a colleague or acquaintance who gets up their nose... It's simply a case of changing the perception of this person, kind of like that old trick for public speaking confidence; Nervous about giving a speech? Easy, just imagine everybody in the room naked... It's just like that, except for three things. One: It can be done on a smaller level (i.e. one person instead of a group.) Two: It's going to be a lot more ridiculous. Three: You're actually going to have the subject run through the thing in their head beforehand, so that "memory" automatically pops up next time they encounter said person. Once you've changed the way that the subject thinks about this person, it will automatically change the way that they react to the person.

What specific things can you change about a person that someone dislikes to make them appear more harmless? Again, you're limited only by your imagination. Have the subject run through a memory about the person and make them appear ridiculous, frail or the exact opposite of the trait that the subject has a problem with. If it's a general dislike or fear of somebody, have them look ridiculous – give them big flappy ears that wiggle dramatically every time they talk. Make their voice ridiculously high pitched or give them an exaggerated speech impediment. Have them imagine the person picking their nose and farting throughout the whole memory. Do anything to make them appear ridiculous.

If it's a person's power and strength that they fear, have them imagine the opposite. Imagine the person as an old frail man wearing 1-inch thick reading-glasses, walking with a zimmer frame. Imagine them as a little kid, and everything they say comes out in a whiny, feeble voice, and maybe they've just wet themselves. You see, you can use your imagination to take away the negative feelings and replace them with laughter and ridiculousness. The fact that the subject can honestly laugh at the idea of this person/thing will allow them to stop being afraid of it, because seriously, how often do you laugh at things that you are afraid of?

The second type of protective visualisation is more tailored to personal health and wellbeing, pain control and self-confidence/calmness. We can achieve these results by visualising a couple of different things:

Visualisation for health/immune system
This visualisation is used to improve general health/immune system strength. Have the subject imagine his internal defence system actively surrounding any problem areas and attacking them. For example, if a subject suffers from frequent colds, you would have them focus their attention around their mouth, nose and throat. This visualisation can be very basic, imagining the healing cells moving to the required areas. Or it can be made more visual by, say, imagining tiny health-soldiers inside the body running to battle another army (the unhealthy bad guys) gathered around the problem areas. Obviously you have them imagine the bad guys losing the war (duh!) If you're looking to help a subject improve their immune system, you can also have them visualise these internal defence systems multiplying, spreading and getting stronger and more prevalent throughout their entire body.

Protective shield visualisation – This type of visualisation is useful to instil a sense of self-belief and confidence, to reduce anxiety and nervousness and to increase positivity. Have the subject imagine a force-field or a bubble that encases their entire body (with this, you may want to check that the subject isn't claustrophobic first, just to be on the safe side.) Here's a quick protective shield script to give you an idea of the kind of suggestions that you should be including:

"As you relax now, I'd like you to imagine that from every part of your body, there is a wonderful powerful force emanating. This force is moving outwards from your core, from your muscles, from your skin, creating a bubble of energy, all around your entire body. This energy shield will protect you from all of those things that are negative, from all of those thoughts that are unwanted. It will allow you to remain confident, calm and relaxed in whichever situation you find yourself in. This protective shield, your own bubble of positive energy can remain with you always, from the moment you awaken until the moment you drift off into a pleasant state of sleep. This shield will be with you every moment of every day, and eventually you will no longer even need to think about it, because this protective shield will simply allow you to go through your life feeling wonderful. Completely free from negativity, as this bubble is full with self-confidence, self-belief, self-worth, relaxation and positivity. I'd like you to get a sense of those feelings now. Feel those feelings inside your protective bubble, feel that self-confidence. Knowing you can do whatever it is that you set your mind to. Feel that self-belief. Knowing that you are able to be the you that you want to be. Feel that self-worth… Knowing that you are always true to yourself and your health. Feel that relaxation, as you drift and as you dream now, allowing the protective bubble, your own personal shield to solidify and to remain an integral part of your body and your mind, for just as long as you need to relax now…"

Energy Ball Visualisation
I personally use this visualisation a lot, and it's a nice technique to use because it doesn't have to be an "energy ball" you can attach any feeling that you like to the "ball" (energy, confidence, calmness, focus, concentration, etc.) Again, this method is pretty universal for most people, because all you need to do is have the subject focus on the centre (core) of their body, and imagine a ball of energy there. Once this is done, you can "anchor" the ball using basic anchoring techniques (that follow a little later in the book,) so that the subject can, if required, use the energy ball as and when they need it. It really is as simple as that, but it works wonderfully. Here's a quick script for you:

"I'd like you to focus on your core. The very centre of your body, and what I'd like you to do now is imagine a ball of energy right there. Right at your core. Now, I'd like you to think of a powerful colour, an energetic, confident colour. Once you have that, I'd like you to imagine that ball of energy in that colour now. Allowing that wonderful, positive feeling to begin to emanate from the centre, outwards with a wonderful, warm, confident energy. Now what I'd like you to do, is imagine that ball of energy beginning to spin. Spinning faster and faster with every word I say and every breath that you exhale. And as the ball spins the colour becomes brighter and brighter. And as the colour becomes brighter, the energy being released from the ball into your body gets stronger, builds and builds. Faster, brighter, more energy, faster and brighter.

Feel that energy now buzzing from your core, all the way to the top of your head, to the tips of your toes. The colour and the energy and that wonderful feeling, circulating throughout your entire body. As if that energy is part of your body now, as if the blood always pumping through your veins is now filled with energy, confidence and positivity. As the ball spins and gets faster and brighter, it's beginning to get bigger and bigger and bigger, and stronger and brighter still. And as your ball of energy continues to spin, that colour getting brighter and that feeling getting stronger. You can allow all of these feelings, colours and all of this energy to become a part of you. You are able to access this feeling of energy, this feeling of confidence, the wonderful feeling of this ball of colour just whenever you need it. And at any point you wish, you can instantly find this energy, this colour at your core, and it may even be more powerful than it is right now. In fact every time you think of it, this ball of energy will be even brighter, even bigger, even faster, stronger and more energising than ever before. And that feels good..."

Pain Control Colour Visualisation
So as you can see, with the energy ball we used a colour, but this pain control colour method is slightly different to that. With this visualisation, we are assuming that the subject has some chronic pain that they wish to be rid of. (As with all pain control hypnotherapy, it is always best to advise your subject to seek medical consultation before using hypnosis to relieve the pain. This is because pain is often there as a warning to tell you that there is something is wrong with your body, so obviously it's in your best interest to find out what that "cause" is – if you can – before taking away the "symptom:" pain. If the subject has already done this, that's fine, but remember that masking the pain could result in further problems for the subject if there is a serious underlying issue.)

The basic principle of this visualisation is to have the subject tell you where the pain is, then have them imagine that area of their body filled or covered with a "painful" colour (have them choose a colour that best represents pain to them.) Have them fill/cover the rest of their body (the un-painful parts) with a different, "positive" colour. Once you have set these two colours, you then have the subject imagine the positive colour replacing the negative colour in some way. You can have them imagine that the negative colour is a beach, and the positive colour is the ocean, and the tide is coming in so the positive colour gradually washes away all of the negative colour. You could have them imagine that it's as if they are covered with paint, and they use a brush to spread the good colour over the bad colour. Perhaps make the positive colour just seep into the negative colour and dissolve it away... Use your imagination (I know I say it a lot, but it's true – be creative! Do things your own way, and you'll get better at improvising when you need to.) Here's a script though, if you're gonna ignore that last part:

"I'd like you to focus on that area of your body where you've been experiencing pain, and I would like you to use your imagination for a moment now. I'd like you to imagine a bubble around that entire area. Now this bubble can be any shape at all, so long as it surrounds the entire painful area. Now what I'd like you to do is imagine that bubble filling up with a colour, a colour that represents pain to you. A negative colour. Do that now, fill that bubble all the way up with that colour and allow that colour to become stronger and stronger. As the colour fills and the intensity increases, perhaps you may notice that pain increasing a little more – but that's OK for now, because it will be gone in a moment. What I'd like you to imagine now, is that the rest of your body, feeling comfortable and pain-free, is filling with a different colour. A colour that represents health, comfort and a wonderful, pleasant feeling. Do this now. Imagine your entire body, filling with this new colour, so that every part except for that bubble of painful colour is now filled with this new, positive colour. Allow the colour to intensify. Allow that wonderful feeling to move through your entire body, wherever that wonderful new, bright colour is helping you to feel good now.

In a moment, I'm going to count from three to one, and when I count one, that bubble filled with the painful colour will pop. When it does, you will find that the healthy, positive colour, being much more powerful than that old negative colour will flow into the negative colour. It will dissolve that pain away, as your healthy positive colour fills every part of your body. Completely free, loose, easy, relaxed and comfortable 3, 2, 1... Pop that bubble now, and feel the old pain dissolving away. That new colour flowing into the space, replacing that old negative colour with this new, healthy wonderful colour. Feel that old colour dissolving away, filling with bright, healthiness. Imbuing that part of your body with a new resilience, a new tolerance a wonderful new feeling of comfort and control. Because just as that colour disappeared, just as easily as that old feeling has dissolved away, allowing you to relax now. To drift and to dream and to focus on that wonderful new colour, flowing throughout your entire body. Spreading comfort, relief, relaxation with every breath that you exhale. Whether you're awake or asleep, standing or sitting, moving or still, that colour remains. Allowing you to feel good, allowing you to know that the thought of the pain that was there, has been replaced by the thought of something new. Something bright, something calm, healthy and completely comfortable, now."

Rehearsal Visualisation
The rehearsal visualisation is exactly what it says, you have the subject visualise themselves "rehearsing" a situation that they are worried about. Whether it's something they're not very good at, something they really don't want to mess up, a high pressure situation or general nervousness... No matter what it is that's causing them trouble, it's a great idea to use a rehearsal visualisation to

"practice" doing the thing before having to actually do it in real life. Especially if it's a scenario that they aren't able to recreate beforehand in order to practice (i.e. performing in front of hundreds of people on-stage, giving a speech at a wedding or delivering a presentation to your board of directors. You can't exactly set these situations up to rehearse in your living room, can you?)

Obviously, these rehearsal visualisations are going to be different every time, so there's no point giving a specific example, but instead I'm going to walk you through exactly what you're going to want to cover. Firstly, you'll need to get an idea of what it is that the subject wishes to achieve. Get them to give you all the steps that need to happen (or all the boxes that need to be ticked,) for them to have a completely positive, successful experience. Once you have this information, you are then able to walk them through the process of a successful rehearsal. Before running through this visualisation, you will suggest that the subject thinks back to a time (or times) where they have done this "thing" before (or when they've accomplished something similar/related.) Then suggest that they feel the positivity and all of the good feelings that went along with successfully doing that thing. (If you like, you can anchor these feelings too, to further strengthen your subjects' experience.) You'll then suggest that they will continue to experience those positive thoughts and feelings whilst running through the full rehearsal visualisation. As you walk the subject through their rehearsal, you can suggest a continuous increase in these positive feelings (and fire off the anchor, if you installed one,) so that the positivity felt during the rehearsal visualisation should almost be making your subject grin from ear to ear. They should be so full of positivity that they might even explode (put a towel down in case – only kidding.)

When it comes down to the rehearsal itself, you will suggest that they enter the situation with their head held high, confident and calm. They will acknowledge anybody that needs acknowledgement with a wonderful smile, beaming positivity. They will then go on to do their thing perfectly. They will do the thing better than they have ever done the thing before in their life. They will remember any and all parts of the thing easily and effortlessly. Subconsciously doing the thing, allowing their powerful subconscious mind to help them to succeed at doing the thing without even having to think about what comes next. They will do the thing confidently with the knowledge that they are in complete control of themselves and the situation. Any outside distractions will fade into the background, and they will be able to take them completely in-stride and continue doing the thing with complete focus, attention and ease. Once they have finished doing the thing, they will feel a wave of happiness, contentment, self-confidence and self-worth. Maybe there will be handshakes, applause, congratulations and compliments, but whatever happens after successful completion of the thing, they will know that they have done the thing perfectly, and to the best of their abilities. Knowing how easy it was to do the thing, they might even wonder why they were worried in the first place, because it turned out that they aced the thing. They completely rocked it, and for that short time when they were doing the thing, they were the absolute best at it. They were the thing-master, and with that experience and with that knowledge, they will find that whenever they have to do the thing again, they will take all of the learnings from these rehearsals, absorb all of these experiences deep into their subconscious mind as a map. This map will guide them towards their continued success, completely aware that they are more than able to excel at the thing, smashing their own expectations and giving their absolute best, easily, effortlessly and confidently.

Even just reading that paragraph, I bet you felt kinda good, didn't you? I know I felt good even as I was writing it, and that's the point! You want to make the rehearsal as positive as possible. Run through the entire visualisation more than once, and each time you should ramp up the positivity. Increase the good feelings and the perceived ease with which they do the thing. Ramp it up and up and up, build that energy and build that positivity until it is sky high. Once you've gone through this visualisation with your subject a couple of times, you can give them the suggestion that they will spend a few minutes, two or three times a week (and just before their "thing") running through this rehearsal visualisation by themselves. This will ensure that they'll be in the right frame of mind when the time comes, enabling them to know they can do the very best that they are capable of, with no self-imposed limitations.

Retrospective Visualisation
The final visualisation method is a "retrospective" one. Retrospective visualisations are a great way to help people to achieve their goals by visualising themselves as having achieved the goal already. Imagining themselves in that new situation and working backwards, to figure out the steps that they would have had to have taken to get to that end goal. For instance, let's say a subject wants to get a promotion from his job... He's currently a barman at a classy local wine bar, and his short-term goal is to become Assistant Bar Manager. You'd have the subject imagine himself as the Assistant Manager, have him get a feel for it... Being respected by the bar staff, helping customers and enjoying all the positive aspects that comes as part and parcel of this new role. Then, during his visualisation as the new Assistant Manager, you'd have him remain "in character" and think back from that future point, about the exact steps it would have taken to get to said position. You'll do this by working backwards from the goal (future,) back to now (present.) An example for this process-tree would be something like:

Got the promotion.
↓
Attended and passed the interview with his Manager.
↓

Bought a new suit and had a haircut.
↓
Prepared interview answers and questions.
↓
Learned more about the company.
↓
Arranged a time/date for an interview.
↓
Completed Manager-training.
↓
Asked the Manager to sign him up for Manager-training.
↓
Registered his interest to work his way up the company ladder.
↓
Began to always arrive to work early, rather than just on time, and ensuring that no matter his mood, he would always strive to work as efficiently as possible.
↓
Read an online guide to getting promoted, looking for tips and pointers.
↓
Spoke to the current Assistant Manager (who was planning on leaving his position) about what he would need to do to get a promotion.
↓
Had the initial thought: I want a promotion.

That is a rough example of what someone's process of achieving their goal *could* be... Now there may be more steps, there may be less. You have to analyse the subjects' steps and determine whether they are logical and achievable or whether you believe they may have missed something out. If the example above went: Had the initial thought → Did training → Got the promotion, you would obviously realise that it probably wouldn't be that simple, that he'd missed a bunch of steps out. At which point you would have to probe deeper and ask the subject; "how did you end up getting the promotion, because surely you didn't just do the training and automatically walk into the job did you?" You could also ask; "how did you know to do the training? How did you arrange that? What did you do to pass it, or did it just happen all by itself?"

Once you have a process-tree that seems like it could actually work in real life, you have to go back over each step with the subject and ask them to visualise exactly what they did to successfully complete each step. What were the things that they did, that if they *hadn't* done them, they may not have succeeded? It may help you to write down all of this information, so that both you and the subject can remember it, because there may be a lot of information and subtleties. Once you have the entire process mapped out from start to finish, you then have the option to run through the entire process with the subject. Have them visualise every step in as much detail as possible in the correct sequence, whilst ensuring that you include everything that the subject mentioned during the breakdown of the processes. Again, as with the rehearsal visualisation, you can give the subject the suggestion to run through this visualisation in their spare time once or twice a week (the more repetition the better!) Once this process has been completed, this "goal visualisation" will work much better than plain old goal-setting. This is due to the fact that the subconscious mind will process and store all of these goals, this creates a map, a list of directions that your subject can actively work towards to attain their goal.

Knowing that things may change, or not quite go to plan along the way (as frequently happens in our human endeavours,) you can inform your subject that they have the ability to "reroute" these directions if need be. So if one of the steps doesn't take them to the place that they expected, they can take a moment to repeat the initial process themselves. Imagining the goal and working their way back from the goal once again to this new point in time to see if anything has changed and if there are any new steps to include or old steps to remove.

AVERSION
What does it consist of?

Being averse to something means not liking that thing. Aversion in hypnotherapy means you are aiming to cause your subject to dislike something. Aversion is a great technique to include when you have a subject that wants to quit doing something that they kinda like (i.e. smoking, eating 20 cakes a day, binge drinking alcohol, taking drugs, etc.) I frequently utilise aversion techniques when performing weight loss and smoking cessation sessions, and it works well in such sessions alongside metaphors, direct suggestions and future-pacing techniques.

The basic idea is to link the thing that the subject wishes to give up with something negative that they absolutely hate. So if I had a subject who wished to give up eating chocolate, I would find out a type of food that they hate and have them imagine eating chocolate, whilst experiencing the negative effects of eating the hated-food. If I had a subject who wished to give up smoking, I'd have them imagine smoking and have every drag on the cigarette taste like they're inhaling the smoke from a clump of greasy burning hair (urgh!) Once you have the ideal response (the subject looking pale and almost gagging,) I'd then anchor this feeling to a touch, so that every time you touch them in that place, they get the horrible feeling. That's practically it – it's a very simple, yet very effective technique. The NLP version of this technique is known as a "compulsion blowout," (if you'd like to do more research.)

How does it work?

This technique works by associating (or anchoring) a negative response to something that the subject wishes to give up. If performed correctly, the aversion-response will be triggered any time after the session, if/when the subject tries to do the thing that they're not meant to be doing. Just the thought of doing it, however, should be enough to dissuade them from even trying...

Firstly you need to establish *exactly* what it is that the subject wishes to stop doing. You don't want to stop him from enjoying all sweet foods if he just wants to stop eating cream cakes, right? This should be figured out before you begin the hypnotherapy session, during your consultation/information gathering section. Once you figure out what your subject wants to give up, you then need to find out something that your subject absolutely hates the smell/taste/feeling of (depending on what you're doing the session for.) If your subject can't think of a taste/smell that he particularly dislikes just use a universal one: Burning hair, dog poo, a pig farm, stinky farts, sulphur, rotten eggs, vomit... Be creative, there's always something that'll make a person retch, you've just got to find it. Feel free to be as disgusting as possible and the more descriptive, the better! If they want to give up eating hot dogs, don't just say "imagine eating that hot dog and it smells like rotten eggs... it smells really gross." You need to make it more realistic, you want to make them feel SICK! Have them "imagine that the sausage in that hot dog in your hand has been replaced with a huge, stinky, sticky dog poo, it's all over the bun and smeared all over your fingers, that horrible stench is so strong, getting stronger with every breath, and instead of mustard, this hot dog you hold in your hand is covered in puke with bits of carrot and spaghetti in it... Getting closer and closer to your mouth..." Sounds terrible, right? Can you imagine eating a poo hot dog with extra vomit? *gags* But as I mentioned before, it doesn't have to be anything so gross, I once helped a woman stop drinking 8 cans of energy drink a day by suggesting that the energy drink was a different flavoured one of the same make... This was enough to make her gag and enough to cause an aversion to her favourite flavour, so you've just got to find the thing that works for your subject at the time.

So, you've got the thing that wants changing and you've figured out what you're going to use to cause the aversion. Now it's literally just a case of doing it. Have them imagine doing/eating/smoking the thing that they normally do in a scenario where they'd normally do it. Have them run through this "normal scene" in their head once. Then you're going to change it and have them run through it again, but this time the reaction is going to be different. The taste, smell, feeling is going to be terrible. It will still appear like they are doing the thing they normally do, but all the pleasure and any good feelings will be completely removed and replaced with terribly disgusting or uncomfortable counterparts. You do this very simply by giving the direct suggestion that the next time they imagine doing/eating/ smoking that thing, it's going to taste/smell/feel terrible, just like *[whatever it is you're replacing it with]*.

I find it is very effective to repeat this section a couple of times to really ramp up that association and aversion-response. (Also because it's hilarious to see someone gagging and retching for "no reason" – not that I'm cruel or anything.) So you get them to the maximum level of discomfort (you should probably stop just before they look like they're going to vomit, because it can happen, trust me.) Once you get them to this level you employ your anchor. You press down with a finger/thumb somewhere on their body (i.e. on their shoulder, knee or the back of their hand,) whilst their uncomfortable feeling is at its peak. When you release the anchor, you suggest that the feeling is gone completely, and immediately take away your finger from the anchor point. Repeat this process a couple of times and you will have a very strong negative anchor. You can use this anchor at any point during the therapy session when giving negative suggestions about the thing that they are giving up.

You don't *have to* use the anchor, it's just a technique that I have found works really well alongside this aversion therapy. If you don't want to use it, simply use the aversion part on its' own, it will still be very effective at causing the subject to react differently to the thing that they…used to like.

Sample script
"And just as you are relaxing now, I'd like you to imagine what it is like to smoke a cigarette. I'd like you to imagine yourself, as if you are in one of the places where you normally smoke the most, and I'd like you to imagine lighting up a cigarette… Holding it in your hands the way that you normally hold it… Feeling the cigarette against your lips as you take a drag, taste and feel that smoke in your mouth, travelling down into your lungs as you inhale… Feeling the feelings that go along with that, and exhaling that smoke… Smelling the smoke curling up from the burning cherry end of the cigarette, up over your hand and all around you, the smell of that smoke.

Now you can forget about that image and go on relaxing for a moment, and we're going to do that once again. This time however, when you imagine the taste and the smell of smoking that cigarette, you'll find that it's going to taste like burning, greasy hair, sulphur, burning rubber and rotten eggs. All combined together into a horrendous stench and a terrible, gross, rancid taste, like the taste of stale vomit right at the back of your throat… I'd like you to imagine yourself, as if you are in that place again where you normally smoke the most, and I'd like you to imagine taking out a cigarette, placing it between your lips and lighting it up… That taste instantly hitting the inside of your mouth like you're eating a clump of burnt hair… Feeling the cigarette against your lips as if the butt has been soaking in a damp, dirty, full ash tray for weeks. That taste getting worse and worse with every drag that you take...

Take another drag and taste and feel that repulsive smoke in your mouth, travelling down into your lungs as you inhale. Tightening, squeezing your lungs from the inside, making them feel uncomfortable as the taste and the smell double in intensity, so horribly rank... Feeling the feelings that go along with that, and exhaling that disgusting smoke, and that smoke that you exhaled is sticking all over your clothes and your hair. Making your entire body smell like that burning hair, rotten eggs, horrible disgusting stench. That rancid smoke curling up from the burning cherry end of that cigarette, up over your hand, into your pores, turning your fingers and fingernails yellow. Turning your teeth brown and making your breath smell terrible and rancid. *[ANCHOR]* The taste and smell of cigarettes are becoming repulsive to you now. Getting stronger and worse and horrible, making you feel sick with the stench of that smoke, with the gross feeling of that cigarette between your lips and in your fingers. And that smell and taste is completely *[RELEASE ANCHOR] gone now! Find you can* breathe now, clean, fresh air, with every breath that you take, the stench of those awful old cigarettes is gone, completely.

Imagine now for a moment that you are in a room filled with amazing flowers, and wonderful foods, and the smell is positively delightful, as you stand there on your own, just enjoying the wonderful smells of nature, and all of your favourite foods, right there in front of you. And now I would like you to imagine that a dirty old man is standing beside you with a filthy cigarette, puffing it right in your face. The smell of these awful cigarettes completely filling the room, getting up your nose, making all that nice food smell of smoke. Completely ruining your experience, the smell of burnt smoke entering your nose, making you feel sick *[ANCHOR]*, and as it burns it makes you feel worse, and worse, and it makes you want to wretch. This cigarette smoke makes you want to be sick. And he's blowing it in your face, and that smell is getting worse and worse. Burnt hair, sulphur, rotten eggs, rancid, horrible smoke filling the room, but you can forget about cigarettes now, *[RELEASE ANCHOR]* and take a wonderful, clean breath of fresh, clean, air and relax. Deeper and deeper, and this wonderful feeling of relaxation reinforcing all of the suggestions that I have already given you, as you travel deeper and deeper into this wonderful world of peace, and tranquility."

[Note: As mentioned previously, you are able to repeat this a couple of times or include different scenarios, as demonstrated in the last paragraph, to increase the overall effect of the aversion therapy.]

PATTERN INTERRUPTION

What does it consist of?
Pattern Interruption is a method of changing a person's state by interrupting something that they would ordinarily do "habitually." Flick back to the induction section and take a look at the handshake induction again, this is the most obvious example (from a pure-hypnosis perspective) of a pattern interrupt. You go to shake someone's hand, and instead of shaking it, you take their hand with your free hand, their natural "handshake" pattern has been successfully interrupted – at which point you are able to give them a suggestion (such as "look at your hand" or "sleep") and this suggestion will be more successfully delivered than if you were to simply give them the suggestion "cold."

How about another parental example: When a child falls over and scrapes his knee, you know what's coming; tears and screaming. If you take the attention of the child, however, and divert it immediately to something different...like pulling a funny face, dancing, playing an impromptu game... Well, somehow that pain just isn't quite as intense anymore. Somehow, a little blubber and sniffle will suffice. The child will pick himself up, dust himself off and get back to doing child-stuff without making your ears bleed. Pattern interrupts, ladies and gentlemen – helping parents trick their children since the dawn of time.

Another "non-therapeutic" pattern interrupt worthy of note is a method used initially (as far as I'm aware) by our friend, Dr. Erickson. This pattern interrupt can be set-up in a rather sneaky way, simply by asking a non-hypnotised person; "can you shake your head to signify a NO response?" There are only two expected responses to this seemingly innocuous question, both are cleverly dealt with using an unexpected response (pattern interrupt.) If the person says yes and nods his head, Erickson would respond by saying; "That doesn't mean no..." and if the subject shook his head and said no, Erickson would respond with; "Oh, you can't?" – Both of these responses, if un-expected, would cause the subject to have a moment of confusion (which is what we are aiming for when using this process,) meaning they would easily go into a state of trance, if you were to capitalise on this "confused state."

Aside from confusing people into a state of hypnosis, pattern interrupts can also be utilised in a therapy-context. Have you ever had a time when you were telling a story to someone, a story or memory that you knew completely off by heart, and this person interrupted your story for a moment with something completely unrelated... Perhaps even a short anecdote about going on a river-boat trip with their family when they were a child, and your friend actually *fell in the river* by accident before they even *got* to the boat. All of your friends clothes were absolutely ruined, their siblings were rolling around on the grass in fits of uncontrollable laughter. Tears of laughter streaming down their faces, almost peeing their pants with laughter. Their parents were screaming to your friend to get out, quick (and trying not to laugh their arses off too – because that's not the respectable-parent thing to do, obviously! *ahem*) The parents eventually managed to get your sobbing child-friend out of those sopping wet child-clothes that were saturated with stagnant river-water, and they found an ACTUAL live trout flapping around in their underpants! What are the odds of that happening? Then you find you've totally forgotten what I was talking about before, when you *try* to remember back to what I was talking about before the fish story... Something to do with hypnosis though, right? But what was it specifically?

That was an example of a pattern interrupt. Your pattern was "reading about hypnosis," I interrupted the pattern with an anecdote about rivers and fish and all that jazz (I even practically told you I was going to do it beforehand too) and then you still *probably* couldn't remember what the hell was happening, because it was all kind of happening... so darn naturally.

The "pattern" that we are interrupting can in fact be thought of as a "habit" (but pattern interrupt sounds way cooler than habit interrupt, and as you know, hypnotherapists are obviously all about being cool, hip and down with the kids... Liek OMG totally, right? Uh, I must've had too much coffee.) Habits are generally useful to us because they allow us to go about our daily business, easily repeating things that we've done numerous times before, but without even thinking about it (kind of like autopilot-mode.) Habits allow us to get all the mundane stuff done (getting dressed, brushing teeth, making a cup of coffee, pretending to pay attention to people we don't like,) whilst allowing our conscious mind freedom to think about other tasks, to plan future events, to procrastinate about anything under the sun, etc. Patterns, though useful a great deal of the time, can also be negative (think: "bad habits.") Nail-biting is a pattern... Eating junk when you get in from work is a pattern... Smoking can even be classified as a pattern... So we can utilise pattern interruption to derail the pattern as it happens (or as it is imagined/described to be happening.) This allows us to perhaps figure out why it's a pattern in the first place and also, more importantly, to change or remove the negative pattern entirely.

How does it work?
Patterns are easily interrupted by using unexpected responses or movements. As described previously, when you successfully interrupt a pattern, your subject will experience a fleeting state of confusion (and when I say fleeting, I mean...fleeting. The window of opportunity to utilise the window of confusion that you have created will usually vary from between 0.5 – 2 seconds...in my experience.) This state of confusion is pre-occupying the conscious mind, thereby opening up the subject to subconscious suggestion (which, as I'm sure you've realised by now, is what we want during a hypnotherapy session.) The feeling of being confused is

not a naturally pleasant experience, so the subconscious mind is more than happy to forego this unwanted-state by accepting a new state/idea/suggestion from another person (you.)

When you interrupt a pattern, your aim is to introduce a new, unrelated step into the pattern... This is a bit different to the pattern interrupt examples that I cited in the previous section, but is relatively easy to accomplish and very effective. Let's use nail-biting as an example pattern. To go from not-biting to biting your nails requires some kind of process and there will be a number of steps required for the transition to happen. It's highly likely that no two people (ever) will have exactly the same process. Some will have long processes, some short, some logical and some will appear absolutely nuts (to everyone except the subject whose habit it is.) I actually used to bite my nails a lot, so here's my nail-biting process, or; "How to bite your nails, if you are Rory Z Fulcher:"

Step 1: Become nervous/upset/bored
Step 2: Increase negative state internally
Step 3: Bring hand to your mouth
Step 4: Tilt head slightly to one side
Step 5: Bite nails

So, to stop this pattern using the pattern interruption technique, where do you think you would introduce a new step, and what would it be? What new action/thought would stop the subject from proceeding through the steps? Have a think about it before you read on... What could you do to stop the process?

Let's say, for example, that we put a new step in, I'd probably go ahead and stick it in between step 4 and step 5. My new step(s) will be:

Step 4a: Miss your mouth, reach round and rub the back of your neck.
Step 4b: Experience a nice feeling, drop hand.

So how does the subject get to step 5 when they've already put their hand down? They'd have to put it back up to their mouth to start biting, and when they do that, they'll rub their neck again. You've put a block in the habitual process by adding an additional step, also you've attached a positive feeling to the new step in the pattern. This will be very useful in making the subject forget about that old, negative way that they used to achieve the good feeling, and more easily accept this new pattern. The step that you add into a pattern *can* be physical, but it doesn't have to be... If a pattern is happening due to a series of thoughts, we would aim to change the pattern of the thoughts instead, and if it's feelings, change the feelings.

How, then, do we actually get this "new step" into the pattern, and how do we make it a permanent fixture there? Well, to incorporate your pattern interruption and program the pattern for future use, you're going to run through this process with your subject. First, have them explain the thing that they wish to change, figure out how they do this thing. Figure out the pattern, every single step and ensure that you remember (or write down) these steps so that you know where to interrupt the pattern. Once you've done this, have them actually go through the process and "do the steps" for real, up until your chosen point where you will interrupt their process and implant your new step(s). To implant the steps in the nail-biting example, I'd stop them when they tilt their head and physically move their hand to the back of their neck, whilst suggesting that "as you rub the back of your neck, you get an instant release of calmness, a sense of that really good feeling of release that you used to get from biting your nails" (or whatever it is that you want to anchor to that particular gesture.) I'd suggest that as soon as they're sure that the feeling is as strong as it could possibly be, they should remove their hand, and lower it back to their lap/side. If the subject can't/doesn't want to physically do the process during the hypnotherapy session, have them run through the process in their imagination, visualising it instead.

[Note: If you're "anchoring" a positive feeling to the new action/response, you may want to pre-install your own anchor that you can "fire off" at the same time as they do the intended thing. We will cover this in the next section, which is all about anchoring.]

So, having the subject do something different during their pattern is a great way to cause the pattern to change into something more productive. The addition that you include during your interruption will more-than-likely become a permanent part of their pattern, allowing them to modify their behaviour and fix their problem. You can also simply interrupt a pattern and not allow the subject to complete the "loop." This often makes people a little uncomfortable, because most people like to complete their habitual patterns...but it works. Repeat the process of beginning the pattern (or describing it) getting to a certain point, and then completely changing the conversation, or completely re-directing the subjects' actions to something different. Do this over and over and the subject will come to subconsciously realise that "wow, I don't actually need to complete this pattern, and yet somehow I still feel good," because the subconscious is pretty good at picking up on important information just like that.

Pattern interrupts are also a very useful tool to create a "change of state." Remember I mentioned the example of a little boy falling over and hurting himself? The parents interrupted the pattern (the pattern here being; fall, hurt yourself, cry,) with something different (like pulling a face or playing a game.) Well this is a classified as a change of state. The boy had begun to enter a distressed state due to his focussing on the pain. The parents easily changed the boy's state to laughing and feeling good, simply by interrupting his pattern with something different. This state change is a really useful thing to do when your subjects (or even you, yourself) experience a negative, un-resourceful state. Laughter is a brilliant way to change a negative state, and if you're feeling down and depressed, suddenly deciding to laugh will definitely cause a change of state, right? By the same token, if a subject is telling you all about his problems and you suddenly laugh... What do you think will happen? Boom, state change. It might be a change from an un-resourceful, negative state to a state of anger (directed at you, for appearing to laugh at his problems) but the state will have changed nonetheless.

Another great way to interrupt a pattern is to ask a completely unrelated question. Imagine you're a therapy client, and the therapist asks you these questions: "OK, so how long have you been afraid of chairs? OK, since you can remember... Can you remember a time when you weren't afraid of chairs? No? What is it about chairs that scares you, specifically?" Pretty normal questions to be asking somebody who has a phobia of chairs, I think you'll agree. How about if the next question was: "So, being afraid of chairs, how many times a day do you think about jumping into puddles?" Boom, state change from thinking about chairs and feeling uneasy to feeling confused (and probably a little uneasy – thinking the hypnotist may have lost his marbles, but that's fine.) So here we've learned that if your subject is in an un-resourceful state, you can interrupt this state by doing/saying something unexpected, allowing you to change their state, thereby allowing you to help them change the way they experience their problem (by looking at it from a different perspective, whilst not being distracted by the unhelpful state they are usually in whilst thinking about the matter in hand.)

Sample script?
There's not really a script for a pattern interrupt, simply because everybody creates their habitual pattern in a different way. Therefore you're going to have to figure out the best time to interject and what it is that you are going to introduce to the pattern to modify it. Also, when we are thinking about interrupting a pattern off the cuff (i.e. during your pre-talk to change the state of your subject) you can never know exactly what they are going to be talking about when you decide to interrupt the pattern, so you won't know what you're going to use as your interruption until you're about to do it. Perhaps whilst your subject is describing the way that being anxious makes them feel upset, they may look out the window for a moment, and maybe you'd choose that moment to slap your hand down on your desk, and laugh to change their state... See what I mean? It is down to you to get creative with interrupts, using them when you think your subject either needs a change of state or a change of a habitual behaviour pattern. Sorry, but this one's on you (but I'm sure you'll do just fine!)

ANAESTHESIA/ANALGESIA

What does it consist of?
Anaesthesia and analgesia are two different methods of temporarily "removing" pain. With anaesthesia, the subject will feel no pain and in fact, they will feel nothing at all in the area that has been "anaesthetised," it'll be completely devoid of feeling entirely. Analgesia is different because although there will be no pain-sensation, the subject may still be able to feel that part of their body... Perhaps in the form of a pressure, or even a tickling feeling (it can be different from person-to-person,) but the pain will be gone.

Long before proper chemical anaesthetics were used in dental surgeries, patients were forced to grin and bear it (literally.) Luckily for some of them, hypnotic-anaesthesia was just being developed/figured out and subsequently, it became widely used as the dentists' anaesthetic of choice for quite a few years. This proves that hypnotic pain-relief is a very useful tool to have in your arsenal, should you ever require it. It also proves that hypnosis, when done correctly, is a powerful tool indeed! Sadly, when chemical anaesthetics were discovered, hypnotic-anaesthesia fell by the wayside, because although the chemical version often caused side-effects, the process was much simpler (and didn't require the dentist to go out and learn hypnotherapy – bloody lazy, I say!)

In the "hypnosis world" you will often hear of this technique being referred to as "glove anaesthesia," and as the name implies, the hand is usually the area where anaesthesia/analgesia is initially induced. Once achieved, this numbness can then be transferred to different parts of the body.

Once again (just so you remember this very important point,) pain is a way of telling you that something is wrong with your body, so we must remember that before we simply go around "switching off" peoples pain receptors, to always ensure correct medical protocol has been attended to beforehand. Ensure that the hypnotic pain-control is the best course of action for your subject to take.

I would personally suggest that you do not attempt to induce anaesthesia/analgesia for use in any dental/surgical capacity until you have a great deal of practical hypnotherapy experience under your belt, including experience with anaesthesia techniques. To give a guideline, I would suggest that at least 1,000+ hours of practical hypnotherapy experience would be a good amount of experience to have before you even consider doing this. Even then, it would probably be worth your while to seek out a mentor who is experienced in the art of surgical hypnotic anaesthesia, who is willing to "sit in" and to guide you during the process. This is simply to ensure the safety of your subjects whilst utilising your tried-and-tested competency and confidence in the art of hypnotherapy.

How does it work?
Natural anaesthesia usually happens when a person is unaware of an injury/pain that they have received. I'm sure you can probably remember a time when you've accidentally cut, scraped or bashed yourself on something without even realising until later on, when you see a cut/bruise. Up until that point you had no idea that it you'd hurt yourself, but upon realisation (actually seeing your "boo boo,") it may have started to hurt... This is natural anaesthesia, and it's practically the same as hypnotic anaesthesia. As with the preceding example, it's something that most of us have experienced in the past, and is something that we're all capable of doing. Before you induce anaesthesia in a subject, it is a good idea to give them a similar example and to make them aware that they have the ability to control their own subjective experience of pain (or pretty much any sensation in the body, for that matter,) because they do have the ability to do this, they probably just don't know it yet, so tell them.

There are various ways to induce hypnotic anaesthesia/analgesia, I have found that the most popular method in hypnotherapy circles is the ice/cold method and this is the method that I typically choose to use, personally.

We have the subject imagine that they are lowering their hand into a bucket of ice-water. Starting at the fingertips (duh) and gradually lowering the hand until it is completely "submerged" up to the wrist/forearm. Whilst this is happening, the subject is being given suggestions of coldness and numbness. We continue to give, compound and intensify these suggestions (because anaesthesia = numbness. If you've ever had a tooth pulled, you'll know this.) You can then go on to suggest that the water is so cold, it's turning to a block of ice... Or just continue giving suggestions of coldness, but make sure to tell the subject that it is a comfortable feeling and that they will experience no ill-effects from this exercise (the mind is powerful. If you can take away pain with the mind, it stands to reason that you can probably cause it too! Be careful, you don't want to give your subjects hypno-frostbite!)

If you don't like the ice-bucket idea, then have them imagine their arm is being covered in ice cubes or snow... Have them imagine that they're being sprayed with a freeze spray... Have them imagine that they're at the South Pole and they're completely covered up in warm, thick clothing, apart from one of their gloves has come off... (Use. Your. Imagination.)

Another way to cause the subject to imagine this state of anaesthesia is to have them imagine they are getting an actual anaesthetic injection into the area. You can have them imagine being in a hospital environment, having the area prepared for an injection and the injection itself. This method will obviously work best if they have a frame of reference, i.e. if they've had an anaesthetic injection in the past, so that they know how they should be feeling.

You can directly suggest that their hand is going numb just by focusing on it. Have them focus on a single spot and work outwards from there. You can have them feed their experience back to you either verbally, or by nodding their head/moving a finger (on the hand that you're not numbing.) Do this by saying something like; "once you feel that numbness in the area that I suggest, move the index finger of your other hand." Utilise anything from the surroundings to increase the sensation. The bottom of the hand getting numb where it's resting on the chair... A twitch of the hand... You could blow on the hand slightly, suggesting a tingling feeling... A change in colour (with this, you may actually see a colour-change happen in some cases, and you could describe it to them. If it doesn't *actually* happen you can still have them imagine their arm becoming paler or blue-tinted, as would happen if they became very cold.)

A final method to use is having them imagine that the arm is made from something else, some inanimate material, perhaps wood, plastic or metal. Whatever you like, but always feeding back the numbness. It can even be a good idea to combine a couple of these techniques for optimum effectiveness.

Once you have achieved this state of anaesthesia/analgesia, you are able to test it with a pinch to the back of the hand. If you've got full on anaesthesia, they will feel nothing. If they feel something but not pain, then you've got analgesia which is great too. If they say; "OUCH!" then you might want to try again. If you're intending on using this technique for something "high-risk," such as during a dental/surgical procedure, then obviously you are going to want to pre-program the anaesthesia beforehand. I suggest that you do this over a couple of sessions, thereby ensuring that your method is working effectively with this subject. You can also suggest that each time the subject experiences the anaesthesia, it will be even stronger and more effective than the last time, and that cold, numb feeling will happen even easier. To speed up this process you may even anchor the feeling to a certain word/phrase so that you can more easily activate the suggestion next time... I like to simply use "anaesthesia."

You are able to transfer the anaesthesia using touch... So once you have achieved the glove anaesthesia (i.e. once their hand is numb,) perhaps you would like to transfer the anaesthetic to their left shoulder. You simply tell them that; "in a moment, when you are sure your hand is completely numb, you can allow it to raise up and your hand will touch your left shoulder. When this happens, this cold, numb anaesthetic feeling will automatically move into that area, all the way throughout your shoulder. That numb feeling will be just as numb, or maybe even more numb than the feeling in your hand, and will continue to increase with every breath that you exhale. Allow that hand to move towards your shoulder, and allow it to touch and allow that wonderful numb feeling to fully cover your entire shoulder, now."

Obviously, once you've finished, you want to take away the anaesthesia and bring the body back to normal. This is simply done using suggestion. Suggest that the part of the body is getting warmer. That the blood is rushing through the area allowing the feeling to come back, allowing the colour to return to normal. Imagine, basically that that part of the body is returning all the way back to its normal, healthy state, working as it should, completely normally, comfortably and feeling wonderfully at ease (you can have them move the part of their body if you wish, to ensure that it's all "working" correctly.) Always ensure that you do remove the anaesthesia afterwards! You may also give suggestions of improved health, healing and functionality of the areas that you worked on, to help alleviate any problems or to facilitate more efficient healing and improvement of the area in general.

Another helpful note on anaesthesia, especially with regards to surgery, is that you are able to suggest that there will be no blood. For instance, to demonstrate anaesthesia in a subject, the hypnotist will often stick a hypodermic needle through the skin of a subjects hand (either the back of the hand, or the skin in between the thumb and index finger.) Again, I advise that you don't do this without the relevant medical training, support and insurance. Once the hypnotist has effectively stabbed the needle through their flesh, he then usually will have the subject open their eyes and take a look at the needle as it remains in their hand (much to their amazement...because they didn't feel a thing!) The hypnotist will then suggest that upon removing the needle there will be no blood, no pain, perhaps just a small depression in the skin where the needle was...but no blood and no pain, and it works. This is another test which effectively proves that hypnotherapy can alter the physiological as well as the psychological. Powerful stuff, folks!

Sample script
[Note: In this example script, I have reduced the length of the "numbing process," because it is simply a case of repeating suggestions of coldness, numbing and reduction of sensation. The ice-bucket part can be drawn out for a good couple of minutes so that the subject really gets into it and focuses on the process, but in this sample script I have provided a simple, short outline of how to do this. You can then add (and repeat) any sections to your heart's content, until you feel that the process is long enough to meet your subjects' requirements.]

"As you relax now, you might remember back to a time where you accidentally hurt yourself but didn't realise until later on. Perhaps you got a cut, scrape or a bruise, but until you actually saw the injury way after it happened, it was almost as if it had never happened at all. Because you are able to control or even turn off your reaction to sensations in your body. We are all able to do this, and because your mind is an amazingly powerful thing, you can accept now that your mind is able to control these sensations and to turn them down or to turn them off completely. You are able to control your mind, just like when you recall a memory. Just like when you decide to focus on your breathing, and you can know now that any time you wish, you are able to create a sense of numbness, a sense of no-feeling in any part of your body that you so wish.

I'd like you to concentrate on your right/left hand now, focus completely upon that hand and allow the feelings and sensations in that hand to be your only thoughts now. And as you focus on that hand now, I'd like you to imagine that all of the sensation, all of the feeling in that hand is beginning to fade away, as if you were turning a dial from 10 down to 0, and with every number that the dial turns, the feeling, the sensation just fades away now.

As you continue to focus your attention on that hand now, I'd like you to imagine what it would be like if that hand were to be placed in a bucket of ice-water. Imagine now, you don't even need to move, just imagine that there's a huge bucket filled with water and lots of ice, just below your hand. I'd like you to imagine that you are slowly lowering your fingertips into the water, and this ice water is so ice cold that there is no pain, just cold, numbness. It actually feels nice as you continue to lower your fingers all the way into the bucket now, colder and colder with every breath that you exhale. Imagine as if the cold of this ice water is being sucked directly into every pore of your hand. As you lower your hand slowly down even more as it numbs into the ice water now, all the way down to your wrist. That numb hand completely submerged in freezing ice water. Imagine now that the water is becoming colder, allowing your hand to become even more comfortably numb. Allowing all of that feeling to completely fade. Allowing any sensation to just simply pass by unnoticed, almost as if your hand is completely separate from your body. Almost as if your hand is an entirely separate thing altogether. The colour of that hand turning pale as it becomes colder and colder, more and more comfortably numb with every breath that you exhale. No feeling, as if your hand is completely inactive. As if your hand is asleep. No feeling, no sensation.

As you focus your attention on your hand, you can give your hand the instruction now to become completely numb. More numb than ever before as you focus on your hand numbing. Tell it now to become numb, completely asleep, no feeling whatsoever now. You can't feel it at all, not a single feeling in that numb hand, no feeling in that cold, numb hand you can't feel it at all because it is so numb.

*[Transfer – If you don't need to move the anaesthesia, skip this **bold** part:]*

[In a moment you're going to transfer this numbness and lack of sensation to that part of your body that we spoke about before we began. This will completely transfer the anaesthesia to this other part of your body, just like in your hand. So when you are sure that your hand is absolutely numb and the feeling is all gone, you're going to automatically raise that hand and it will touch to that part of your body that you want to feel numb. As soon as that hand touches that other part of your body, this numbness will transfer to the new body part instantly and automatically.

So you can allow that hand to lift now and touch that hand to the part of your body that you want to become numb and cold. No feeling or sensation. As you touch this new area, imagine that pale, bluish colour of your cold, numb hand spreading onto this new area. Allowing the skin to react, to cool, to numb, allowing the colour to spread and fill and numb and cool. Imagine all of the numbness, all of the sensation of loss of feeling are being transferred into this part of your body now. Allow all of that feeling to completely transfer over, to completely fill and numb and cool and numb that part now.]

As you continue to focus on this part of yourself that has become numb and cool, so completely numb. All sensation disappeared, all feeling gone, numb, so relaxed and numb now. You can continue to breathe and with each breath that you exhale, that part of you can become even number. So numb that it almost feels like that part of you is floating, disconnected from your body, completely numb now. And as you enjoy this wonderful sensation, you can breathe deeply and allow yourself to relax completely.

[Anchoring section:]
As you focus on this sensation, this <u>anaesthesia</u>, know that any time you wish, you can achieve this feeling of <u>anaesthesia</u> in any body part you wish. Simply by suggesting <u>anaesthesia</u> to yourself, focusing on creating these feelings that you are feeling now. Focusing on <u>anaesthesia</u>, allowing that part of your body to cool and numb and create <u>anaesthesia.</u> As you focus on the word <u>anaesthesia</u>, these feelings can double and cool and numb, and any time that you wish to provide yourself with <u>anaesthesia</u>, you can focus on the word; <u>anaesthesia.</u> Focus with this intention, and the <u>anaesthesia</u> and all of these feelings that come with it will happen. Focus now and repeat the word silently in your head; <u>anaesthesia</u>. As you focus on the feeling as you focus on the numbness as you focus on the cool detached feeling, or lack of feeling and repeat; <u>anaesthesia</u>. Numbing, cooling and numbing and cooling. Comfortably numb, calm, numb, cool and relaxing.

Numbness increasing and increasing as you focus on the anaesthesia becoming stronger with every breath you exhale.

Each time you experience this state of anaesthesia, it will be stronger and more effective. You will have more and more control over this state with every time that you experience it, becoming more proficient, more easily accessible and much stronger. I'd like you to imagine now what it will be like the next time that you are here with me. The next time that you're experiencing this feeling of anaesthesia even stronger than you are now experiencing that. Imagine how powerful that feeling feels. Feel it now, and know that your mind is learning now how to harness and control these feelings. You can realise now that you are more completely in control of yourself every time that you practice this anaesthesia. Completely in control of your mind, your reactions to sensations and your reactions to everything. And knowing this will allow you to more easily bring about this state of anaesthesia whenever you require it, and each time this natural anaesthesia will be stronger and better and easier to accomplish.

[Remove anaesthesia:]
And now, just as easily as all feeling disappeared, the natural, normal wonderful warm feeling can begin to return to every single part of your body now. Comfortable and feeling good, as if you've submerged the area in a lovely, warm bath, and it's beginning to warm right up again. As if you've wrapped it up in a nice, fluffy warm blanket and all the comfortable, warm sensation is beginning to return once again, feeling really good, natural, comfortable and normal.

The blood flowing steadily and easily back into the area, allowing that area to return completely back to normal. Allowing your entire body to regulate its' temperature to a normal, comfortable, natural level. That comfortable temperature that is right for you and that helps you to relax. So warm, so comfortable, feeling really good now..."

RECONNECTION
What does it consist of?
"Losing touch with yourself" can often cause a person problems. Life changes, we end up doing different stuff than the stuff that we used to do. Sometimes we even forget to do the stuff that we used to love to do, and in some cases we even lose track of the memories of doing those things or being in those positive situations that made us feel great. Over time, if a memory is not accessed, the clarity of this memory will gradually fade. The lines begin to blur, getting smaller and smaller. This is a downward spiral and perhaps the memory could even become a non-entity. Love is not enough to keep a memory active, you actively have to keep accessing the memory, so it stays right where it belongs. As such,

revisiting positive, life-affirming memories whilst in hypnosis is a great way to have your subject re-connect with a great deal of positive experiences from their past. Whether you have a head like a hole or can remember 1,000,000 things at once, there are always memories that need to be actively remembered. Me, I'm not that great at memory, but it only takes a little discipline to get better (and it's worth doing, especially if you're consciously finding it harder to remember things than you used to.) You can imagine, though, that forgetting these important memories would suck. Losing your past can hurt.

The reconnection technique can be used with subjects who are feeling down and depressed, anyone who, when you ask him, struggles to recall a single positive memory from his entire life, but he'll easily recount numerous negative memories and recollections. So your aim is to have him remember positive experiences and to experience those positive feelings that went alongside them. It is also possible to utilise this technique to re-connect someone with something that they used to do. Some hobby, talent or pastime that fell by the wayside. Deep down, they still know how to do it, they still know all the moves, but perhaps they just need a reminder. What better way to remind them, than having them remember themselves doing the thing and enjoying it immeasurably. The best use for this technique however, is for people who are "stuck" and can't achieve a goal that they're trying to accomplish. Let's say someone is having trouble remembering information for an upcoming test at college, we would have him remember times that the subject did successfully remember things… The alphabet, his home phone number, the names of all his school friends, the recipe for his favourite meal… Once the subject has remembered these things, you are able to link this "learning state" to the problem area, thereby causing the subject to be in a much more desirable state when it comes down to his studying.

How does it work?
By accessing past memories of success, the subject is caused to experience the "positive state" which they were in at those times. You are then able to amplify the state and the accompanying feelings and thoughts by suggestion and compounding various memories, one after another. Once this positive state has been accomplished and "ramped up," you will then suggest that this state is an ability. The ability to be happy, the ability to learn, the ability to remember. Whatever it is that you're aiming to help the subject accomplish. Once you have "given them" this ability, then you can have the subject imagine their current problem whilst utilising this ability, focusing on their ability and letting them know that this new "problem" is exactly the same as those old things that they easily and effortlessly accomplished. You're practically causing the subject to remember that they can do this thing.

Sample script

"I'd like you to remember back to a time where you learned something, and it stayed right there in your head. How about learning the alphabet, that's in there. You focused on it and practiced reading it and speaking it, and somehow it just went into your head and that knowledge just stayed there. Numbers and counting, that's something you didn't know until you learned it. And now it's as easy as 1, 2, 3... You don't even need to think of it, because the information that you wanted to remember just automatically gelled into your memory with practice and repetition, and you know now that's the right way to do this. You could probably count to a million without batting an eyelid, and remembering all of that is as easy as 1, 2, 3.

How do you know where you live? You remembered your address by writing it out a couple of times, and once you practiced it, you got it. You can remember dates that are important to you... You can remember faces of people and the names associated with those faces... It might have taken you a little while, and you might've had to have practiced those names and those dates, rehearsing all of that information. But you focus on the information, repeat it, speak it, write it, watch it, learn it, and it all goes in there because you know that repetition is a great way to learn and you know that you are able to learn. In fact you are an expert at knowing how to learn. You're the master of learning, because you can already remember so much that has happened in your life, people, places, things, information, information, filling up your head without even trying. It's in there, ready to be pulled out just whenever you need it.

That ability, that learning ability is right there inside you now, doing what it does without you even trying to consciously remember. So imagine how much better it works when you consciously tune in to that inherent learning ability, knowing that you know you can learn and remember and recall information so easily. Just causing that information to be sucked up into your brain by repeating it, speaking it, writing it, watching it, learning it, and it all goes in there, because you know that repetition is a great way to learn, and you know that you are able to learn... In fact you are an expert at knowing how to learn. So I want you to imagine now that thing you've been struggling with, but imagine it whilst knowing that you have this ability to learn. Imagine just how easy it is going to be to learn these things, by using the methods that you can remember the way that you will learn best. Utilising this ability to learn and allowing all of this new information to join the rest of the information inside your head, which itself used to be new information until you easily and effortlessly learned it and it became a part of you."

AGE REGRESSION

What does it consist of?

Age Regression (or simply; Regression) is a technique used to take the subject "back in time" (in their head) to an event in their life that could be causing them a problem in the present. Regressions are quite frequently used for remedying phobias and fears. It can work wonders for depression, psychosomatic issues, unexplainable guilt or shame, relationship problems... Regression is a very useful tool for a well-rounded hypnotherapist to know, especially if the problem that you are dealing with is proving difficult to fix using other methods. Regressions can also be used if the subject is unaware as to why they have this problem in the first place, as it could be due to a "repressed memory" – i.e. a traumatic past event that the subconscious mind is "hiding" from the conscious mind, so as to protect the subject from the memory itself (yes, the subconscious mind is able to do this. The subconscious mind always strives to protect us, but sometimes the way in which it does this can actually cause larger problems to arise.) These memories can be things that were never emotionally dealt with and then "forgotten" (repressed,) and they could have easily caused long-lasting changes in the behaviours and convictions of your subject. Sometimes the only way to change these things is to figure out what caused them in the first place and allow the subject to finally express their emotions and feelings about the event.

Regression is a very powerful tool and it should be treated with a great deal of respect (as with all aspects of hypnotherapy – but regression especially so.) Regression has been in the press over the years, having been successfully used to discredit cases of child abuse and alien-abduction (uh-huh) that the supposed-victims were *sure* had happened, but it turned out that the memories, once re-experienced were in fact completely different. It works the other way too, someone that has no recollection of any traumatic events could go back and discover that they were abused as a child. These things can happen, so be very careful if you decide to use regression as a part of your therapy, there's a steep learning curve with this one.

Following on from the last paragraph, not everything that a subject experiences in a regression should be taken as fact. There is a phenomenon known as "false memory" which can happen during regressions (they happen without regressions too in general day-to-day life.) Obviously your subjects are in a highly suggestible state whilst in hypnosis, especially deep, regression-level hypnosis and as such you must aim to keep your suggestions and questioning as content-free as possible. Do not ask "leading questions." I.e. if a subject, during a regression describes being in a room with her father and then begins to cry... Do not ask "what did he do to you?" or anything like that. "What is happening now?" is a good phrase to use, and similar content-free probing questions:

"How does that make you feel?"
"Where are you?"
"Who is with you?"
"What does it look like?"
Etc.

Do not imprint your own thoughts, beliefs, assumptions and suppositions upon the subject whilst regressed, keep it clean and content-free from your end. No leading and no implications. If you adhere to this rule, false memories are a lot less likely to happen, but we must always remember that memories whether true or false are equally easy to create. Our own subjective experiences may not accurately reflect what actually happened in a real life situation, for example; imagine being a child and walking into a room where the mother is beating the father... Obviously this could give the child the impression that the mother was a foul and evil person, but perhaps before the child walked in, the father might have struck the mother first. As I say, all of our memories are "subjective" and sometimes these memories might not tell the full story, so be careful when using regression techniques.

How does it work?
To utilise regression successfully, your subject needs to be in a fairly deep state of hypnosis, you can achieve this using a variety of deepeners, visualisations and fractionation helps too. Regression can be used during a lighter state of hypnosis, but this type of regression is usually going to be what is known as a "pseudo-regression." During a pseudo-regression, the experience of the subject will be more akin to viewing a video of the memories on a screen, as opposed to experiencing them fully as if they were inside the memory. They may be able to see (and even feel, to some extent) the past experience, but at this level they will still be aware of the present, the environment in which they are in. At this level, the subject has a lot more control of the memory, as opposed to a deep, full regression. Your subject will probably remember everything that happened during this pseudo-regression process.

Get the subject into a deep state (or a somnambulistic state) and you should be able to achieve a full regression, which means it will be more likely that they will be able to totally experience their past memories, as if they're actually there inside the memory. The depth of hypnosis required for regression needs to be sufficient to produce amnesia upon suggestion, so if the subject does not react well to a suggestion to "forget something" (such as a number) then you probably won't be able to regress them successfully. It is a good idea to test this beforehand by either directly suggesting that they will forget a number and having them attempt to count, or you could utilise part of a Dave Elman induction, in which he has the subject count backwards, and each number that they count relaxes the subject, and with each number they count, the numbers begin to disappear until those numbers are completely gone... You can have the subject indicate when this happens by lifting a finger. Once you have achieved amnesia, you may continue to deepen the state a little more so that the subject can maintain this depth throughout the regression process.

During a regression you may notice a change in their posture, facial expressions, voice-tone and language patterns. It can be as if the subject is actually there, inside the memory *as* their younger self, and it can be a little weird hearing a grown man speaking in a child-like tone, using childish words, etc. But at least you'll know you've got him to the right place. If you are having the subject experience a traumatic event, you may notice that they will outwardly appear fearful, they may cower, they may even sweat, cry or scream, so be aware that this may happen just so that it doesn't shock you if/when it does happen. I would also advise against touching the subject during a regression. If they were abused as a child and you have them re-experience this, touching them would definitely not be a good course of action, so be aware of that.

Although your subject may not recall 100% of the actual details of the memory during the regression, they will certainly be able to experience the feelings and emotions that were present during the event (which is what you want.) Often, subjects will struggle to recall what happened during the regression itself and if you were to ask them afterwards, they might have little-to-no recollection of the regression happening whatsoever. This is quite similar to the way that we often forget dreams straight after they have happened, but again it is a fairly common reaction. I tell you just so that you are aware it can and does happen.

Once you have your subject in a deep enough state of hypnosis, at this point your goal is to actually find the "problem memory" itself. Then, once you've done this, you are able to suggest a way for the subject to deal with the memory in question. To get the subject to the correct memory (i.e. the memory that needs to be reviewed,) you are able to use a couple of different techniques. The first technique is a visualisation that allows the subject to pick and choose the point that they go back to. We have them imagine a library of memories with a huge bookshelf stretching back a long way. Each book on the shelf is suggested to contain memories of their past, starting at today and working backwards all the way to the date of the subjects' birth. You have the subject find the right date and open the corresponding book, to experience the memory that their subconscious deems to be the problem.

The second method used to find the memory is to use what is known as an "affect bridge," this method is a super quick way to regress a person back to the event that may have caused the problem (and this is the method that I will personally always use when doing regression work.) The affect bridge is a very useful method to use if the subject has no idea as to the initial cause of their problem. With this method, we have the subject experience the negative feelings related to the problem that they wish to fix, then we intensify these feelings with suggestion. Once the feeling (or "affect") is heightened, we suggest that the subject use the feeling as a bridge back to the first time that they ever experienced this feeling. This usually tends to send the subject back to the situation where they subconsciously picked up their problem. (If they can't find the first time, have them go back to the time where the feeling was strongest.)

The affect bridge technique is not for everyone, because obviously the subject is asked to physically experience the emotions and the stronger the emotion experienced, the better the affect bridge is going to work. This can be quite a shocking experience if you're not used to dealing with emotional responses, but it is very effective.

Another thing to point out is that there can be more than one past event that has contributed to the problem. The first event that caused the problem is known as the "initial sensitising event" (ISE.) Any further occasions that added to the problem are known as "secondary sensitising events" (SSE.) For example, an ISE could be that a subject was beaten as a young child once, when his father came home drunk. The SSE could be subsequent acts of violence that happened thereafter, or even threats of violence from the father or other people. It is certainly worth figuring out if your subject has more than one sensitising event to deal with, and you are able to do this in the same way as you figure out the ISE. Often you will find that there is more than one event to deal with, so don't just assume that there's only one.

A good method to use during the regression to figure out if you have an ISE or an SSE is to ask the subject whilst replaying the memory; "is this feeling familiar or is it a new feeling?" If the feeling is familiar, you probably have an SSE, if it is new, it's more likely to be their ISE. So if you keep getting SSE's, keep working back, eventually you will get to the ISE (it may take some time, but be persistent.) Just to make sure that you have gotten to the ISE, you can attempt to regress even further back, and usually you will find that the subject has "nowhere to go." To do this, when you think you have the ISE you can suggest that the subject; "continue to focus on this feeling, and I'm going to count backwards from three to one, and when I reach one you will find yourself back at the very first time that you experienced this feeling... 3, 2, 1."

Once you have regressed to the memory in question, you are then able to suggest a way for the subject to deal with said memory. You can do this by having the subject allow themselves to react to the memory completely and fully, as if they are there, and work through the emotions – a kind of "catharsis" (emotional release)... You can have the subject talk through the memory, explaining their thoughts and feelings... You can have the subject speak to any participants in the memory, and have them tell those participants their thoughts, allow them to get anything "off their chest" that they never got a chance to say to the person in question... Sometimes simply re-playing the memory (if it was repressed and forgotten,) will be enough to help the subject. But with regression it is often a good idea to actually work through any issues that arise with the subject, or it could make matters worse.

A technique that is very useful during regressions is the "informed child" technique. I'm including this technique here (instead of in its' own chapter) because you'd pretty much only use it during regressions. It consists of regressing the subject back to just before the initial event, then having the subject explain to their "child self" what is about to happen. Giving their younger self the "tools" to deal with it more effectively, by changing their perception of the event and of themselves. Often a subject might have picked up the idea that there was "something wrong with them" (whether it was something they heard, saw or something that happened *to* them,) and this idea that there was something wrong with them could have affected their entire life and often become like a self-fulfilling prophecy.

With regards to the informed child technique, it's pretty much a case of "if I knew then what I know now, things would have turned out better," and often, that can be pretty much true. So we have the subject go back to just before the traumatic event (i.e. five minutes before) and have the subject talk to their younger self, giving them the information that would have helped them to get through the experience that happened, whilst making as little negative impact on them as possible. You must take the subject back to before the event happened for the suggestions to take effect. Their "younger self" needs to be in a calm state, the state that they were in before the event ever happened and before they had formed any opinion of the problem in question. You must ask the subject how they are feeling at this point, if they are still not feeling happy/comfortable/loved then you should regress them further back, ensuring they are in a positive state before "informing" them of what is to come. The pre-ISE subject will easily accept your suggestions about the event, but the post-ISE subject will completely reject the suggestions, as they will have already formed opinions about it.

Once you have regressed them to the correct point, have the subject inform their child self that there is nothing wrong with them, and ensure that the child understands they are safe and strong (elaborate upon this section with more positive reinforcements specific to your subject and his problem.) Once this has been achieved, you then have the subject (as the child) experience any and all events (both ISE and SSEs) that have caused the problem whilst maintaining their new (informed) perspective. Then bring them all the way back to the present day.

You can then future pace the subject and have him accept himself, knowing that there is nothing wrong with him and accepting that. Knowing that it was all just the cause of an uninformed child's thought that influenced and affected his thoughts, feelings and behaviour throughout the years. There never was anything wrong with him at all. Once this is accomplished, you usually find that many negative beliefs are dispelled and disappear completely.

A great deal of the time, your subject might go back to some minor event that happened during their childhood, and although seemingly innocuous, the event may have been given great significance by the subject at the time. If this happens, you might just use a "watered down" version of the informed child technique and have the subject experience the memory again but with an adult set of knowledge. For example, let's say it's a fear of moths and the memory was that a parent opened a box and screamed because a moth flew out directly into their face. You'll agree, this is not a reason to be afraid of moths for your entire life, but the subconscious mind of a child does not know this. So walk them through the memory with an adult perspective, have them change the way they react to the memory.

You can even change the portrayal of the memory itself using the "submodality shift" technique; change perception of the memory from 1st person to 3rd person, drain the colour, make it as if they're watching on a screen, make the screen small and move it far away, turn down the sound, turn down the sound of the thoughts, change the feelings associated with the negative memory... All of these "submodality shifts" will help to reduce the impact of the memory itself. A useful thing to do with this technique is to "calibrate" the subjects' reaction to the memory beforehand... Use a scale of 1-10 to find out how bad the subject thinks the memory is, and with each "submodality" that you change, you then re-calibrate and find out if the change made any difference on the scale of 1-10. If they start out with the memory at a 9 or 10 (bad reaction) you want to aim to bring the memory down to a 1 or 0 (good reaction/no reaction at all.)

Another (similar) useful tool to use during regression is a technique known as dissociation (frequently referred to as the "fast phobia cure,") whereby you have the subject imagine that the negative memory is on a screen in a cinema, and you have them imagine that they are watching it from a 3rd person perspective, high up in the projection room (which removes the feelings of being part of the memory itself,) you can play the "movie" backwards, you can even have them imagine a funny soundtrack to the movie. You anchor the state of watching the "movie" whilst having a positive/neutral reaction to it, and then you progressively bring them closer to the screen whilst keeping the emotions to a minimum utilising your positive anchoring. Eventually you re-introduce them into the memory but with all of the negative feelings removed. These two methods are well-documented NLP techniques and although we are not covering them in-depth in this book (hence the very brief explanations,) I highly recommend that you research these two techniques because they are very useful therapy tools to know, especially when dealing with fears and phobias. It is 100% worth researching NLP as a whole (I personally use NLP techniques in practically all of my hypnotherapy sessions alongside many of the hypnotherapy techniques outlined in this book.)

Be aware that during a regression, you might have to repeat the process of removing negative emotion/feelings a few times, but you must ensure that you take away as much of the emotional response to the memory as possible. Whichever technique you choose to use, you need to check that the negative feeling/belief that was causing the problem no longer exists, if it does then you need to go back and repeat the process again until it is completely gone. As mentioned before, your subject might never feel "positive" about this memory, but if you can at least neutralise the negativity, then you're doing a good job.

Again, as with anaesthesia, I would personally advise that you do not use regression (with a therapy subject) until you have a great deal of practical hypnotherapy experience under your belt, including many hours experience with regression techniques. Obviously you will need to practice the techniques before you utilise them in an actual therapy session with somebody that has a deep-seated problem. My advice is that you practice with a "test subject" or volunteer, and instead of regressing your test subjects back to a traumatic/repressed memory from the past, simply regress your subject back to a more recent, positive event. Some time that they were super-happy or having a lot of fun. Have them run through the event, describing it to you, telling you their thoughts and feelings. Then bring them all the way back to the present, suggesting that they bring all of these wonderful, positive feelings back with them so that when they are awakened from hypnosis, they will feel just as good as they did during that memory.

Obviously in the scripts that follow, I have not included any therapy-work, because the intervention that you use depends on the subjects' problem. You will have to pick and choose at the time which techniques to best employ. I have included two sample scripts which will allow you to take the subject back to the memories in question and to bring them back to their present state afterwards (hopefully after you've successfully remedied the problem-memories.)

Sample script – Regression #1 "Library"
"I'd like you to imagine that you are standing in a beautiful garden, an amazing place where you can just relax completely. In front of you, right in the center of this garden, is a wonderful, old stone library building. I'd like you to imagine

walking through the garden towards the 5 steps at the entrance of this library, enjoying the sensations of this wonderful garden as you walk. The sights, sounds, smells and feelings...

I'd like you to imagine that you've reached the steps now, and you are climbing easily and effortlessly towards the entrance to the library. As you reach that door now, you can easily push it open and step inside the library entrance hall. Notice the beautiful surroundings inside the library. Solid oak furniture, a wonderful polished marble floor and rows and rows of shelves and books. Thousands and thousands of wonderful books. You, however, are here to visit your own individual library room which is just over to the right, behind a locked door. Make your way across the library to this door now, and notice in your hand, you have a key – the key to your own personal library. As you reach the door, you may notice that it has your name imprinted on a beautiful plaque there. Slip your key into the lock now and turn, feel the lock click and release, turn the handle and open the door. Step inside and as you walk into the entrance room of your own personal library, you may notice a comfortable carpet on the floor beneath your feet, and a wonderful feeling of comfort, familiarity and tranquility. Just ahead of you is a beautiful, wide staircase which will take you down into the library itself. There are 10 steps down into your library room, and with each step down you are able to relax even deeper into this wonderful state of hypnosis. Take the first step down to 9 and relax... Down to 8, drifting and dreaming... Down to 7, as you exhale away any tension... Down to 6, and inhale relaxation... 5, even deeper now... 4... 3, so relaxed, so calm... 2, and 1 you're at the bottom now, in your own personal library.

The room is only as wide as the staircase, but it is well lit, and you can see that it stretches all the way off in front of you, into the distance. Looking at the books on the shelves closest to you, you may notice that the spines of the books have this years' date, along with different days and months written beneath. As you look further down the corridor, you can notice that the dates on the books are going backwards... The further you walk down this corridor, the further back in time these books document. All the way, far down the corridor to the very beginning of your life – the day that you were born. And the strange thing about this library is that all of these books are about you, about the things that you've done and the people you've known throughout your entire life. Each book contains a day of your life... Some books are thicker than others, and that's fine.

I'd like you to pick up a book from this year and just take a look inside. Flick through and you'll either see a picture or read about some pleasant event that happened in your life this year. Once you have a sense of that, I want you to tell me what you see... *[Wait for response – you may need to encourage them to find a book/memory]*

OK, now what I'd like you to do is place that book back on the shelf. If you need to find books from further back in time, you can just think yourself down the corridor, and you will appear directly in front of the books that you require. So I'd like you to find that you can move further down the corridor now, to some books from an earlier time in your life. I'd like you to pick another book that has a similar pleasant event inside. Flick through the pages and tell me what it is that you see. *[Wait for response]*

Good. Now I'd like you to close the book, place it back and take yourself all the way back up the corridor to the foot of the stairs. Once you're back there, you can lift a finger on your right hand to let me know that you're there.

Now I'd like you to go back to a recent time that you've experienced *[the problem]*. Allow that book to just appear in front of you all by itself and allow it to fall open at the page in question. Once you have that memory, allow that finger on your right hand to lift to let me know when you're there.

OK, so I'd like you to tell me what's happening there... Get a sense of that, get the feelings and emotions now. I'd like you to allow those feelings and emotions to become stronger and stronger, and I'd like you to tell me what those feelings and emotions are now... *[Wait for response]* I'd like you to use those feelings as a guide to take you back, all the way back down the corridor of books back to a book that has a memory with the same kind of feelings and emotions. All the way back to either the first time or the worst time you experienced these feelings or emotions, and I'd like you to allow that book to just appear in front of you all by itself and allow it to fall open at the page in question. Once you have the page, you can allow that finger to lift again to let me know that you're there.

[If they struggle, you can either continue to coax it out of them, or go for a different memory. At this point you are able to have the subject describe the memory. Remember do not "lead" them. Your aim is to facilitate them telling you their best rendition of the memory without corrupting the information. Once you have figured out what happened, you can then use some of the techniques mentioned in previous and following chapters to deal with any issues related to said memory.

Remember, there are ISE's and SSE's, you can and should deal with the SSE's too but your main goal is to find the initial event (ISE) that caused the problem – 99% of the time, it'll be the one that is as far back as they can go, using that feeling/emotion as a guide. Once this is done, bring them back to the present, and then take them back again if you need to find SSE's...]

Now I'd like you to use the same feelings and go back again to any other significant time that you have experienced these feelings in the past. Go there now and allow the finger to lift to let me know when you're there... Now tell me what's happening. *[Repeat this section as many times as required and deal with negative memories separately each time. Once you are finished, bring them back...]*

OK, I'd like you to find yourself returning now, returning all the way back to the current year and the present day *[tell them the date]*, all the way back to the foot of the stairs of your personal library room. Now that you are back, find that you begin to climb those stairs up towards the main library, and you are able to bring all of those positive memories from your life back with you. Bringing all of the positive understandings and solutions that we have discussed here in your library, and anything that you wish to leave, anything negative that you do not want any more, anything that you do not wish to remember, you are able to leave that behind now. Bringing with you exactly what you need to allow yourself to live a full, happy, healthy life, just the way that you want it to be.

As you reach the top of those stairs now, notice that there is a bin over by the wall. Put any of those things than you no longer wish to have into that bin, and they will automatically disappear, gone forever. Left behind. Once you've done this, walk back across the comfy carpet to the door of your private library... You can walk through and close the door and lock it once again. The key disappears from your hand as you find your way back to the main door of the library now, and walk through. Down those five steps into wonderful relaxation, back into the garden of your dreams where you may find a wonderful, relaxing place to sit. And as you sit there and as you relax, you can take this time to reflect on this experience and to simply enjoy this wonderful feeling of peace, relaxation and tranquility.

Sample script – Regression #2 "Affect Bridge"
"I'd like you to focus on that feeling that comes with the problem, focus on that feeling now. Imagine that feeling and feel it just as if you were really experiencing it now. As I continue to talk about that negative feeling, that feeling you don't like, find that it gets stronger and more intense.

[Keep giving these suggestions until you notice the subject begin to respond, you should notice a change in them physically – whether it is breathing, skin tone, sweating, tears, tension of the body, whatever happens, feed that back to the subject to increase the affect.]

I can see that you are experiencing this feeling, this emotion strongly and on a subconscious level because *[feedback reaction]*. I'm going to count from three to one, and when I reach the number one this feeling will be so strong, it will be as strong as you have ever experienced it... 3, 2, 1.

Now, as you are experiencing this feeling, this emotion, I'd like you to understand that this experience can be used as a bridge that is connected to the very first time that you felt this way, the very first time that you felt these emotions and feelings. In a moment when I count from three to one, you will find yourself back to that time. That very first time when you felt this way, you will be instantly transported back to that time, 3, 2, 1 now..."

[At this point, ensure that you have the ISE and deal with it as you see fit. You are then able to continue to use the affect bridge in exactly the same way to find SSE's.]

"Using this feeling once again, you can move forwards from that initial event to the next significant time that you felt this feeling... Go there now, and tell me where you are. Tell me what is happening..." *[Find and deal with as many SSEs as you feel necessary and then bring the subject all the way back to the present.]*

"I'd like you to come all the way back to the present now. All of those feelings and emotions a distant memory, because you feel good now. Comfortable, relaxed, calm and at ease. This wonderful feeling of tranquility allowing all of these positive suggestions to stick. Allowing this new reframing of all of these past situations to remain deeply locked in your subconscious mind. Allowing all of these positive changes to happen and to continue to allow yourself to remain strong, confident, calm and in control of your thoughts, feelings and actions. All the way back to the present day now, as you drift and relax and dream."

ANCHORING (NLP)
What does it consist of?
Anchoring is the one NLP technique that I have forced myself to include in this book, simply because I use it all the time and find it to be an invaluable tool during hypnotherapy sessions. Anchoring is the installation of an association between a feeling (happiness, energy, calmness, etc.) and some kind of sensory experience (touch/sight/sound.) Anchoring (as with most hypnotic phenomena) often occurs completely naturally and without even thinking about it. I'm sure you've had a time where you've smelled a certain perfume/scent and been instantly reminded of somebody from your past... Well, that's an anchor (an olfactory-anchor, in fact) and what we're doing in hypnosis is creating something like that, where the subject responds to an external stimuli with an internal action. Sometimes these anchors "fire" and we have no idea as to why our mood

suddenly changed, or why we suddenly began thinking of an old acquaintance, and that is the power of anchors. Anchors can change our state instantly, with almost no effort at all. When these anchors are created naturally however, you don't actually have do anything to cause the anchor to happen. You didn't create it and it is beyond your control (as it is a subconsciously activated process,) but you do generally find that most natural anchors end up being naturally deleted... For instance, if you smell a certain food and it reminds you of an old friend (due to the fact that you used to eat that particular meal together frequently,) then you decide to eat the same meal with a new friend every week, your subconscious will naturally overwrite that link. The anchor between the scent and your old friend is deleted or replaced by the link to your new friend (or your ten cats, depending on how your life panned out.)

These naturally occurring anchors are generally associated with some kind of emotional state (you don't often tend to think "wow, that smell reminds me of a time where...nothing at all happened, and I was completely bored" right?) So fears and phobias can be classified as anchors. You've anchored your state of being afraid to an action, such as: seeing a duck. The anchor has then been reinforced so often that even if you hear the word "duck" it sends a shiver up your spine... Technically, that is an anchor. The act of smoking a cigarette can be anchored to feeling calm and relaxed, eating a cake can be anchored to feeling comfortable and loved, taking a drug can be anchored to feeling happy and carefree, being hurt physically can be anchored to a sexual feeling... A lot of conditioned responses can be simplified in to anchor-terms, and people may have no idea why they respond in these ways. But as they say; our past can shape us, and boy, ain't that the truth!

So as we can see, anchoring need not be limited to being utilised during hypnosis, as it works rather well in the normal waking state too. If you've ever heard of "Pavlov's Dog," you'll also realise that anchoring is not limited to humans. Ivan Pavlov (a Russian psychologist in the 1800's) was studying the salivation of dogs in relation to feeding. He learned that an external stimulus, if linked with the feeding process, would cause the dogs to salivate even when the feeding-process itself was removed. So initially Pavlov would ring a bell every time the dogs were given food, he repeated (anchored) this process and after a short period of conditioning this response (anchoring it,) the dogs would automatically begin to salivate any time the bell was rung, whether there was food or not. Pretty neat, huh? Obviously, we're not particularly interested in dog spit, but luckily this anchoring process is a very useful tool to use in your hypnotherapy sessions with human beings too.

Remember back to the aversion section where I described the anchoring of a negative response? Well that's a brilliant use of anchoring. You can also do the opposite and have the subject experience a positive response to your anchors too. Anchors can be used solely during a hypnotherapy session, or you can install an anchor and inform the subject that they are able to "fire off" the anchor by making a certain gesture (I personally like to have them touch their right thumb to their right ring-finger, because it's not a gesture that will often happen by accident, unlike the thumb and index-finger which touch all the time, so they have to actively touch those fingers together with the intention of firing off the anchor.) Another use for anchoring is what's known as an "anchor collapse" which is a great tool to use if the subject is in a negative state. You anchor the negative state, create a positive state anchor too and then fire them both off at the same time. If the brain was a computer, an anchor collapse would be the equivalent of hitting CTRL + ALT + DELETE a couple of times (resetting the state.)

How does it work?
Firstly, to create an anchor you're going to need to create the target state within the subject. To do this, you'll simply have the subject "remember a time when you..." whatever... When you were happy, calm, in control, powerful, made good decisions, were dominant... Whatever state you are wishing to anchor, have the subject remember it and to remember exactly how they felt at that time. Have them imagine it as if they were there, have them notice how their posture would have been, notice any feelings in their body, etc. When the subject is in that state, you then need to intensify that feeling as much as possible. This can be easily accomplished by suggesting "I'd like you to double that feeling now, make it stronger, double it again, and again..." You may notice a physical change in the subject when they are "in state" (or you might not, it varies.) If the subject is already in the state that you wish to anchor, use the same process of intensifying the state before you anchor it, even if it is a negative state that you wish to anchor, you still need the state to be at a peak level.

Once you have your target state ramped up and intensified and double-doubled, then you need to anchor it. What are you going to anchor it to? Well your first decision is; are you going to anchor it to something that you do or are you going to anchor it to something that the subject does? You can do either or both. I would suggest that with a positive anchor (say, for confidence,) it would be a good idea for the subject to be able to use it whenever they feel they need a boost of confidence. To do this, you should suggest that; "in a moment, I'd like you to touch your right thumb to your right ring-finger and when you do that, this wonderful feeling of confidence will double and double and double. It will be as if this feeling is coming directly from the connection between that thumb and ring-finger. Do it now and squeeze and feel it double and double, stronger and stronger. And whenever you need to feel this confidence you can touch these two fingers together and this wonderful feeling will instantly come back... Just the same as if you take those fingers apart it will stop now! *[if they don't take them apart, do it for them]* but then as soon as you touch them together again now, that feeling always comes back instantly and doubles and doubles, stronger and stronger!"

If, however, you are simply looking to anchor a state for your own use during the hypnotherapy session you don't need to be so overt about it. You do not need to tell them that "every time you press on their shoulder/knee that the feeling will intensify," because simply by intensifying the state sufficiently and then pressing your hand/finger for 5-10 seconds on that area, you will effectively be anchoring the state to that touch. I would suggest that you do this a couple of times to sufficiently anchor the state. So you're going to want to create the initial state, and anchor it, after anchoring the state once, you should then "break the state." Do this by having the subject imagine something completely different and unrelated (something non-emotional,) so that they are no longer "in state." Once that is done, then you go back to describing the feelings you wish to anchor once again, using the same procedure as before. Anchoring in exactly the same place/way as you did before. You can do this as many times as you think necessary.

[Note: Before your session ensure that the subject is OK with you touching them on the shoulder/knee so that they are not shocked or confused when it happens.]

Once you're happy that the state is anchored, you can break state again and have the subject talk briefly about some inconsequential, non-emotional event, whilst they are doing this you can fire off the anchor and you should automatically see whether it is working or not. If it's not working, go back and do it again (you might occasionally find the odd person who doesn't respond well to anchors – some people who suffer depression are a prime example, but the majority of the time this anchoring technique will work really well.)

Another way to create an anchor is using your voice, you are able to easily anchor a state to a specific word or phrase. Think back to the anaesthesia section where I kept saying "anaesthesia" all the time, to anchor that state of "anaesthesia" for the person who wanted to experience "anaesthesia..." Get it? Same principle as with the kinaesthetic (touch) anchor, except instead of putting your hand on their shoulder, you're simply slipping in a phrase/word at the emotional height of the state...

[Note: When you do this, it can be a good idea to remember back to the techniques mentioned during the "analogue marking" section.]

I have heard of people who use the verbal anchoring technique to conversationally (i.e. secretly) program a subject to have hypnotic-orgasms when they hear the trigger-word. Obviously this process was utilised with the hypnotists partner and not just a random subject who walked into the office (yikes – lawsuit!) but every time during their normal lovemaking process, when the partner would reach climax, the hypnotist would subtly say the trigger-word thereby anchoring the "peak state" to said word. So I'm sure you can guess what happened when the hypnotist "accidentally" said the trigger-word whilst they were both out shopping at the supermarket... Which brings me to an important point: Be careful which trigger-word you choose to anchor your state to, because if you end up attaching a hypnotic-orgasm to "hello" then you might be in trouble.

A much more subtle way to anchor using your voice is utilising tone/pace/volume. For example, if someone is explaining something to you in an excited, strong voice then you are more likely to be led into the state of excitement yourself, whereas if someone explained the same thing in the same words but with a dull monotone, you'd be much less likely to be enthusiastic... Same with anchoring, produce the peak state and then change your voice subtly during the peak state, then next time your voice changes in this way – boom, anchor fires. You can also do this with your body language (this only really works if your subject has their eyes open, but as mentioned before, you can definitely do some eyes-open anchoring if the mood takes you.) When you're ready to anchor, tilt your head a certain way... Lean in towards the subject... Do something different that you haven't done throughout the rest of the session (and repeat it a couple of times to reinforce the anchor.)

With these methods, your subject will subconsciously pick up that there is something different about your message, but consciously (assuming you weren't hugely over the top about it,) they'll be none the wiser!

Also I mentioned "anchor collapsing." Collapsing anchors is a really useful method to get a subject out of a non-resourceful state. Have the subject talk about their negative state, and help them to make that negative state even stronger (what a good friend you are.) Once in peak-state, anchor the state as you wish (a touch-anchor would work best here. Verbal anchors don't work so well for collapsing, as you have to fire them off at the same time.) Once the non-resourceful state is anchored, you will then have the subject describe a time where they were feeling really good, happy, confident, resourceful, etc. Ramp up that feeling and anchor it (in a different place, but one that you will be able to reach whilst firing off the initial anchor.) You can then test the anchors by talking about something related to the negative state and firing off the first anchor, then talking about something more positive and firing off the second anchor. Once you're happy that the anchors are installed properly, you then touch both anchor points at exactly the same time and the anchors and the associated emotions have a tendency to just "collapse." You can then ask the subject to try and get back that non-resourceful feeling, and they generally cannot.

Sample script
Anchoring is a rather physical process and as such there is no "script" for anchoring, you just have to talk the subject into a peak state and then touch them, make your gestures or spout out your trigger-word/phrase... Then break state and do the process again... It really is as simple as that.

I don't even need to tell you again that you need to *go and get a book on NLP*.

So I won't...

Even though I just did, with an embedded command.

Sorry.

POST-HYPNOTIC SUGGESTION

What does it consist of?
All suggestions can pretty much be defined as post-hypnotic suggestions (PHS,) but when we refer to a PHS, we generally mean a suggestion that we make during a hypnosis session which will cause some specific thing to happen after the hypnosis session is completed. Commonly, a PHS is associated with stage/street hypnosis, where the hypnotist gives a funny suggestion, such as; "when I wake you up, you will have the irresistible urge to go around sniffing the armpits of everybody in the audience." The hypnotist then wakes up their subject, who will jump up and grab the nearest person and get a-sniffin' with great gusto (assuming they're a responsive subject.) These suggestions however will not remain active in the subject indefinitely and will "wear off" after a few minutes. When we are giving a PHS during hypnotherapy, the suggestions are a lot more likely to remain active and can even last indefinitely, simply because the suggestions given are going to be highly beneficial to the subject and they will be designed to work alongside the subjects' own personal beliefs and values – rather than just making them look like a tit for our own amusement.

We utilise PHS to give the subject various positive suggestions which are intended to activate directly after their session. We can suggest that they will sleep better, be more relaxed every day, feel happier, feel confident, learn more easily, etc. These suggestions are usually given directly, i.e. "after I wake you up and you travel back to your home, you will find that tonight when you go to sleep, you will fall asleep easily and sleep like a log all night."

You can include triggers with these suggestions, it's kind of like a crude version of anchoring: "Whenever your head touches your pillow, you will instantly be ready to fall asleep." ... "Whenever you see a green car, you will feel absolutely spectacular and have no idea why, and that feeling will last all the rest of the day."

Another great PHS to utilise is a reinforcement of your suggestions, directly suggesting that all of the suggestions the subject has received will remain active and get stronger every day. It's a very direct method, but one that I personally will use at the end of all of my hypnotherapy sessions for added effect.

How does it work?
How to post hypnotic suggestions work? Well they work just the same as all the other hypnotic suggestions work. At the end of the hypnotherapy session your subject will (hopefully) be in a highly receptive state. Their subconscious will be like a sponge, ready to soak up all of the goodness that you can impart upon it, so pile it on thick! Give many positive suggestions, rapid fire. You want to be like a positive, life-affirming verbal-machine-gun at the end of your session: "You're feeling good, all these suggestions are working, you'll sleep well, you're awesome, you're confident, you're calm, blam, blam, blam..." Another good thing to include is the PHS that the next time your subject is hypnotised (by you,) they will easily go even deeper than they are right now, and it will take no time at all. Program to make your own future sessions easier – why the Hell not?

You can give some final suggestions relating to your therapy goal just before you wake up your subject too. "Whenever you go to the cupboard, you'll notice whether you're actually hungry or if you're just bored." ... "Whenever you see a spider, you'll feel confident, happy and in control." ... "Whenever you see someone smoking a cigarette, you'll smile and be happy knowing that you are a non-smoker." ... "Whenever you enter into a new, strange situation, you will feel confident and calm, like an adventurer having a wonderful time." ... "Whenever you don't feel so happy, you will fire off your positive anchor and that will make you feel absolutely wonderful, just like you do now." ... Get the general idea? Layer it up, stack suggestions on top of suggestions on top of suggestions. I'm going to include a universal script for PHS that you could use at the end of any hypnotherapy session. Feel free to add extra parts to it to make it more specific to the subject that you are working with.

Sample script
"In a moment I am going to wake you up from hypnosis completely. Before I do, as you listen to the sound of my voice, understand that all of the suggestions that you've been given during this session, all of these positive suggestions are

travelling deep, deep into your subconscious mind. All of these wonderful new thoughts, feelings and behaviours are bonding and melding into your subconscious mind as a part of the new you, the best you, the you that you know you are able to be. You can be confident, calm and relaxed, every minute of every day. No matter what you encounter, you will easily remain happy, calm, confident and relaxed. Any time that you see your friends or your family, you will be motivated, so highly motivated to make a complete success of yourself in everything you do, because you know you have it within yourself to be wealthy in all the ways that matter to you, whether financially or even emotionally. To maintain health, knowledge and to be a success in only the ways that you know you can be successful now.

As you listen to the sound of my voice, feel a wave of confidence wash over you. Like an amazing wave of energy filling you from your head to your toes with confidence, self-belief, self-motivation... You may find that your memory begins to improve. You might notice that you feel slightly different in subtle new ways, and each small difference that you notice is proof that these suggestions are deep in your subconscious mind having a positive effect on the way that you live, on the way that you see life. Tonight when you go to bed, just as soon as your head touches the pillow you will find that you are ready to sleep, and you will sleep soundly, you will sleep easily and you will sleep deeply. And every time you sleep all of these suggestions will reinforce and become stronger, and every time you dream, all of these positive suggestions will allow you to easily become that best you, that you know you are capable of being exactly who you want to be now.

If you ever return to be hypnotised again, you will find that you can easily go back into this state of hypnosis, ten times deeper than you are even now, and ten times faster than ever before. So deep, so relaxed, and whenever you relax, whenever you daydream, whenever you sleep and whenever you dream, all of these suggestions are doubling and becoming an essential part of you, and that feels good now..."

SELF-HYPNOSIS & AFFIRMATIONS

What does it consist of?
Self-hypnosis is exactly what the name suggests, you teach your subject how to hypnotise himself at home so that he can continue to reinforce the suggestions that you have already imparted, thereby increasing the overall success of your hypnotherapy sessions. Also, self-hypnosis is a useful tool to make positive changes in yourself without having to go and see another hypnotherapist, though

some people prefer to have a hypnotherapist to guide them, rather than doing it all in their own head.

Self-hypnosis consists of putting yourself into trance (very similar to meditation,) and once you are in that state of trance, focussing your attention on positive suggestions (very similar to affirmations such as Émile Coué's famous affirmation; "Every day in every way I am getting better and better." Obviously during self-hypnosis, your subject isn't going to be performing regressions, aversion therapy or anything like that on themselves, so don't worry, you don't have to teach them to do any of that stuff! All they need to know is how to put themselves into a relaxed state and then they can repeat a simple, direct positive suggestion or two (which you will give to them.)

As with meditation, self-hypnosis can take as long as you wish, and it will leave you feeling relaxed and refreshed afterwards.

How does it work?
Firstly, your subject needs to know how to get into trance. Odds are, they probably won't be able to achieve the same depth of trance that they achieved in the session with you (until they've had a fair bit of practice at it, anyway.) You have to let your subject know that even if they don't get quite as deeply entranced, the self-hypnosis suggestions will still be effective. There *is* a difference between just lying down with your eyes closed and being in trance, but it's a blurry line and will only come with practice. After the initial hypnosis session, I would suggest that the subject aims to practice self-hypnosis every day thereafter for at least a week. The subject will eventually be able to achieve this trance state wherever/whenever they like, so if they don't have time to do it at home, tell them to do it whilst sat down on their lunch break, or on the train on the way home (NOT whilst driving, obviously.) Generally, though, it's preferable to do the self-hypnosis in a place where they will be undisturbed and comfortable for about 10-20 minutes, a comfortable chair or even a bed. A light trance is all that is required during self-hypnosis anyway, as you still have to actively guide your thoughts. So although the subject will feel more aware during this process, the effect of self-hypnosis is certainly noticeable and sometimes even profound.

I will include a "script" for you so that you can explain to the subject exactly how to put themselves into a state of self-hypnosis in a moment.

Once your subject has induced self-hypnosis they are to then give their suggestions, the two ways that I personally suggest that people do this are positive affirmations or focused visualisations. Obviously you are going to have to tell the subject what it is that they need to be doing whilst in self-hypnosis, and there are a lot of possibilities there... Too many for me to list, obviously, but the basic idea is to keep it simple and focus on the end result. Remember, the subject won't have a script (unless you want to write them one – could be a good idea,) so it has to be short and easy to remember, make it almost "mantra-like."

With positive affirmations, here are a couple of examples. You would have the subjects repeat the following sentence (or something like it) to themselves during self-hypnosis. For a stop smoking session: "I am a non-smoker. I am becoming healthier every day I don't smoke. I have strong will power and I am in control. I am a non-smoker, cigarettes are a thing of the past and now I am healthy, happy and strong."

For a weight loss session: "I am becoming healthier every day, I am in control of my eating habits. I eat only when I am hungry, when my body required fuel. I am in control, becoming healthier and happier every day."

For a confidence session: "I believe in myself, I am confident, friendly, funny and a wonderful person. I deserve respect and people respect me. I am becoming more confident and happier every day."

For an insomnia session: "Every time I sleep, I can sleep deeper and easier than before. Each time I sleep I will learn how to sleep better, and sleep will come easier to me every day."

Affirmations work really well, but you have to ensure that they are delivered positively, so rather than saying "I will not smoke," you would suggest "I am a non-smoker, feeling great," because the subconscious mind works a lot better with positive suggestions than negative ones (but you should know that, already.) Also, ensure that the subject focuses properly on the goal in question without getting side-tracked, because although he may scoff at the idea of self-hypnosis helping him, if he enters the state and then accidentally starts giving negative, self-loathing suggestions such as "this isn't working, nothing I do is ever good enough, I suck!" it's probably not going to do the poor fellow much good, is it...
Visualisations are a much more powerful tool to use during self-hypnosis, it can be almost like being in a dream, except you are able to control the direction in which the dream unfolds and everything that happens therein. Also your subconscious mind cannot actually tell the difference between something that you vividly imagine and something that you actually experienced in real life. So if you imagine yourself overcoming a problem during self-hypnosis, your mind will create all the resources that you need to actually overcome your problems in real life. This makes visualisation the perfect tool with which to rehearse situations that you are worried about, during self-hypnosis. You can go over the situation in your head and practice running through it completely successfully, so that when

the time comes and you actually reach the real life scenario, your subconscious will know better what to do.

So, to have the subject utilise visualisation techniques, all you need to do is simply have them visualise their goals whilst under self-hypnosis. Have them create a short visualisation sequence that is in relation to their goals, something that they can play over in their mind's eye. You can have the subject include an affirmation alongside this visualisation too.

For a phobia session, have the subject imagine being in a room with their phobia (if applicable,) have them imagine interacting with it completely safely whilst repeating an affirmation such as: "I am confident, calm and in control. I control my thoughts and my reactions."

For an anxiety session, have the subject imagine being in a place where they usually would become anxious, but have them imagine themselves feeling on top of the world, confident, calm and positive whilst repeating a similar affirmation: "I am confident, calm and in control. I am becoming stronger and happier every day."

For a stress session, have the subject imagine themselves in a highly stressful environment, dealing with it like a Zen-master: "I am calm, relaxed and in control. Relaxing more and more easily every day."

For someone who wants to get a new job, have the subject imagine themselves turning up to the job interview in their best suit looking their absolute best, speaking clearly, making the interviewers laugh, etc. whilst repeating the affirmation that: "I am going to get this job. I am the perfect choice and the company will employ me."

Get the picture?

Sample script
"To ensure continued success and the best results possible, I recommend that you practice self-hypnosis for between 10 to 20 minutes per day for at least the next 7 days following this session. Only do the self-hypnosis when you are able to be uninterrupted for 20 minutes in a safe place. Do not do it whilst driving or otherwise being pre-occupied.

There are only a couple of steps you need to remember to successfully do self-hypnosis:

1 – Ensure that you have 20 minutes available
2 – Get comfortable and focus on your breathing
3 – Allow your mind to clear, focus on relaxation
4 – Deepen the state of relaxation
5 – Repeat your affirmations/visualisations
6 – Exit the state

You don't need to be in a super-deep state of hypnosis for self-hypnosis to work, you only need a light trance state, but once you are relaxed you are going to want to deepen the relaxation anyway. You can do this by focussing on your breathing and relaxing more with every breath... Counting backwards and drifting deeper with each number... Tensing and relaxing your muscles progressively from your toes all the way up to your head... Imagine that you are at the top of a staircase, and each step that you step down will help you to relax even more, and the door at the bottom opens out into a wonderful relaxing place... Imagine yourself walking through a forest and with each step, relax even deeper... Use your imagination during this process. Enjoy the process and enjoy the self-hypnosis and you will benefit greatly from it.

Once you're in a state of trance, focus on this affirmation/visualisation: *[give them their own personal thing to focus on during their self-hypnosis session]* Repeat this to yourself over and over, and feel free to change parts to make it more positive, ensuring it is exactly how you wish it to be.

Once you feel you are done (or when you feel 20 minutes is up,) allow yourself to drift back to consciousness. You are able to do this by simply thinking it. Bring yourself back out slowly, acknowledging that all of the suggestions and affirmations that you have given yourself during this self-hypnosis are now in effect, getting stronger every day. It's as easy as that."

DISCLAIMER/CONTRACT OF SERVICES FORM

The following "contract of services form" I have provided is designed for example purposes only and if you intend to copy this form for your own personal/business usage you will need to have it approved by the appropriate authorities beforehand. To the best of my knowledge, this is not a legally binding document (because I wrote it myself, and I am not a lawyer…not by a long shot.)

If you decide to use a disclaimer/contract of services, you might want to use 2 copies (one for your own records and the other for your client to retain.) So here it is, a simple guideline upon which you may base your contract of services form:

"My Hypnotherapy Company Name"
Contract of Service – Page 1

AGREEMENT

I hereby give my full consent to receive a hypnotherapy session(s) with the hypnotist; *[YOUR NAME]*.

I understand that hypnotherapy is not a replacement for medical treatment, psychological or psychiatric services or counselling. I also understand that *[YOUR NAME]* does not treat, prescribe-for, or diagnose any condition.

I confirm that I am not physically or psychologically unfit to attend a hypnotherapy session. As such I confirm that I do not suffer from any undisclosed psychotic disorders, clinical depression and I am not prone to seizures.

I understand that hypnotherapy results vary on a case-by-case basis and that the above named hypnotherapist may not guarantee results.

I am aware that I am free to terminate any or all sessions at any time (whilst observing the cancellation policies in place,) and I have agreed to participate in each session to the best of my ability and of my own free will.

I understand that absolute confidentiality regarding the content of my sessions will be honoured by the hypnotherapist.

I have accurately and truthfully provided any personal information as requested by *[YOUR NAME]*.

Client to PRINT/SIGN/DATE HERE

Contract of Service – Page 2
Disclosure Statement

CONFIDENTIALITY

Matters regarding your sessions will be kept confidential except in the following circumstances: You grant the hypnotherapist specific permission to release information to a specific individual or agency; child abuse; you are an imminent danger to yourself or others; or in the case of the subpoena of records. Any information shared is kept confidential.

You understand and accept that individual hypnotherapy cases may be discussed with other therapy-consultants, but in these circumstances, clients are never identified by name.

FEES AND PAYMENTS

Hypnotherapy sessions with *[YOUR NAME]* are charged at a set rate of £XXX per session.
Hypnotherapy sessions do not have a specified duration, and as such are of variable length.
Payment is required upon booking, prior to your session.

24 HOUR CANCELLATION POLICY & REFUNDS

[YOUR NAME] operates a 24 hour cancellation policy for all hypnotherapy sessions; appointments cancelled within less than 24 Hours will be charged the full rate for that appointment. All timely cancellations are eligible to receive a full refund. No refunds are given subsequent to the completion of a hypnotherapy session.

DATA-COLLECTION FORM

The information that you request from your client is entirely up to you, but here is the information that I suggest is worth including within your data collection form. Feel free to pick and choose whichever parts that you like. I have not laid it out as a form, but as a list:

Personal & Address Details
MR/MRS/MS, First Name, Surname, Occupation, Marital Status, Children, DOB, Address, Postcode, Contact: Home, Work, Mobile, E-mail Address

Emergency Contact
Contact Name, Home No, Mobile No, Notes

Family & Other Details
Brothers & Sisters (Number/Names/Ages/Relationship,) Parents (Alive? Relationship?) Family Notes, Dominant Hand (L/R,) Visual (Y/N/?)

Presenting Problems & Additional Problems (notes)

Medical History
Doctor, Practice, Contact Phone No, Reason of Last Visit, Psychiatric Treatment? Nervous Breakdown? Allergies? Tablets/Medication?

Social History
Background - relationships with others in family/close friends, work etc.

Previous Hypnosis
Good/bad experience? When? Who? What Format? Stage Hypnosis?

Additional Information
Safe Place, Significant Event History (ISE/SSE,) Session Records, Comments, Goals, Homework (self-hypnosis)

AFTERWORD

So, you have reached the end of the book, well done! I hope you didn't fall asleep too many times whilst reading, although I suppose if you did that would mean my written-hypnosis skills are as good as the verbal ones!

Now that you're done reading, there's only one course of action and that is to go and practice these techniques on people. Don't just sit there on Amazon buying more books. Books are a good start, but to actually become a hypnotherapist you need to jump in and get your hands dirty. It is my hope that you have gained enough knowledge during the pages of this book to feel comfortable and confident enough to start dabbling and having a go at helping people to get better. The more people out there who understand hypnotherapy and practice it successfully, the better the world is going to be.

On your journey to becoming a Hypnotherapist you may have fuck-ups (we all do,) you may get sick and tired of people thinking you're going to turn them into a chicken (don't even get me bloody started!) But whatever happens, keep at it. Practice, practice and practice some more and eventually you might get to the stage where you are able to fix someone's life every day...

How good would it feel? Saving a person's life every day of your own life...

Pretty bloody good, that's how.

(...and It'll feel even better if you're earning £100+ an hour for doing it!)

All the techniques, methods and information contained within this book are correct to my knowledge, but I am just as fallible as the next guy... OK, maybe a *little* less fallible, but if I got anything wrong, please don't hold it against me.

I hope you've enjoyed reading this book as much as I've enjoyed writing it. In fact, I hope you've enjoyed it more than that, because it's been ruddy hard work formulating all these jumbled up thoughts into coherent sentences! If you did enjoy it, I'd really, truly appreciate it if you'll write a quick review on the Amazon book page... That way, I actually get to see what you think of the book, and also future readers get to make an informed decision before buying the right book!

If you do want MORE information, or if you're interested in **live hypnotherapy training courses**, keep flicking through the pages. You can also take a look at the other hypnosis books and DVDs that I have available. I'm sure you'll love 'em...

LIVE TRAINING

If you want to become a professionally trained hypnotherapist, you're in luck. You have the amazing opportunity to qualify as hypnotherapist with me as your own personal hypnotherapy trainer. The HypnoTC hypnotherapy diploma course (and international certificate) is one of the most comprehensive practitioner level courses available in the UK (if not the world). So, for full details about how you can qualify as a professional hypnotherapist with me, or to come along to one of our *free hypnotherapy taster days* (yes, 100% free), visit the Hypnotherapy Training Company website, here: **www.HypnoTC.com**

The HypnoTC diploma and international certificate is one of the most highly respected qualifications a practicing hypnotherapist can have. As well as meeting the international training standards of the National Guild of Hypnotists (NGH), the course easily meets and exceeds the UK Core Curriculum and National Occupational Standards too. It has been externally accredited by a number of independent hypnotherapy accreditation organisations, including the GHSC/GHR, BIH and FHT.

There are a lot of hypnotherapy courses out there, but unfortunately many of those courses are being "taught" by second-rate trainers who are only after one thing (money). When booking your hypnotherapy training, ensure that you compare training providers and check the course syllabus, student testimonials and tutors' qualifications and experience (both for hypnotherapy and also for teaching)! My company, HypnoTC, offers one of the very best courses in the world, and provides an unparalleled quality of training, guidance and ongoing support. Both myself and Dr Kate (my co-trainer) are fun, engaging and have years of hands-on, practical experience doing hypnotherapy "in the field" as well as teaching it internationally. As such, you can be sure that you are in safe hands with 2 highly experienced hypnotherapy trainers. For more information and upcoming course dates, visit: **www.HypnoTC.com**

As well as hypnotherapy training, I also offer rapid induction and stage/street hypnosis training throughout the year (mainly in London, UK, but occasionally at hypnosis conventions internationally, such as HypnoThoughts Live in Las Vegas). So, if you're looking to get some hands-on practice and feedback, then this is a great option. My courses attract people from all across the world and I frequently have people flying in internationally to attend my courses (even all the way from the USA, Asia and Australia – now that's commitment!).

If you'd *just* like to learn and develop your rapid induction skills, learning to hypnotise fast, you can come along to my 1-day rapid induction workshop. Full details of that are available here: **www.rory-z.com/rapid-induction-training**

Interested in doing 'fun stuff' with hypnosis too? Then, join me for the stage & street hypnosis 101 weekend. Full details of the course are available here: **www.rory-z.com/stage-hypnosis-training**

1-TO-1 TRAINING & PRIVATE MENTORING

As well as those 'group' training courses, I also offer 1-to-1 training for those who cannot make it along, and for those who're serious about improving their hypnosis skills/business. 1-to-1 training is completely bespoke and designed with your needs in mind. You can book either a half day (5 hours) or a full day (8 hours), which you will personally spend with me, and we'll intensively cover anything you wish to learn about hypnosis, with a whole bunch of practice, and constructive feedback.

I also offer shorter mentoring sessions for those hypnotists who're already practicing but looking to refine their skills or improve their hypnosis business. Mentoring sessions can be held via Skype/Zoom or over the phone and can be booked in 15-minute chunks as required.

To enquire about booking 1-to-1 training or private mentoring, please contact me directly:

- E-mail: **rory@rory-z.com**
- Phone: **(+44) 07858 300 422**

HYPNOSIS BOOKS

As well as *this* book, I have a number of other books currently available in paperback/e-book format:

- **The Instant Hypnosis and Rapid Inductions Guidebook** – Learn to do rapid hypnosis inductions. This book will teach you how to quickly and confidently hypnotise people *fast*, whether for hypnotherapy or for entertainment purposes.

- **The Stage & Street Hypnosis Handbook** – Learn to do stage & street hypnosis. This book is a great introduction to the subject, and is suitable for beginners and even hypnotherapists (Note: it can be useful for hypnotherapists to learn stage/street skills as they can translate well towards helping you develop as a hypnotherapist... even if you never intend to do any stage/street hypnosis yourself).

- **Hypno-Fasting** – 'Hypno-Fasting' is a combination of two tried-and-tested, highly effective weight loss approaches (including a lot of information that can be applied to your hypnotherapy work with weight management clients), and is a great way to lose weight quickly, and permanently... It's also an Amazon #1 best seller!

- **Sam the Sleepy Sheep** – This award-winning book has been specifically designed to help put children to sleep. The book uses sleep-inducing hypnotic language patterns to easily and effectively get children to close their eyes and quickly drift into a natural, deep sleep.

HYPNOSIS DVDS/VIDEOS

Some people prefer to watch things as well as reading about them. This is where these hypnosis training videos can be very useful:

- **Rapid Hypnosis 101 – Learn to Hypnotise FAST** – Learn to do rapid hypnosis inductions with this instructional video. Filmed at a live rapid induction training course, this is the next best thing to training with Rory Z in person.

- **Stage Hypnosis 101 – Learn to be a Comedy Hypnotist** – Learn how to do stage & street hypnosis techniques using this awesome instructional video. It covers inductions, deepeners, susceptibility testing and how to perform hilarious comedy hypnosis routines.

OTHER USEFUL HYPNOSIS PRODUCTS

- **Hypnotic Language Cards** – If you are interested in learning about conversational hypnosis or Ericksonian/indirect language patterns, the HypnoTC Hypnotic Language Cards are your best place to start. The language patterns presented in these cards are ideal whether you're looking for added effectiveness in hypnosis, NLP or coaching sessions, adding an edge to your public speaking and storytelling skills, or perhaps for the increased ability to subtly influence people in your normal daily interactions.

- **Core Values Cards** – These 'Core Values Cards' are designed for therapists to use with clients, but can also be used by individuals to discover their own core values. Knowing the core values of your client is integral during the therapy goal-setting process, and will increase the

effectiveness of your therapeutic approach.
- **Hypnosis clothing** – Hypnosis-branded clothes are the perfect way to let people know that you're a hypnotist or hypnotherapist and they are *great* conversation starters!

All hypnosis books, videos and products are available to purchase on my website, here: **www.rory-z.com/hypnosis-products**

NEW ONLINE HYPNOSIS TRAINING COURSES

As well as all of the above training options, I also have a vast range of online hypnosis and hypnotherapy training courses (and also *digital download* versions of both of my Hypnosis 101 DVDs). So, if you'd like to check out our range of online courses (which is always being added to), you can get immediate access right now, here: **www.hypnosis-courses.com**

As you are *obviously* serious about learning to use hypnotherapy effectively in order to help people, the best online course for you to get started with would probably be the **'Hypnotherapy 101'** course, which consists of over 6.5 hours of intensive video training as well as a comprehensive 150-page course manual. It's definitely the next logical step to take after reading this book, and will really help you get to grips with becoming a competent, confident hypnotherapist! Check it out on **www.hypnosis-courses.com**.

THANKS FOR READING!

I hope you've enjoyed reading this book as much as I've enjoyed writing it. Whilst you're here, if you can spare a few seconds right now to leave me a *quick* Amazon review **I would totally appreciate it**! I absolutely love receiving Amazon reviews and it'll be great to see what **YOU** think of this book, whether a few words or a few paragraphs!

in hypnosis voice

"...imagine how easy it would be to *go on Amazon* and *do it right now...*"

(Hehe)

If you have any questions or comments about this book, my other products, training courses or mentoring, don't hesitate to get in touch, because I'm always happy to help. You can get in touch with me personally via the contact form on my website, **www.rory-z.com**, drop me an e-mail to: **rory@rory-z.com**, or give me a call on: **(+44) 07858 300 422**

Thanks for reading and good luck on your hypnotic journey... Now go out there and do it! Practice, practice and practice some more!

Rory Z Fulcher

Printed in Great Britain
by Amazon